HSK 3 Chinese Grammar

HSK 3 Chinese Grammar

A Chinese Grammar Wiki Book

Editor-in-Chief John Pasden

Foreword by Dr. David Moser

SHANGHAI

Published by AllSet Learning, Shanghai, China.

For information about educational or bulk purchases, please contact AllSet Learning at sales@allsetlearning.com.

1st print edition, 2019.

Paperback ISBN: 978-1-941875-47-6
eBook ISBN: 978-1-941875-48-3
ASID: 20190731T210923

For anyone who needs to pass the HSK
but also wants to *really learn* Chinese
and get a solid grasp of its grammar.

Table of Contents

Foreword

Learning Chinese used to be a frustratingly "front-loaded" endeavor. One had to first learn pinyin, the four tones, how to write thousands of characters with the correct stroke order, how to use the 214 radicals to look up unfamiliar characters in a dictionary, and, of course, how to limn the mysterious principles of Chinese grammar. This process entailed inordinate sacrifices of eyesight, friends, and years of precious life spent "learning to learn Chinese," before the hapless student could be weaned from a diet of pre-digested pabulum and delve into the messy, glorious world of real texts.

The Chinese Grammar Wiki is on the cutting edge of a growing arsenal of digital and web resources that have made this front-loaded Sisyphean nightmare a thing of the past. This very cool tool, developed by John Pasden and the folks at AllSet Learning, is in accordance with the new "learning grammar as you go" principle of Chinese study in the digital age. Learners can now boldly embark on the ocean of Chinese very early on, with navigational tools like the Grammar Wiki to reduce the risk of getting lost at sea. For the intrepid, motivated learner, studying Chinese can now be an adventure, instead of a five-year stint in solitary confinement. And from the very outset, students can begin to move toward the goal that was formerly so elusive: the acquisition of 语感 (yǔgǎn), the "feeling for the language."

In my opinion, the Chinese Grammar Wiki has at least three very strong characteristics:

Modularity. This is a long-standing commonsense feature of website design, but it's absolutely crucial for a grammar tool like this. The Wiki has conveniently carved up Chinese grammar into useful modular chunks with the beginner in mind, so that searching for a structure or topic is intuitive, quick, and yields a clear explanation that enables the user to forge ahead, enlightened and empowered. The structure and site map is user-friendly at every level, which means that the Wiki can be easily "plugged in" to existing Chinese syllabi, or simply employed by the student independently to explore texts and materials outside of class.

Interlinking. The Wiki is structured so that alongside the grammar points on most pages there are helpful links to related or similar grammar points within the Wiki. For example, in exploring the grammatical points for 比 (bǐ) involving comparison, you will find explanations of the basic 比 (bǐ) structure, examples, and common errors, but in addition you will also see links to other "comparison" structures using 没有 (méiyǒu). This interlinking feature gives the user a fuller picture of various grammatical structures that serve similar functions in the language.

Universality. One of the strongest points of the Chinese Grammar Wiki is that the grammatical explanations have been tailored so as to contain the right amount of information, at the right level of specificity and complexity for the majority of learners. Designing a grammar resource with such wide applicability is not an easy task, requiring not only technical know-how and careful thinking, but also a strong intuitive sense of what the average student needs to know. Linguist Edward Sapir said “all grammars leak,” and this mutable, watery quality of language means that no grammatical framework is going to contain only tidy, airtight rules that cover every situation. In explanations, there is always a tradeoff between succinct simplicity and the real-life complexity, and the Wiki does an admirable job of striking a satisfying balance between these two yin-yang poles.

Being digital in nature, the Chinese Grammar Wiki is very much a work in progress, and the designers always welcome input and suggestions. Product development is always an interactive process, and the more people use the resource, the more useful it will become. I encourage Chinese students at all levels – and even Chinese teachers – to check it out and discover what the reference tools of the 21st century will look like.

No matter what well-meaning pedagogical Pollyannas might tell you, Chinese is still “damn hard.” Thankfully, there now are digital resources like the Chinese Grammar Wiki, which goes a long way to making the struggle easier.

David Moser
Academic Director, CET Beijing Chinese Studies
Beijing Capital Normal University

Introduction

The **Chinese Grammar Wiki** began life as an Excel spreadsheet full of grammar points organized by difficulty level. This list was needed to track the progress of AllSet Learning's clients and to design personalized grammar practice where it was most needed. But as the lists continued to grow and evolve, it quickly became apparent that it made sense to put the grammar points online, so that the newest version would always be front and center. For ease of editing, what could be better than a wiki? And if AllSet Learning teachers were to have access, why not open up access to *all learners*? The Chinese Grammar Wiki was developed internally for about a year before becoming public in January of 2012. Since then, it has grown tremendously, both in content and in traffic.

Probably the most important feature of the Chinese Grammar Wiki, which has always been kept at the forefront of its development, is its focus on learner level. An absolute beginner can't absorb a multitude of uses for every grammar point she encounters, and she shouldn't be expected to. And she certainly shouldn't be given frustratingly difficult example sentences when trying to grasp the most basic grammar concepts. That's why example sentences on the Chinese Grammar Wiki are plentiful, but relentlessly edited to be level-appropriate. And for the learners that can't get enough, relevant articles of all levels are always just a link away. Although the wiki aims to be 100% comprehensive, it's no coincidence that there are fewer A1 grammar points than A2 grammar points, and fewer A2 grammar points than B1 grammar points. Considerable thought and care has gone into curating and pruning the lists of grammar points.

The Chinese Grammar Wiki is not a Chinese course. Rather, it is a companion resource that can complement any Chinese class. Don't expect to read it from start to finish, or to go through the grammar point lists from top to bottom. But do expect to come back often. And expect to get sucked into the curiously logical world of Chinese grammar.

John Pasden
Editor-in-Chief and CEO
AllSet Learning, Shanghai, China

HSK Levels and CEFR Levels

Since the company's inception in 2010, AllSet Learning has used the Common European Framework of Reference (CEFR) levels for its clients and study materials. CEFR has a great reputation for being practical and descriptive of communicative proficiency (we especially like the "Can Do" statements) while mercifully keeping the leveling and sub-leveling to a minimum. The A1-A2, B1-B2, C1-C2 progression is intuitive and helpful for both learners and educators, and can also be fairly easily converted to the American ACTFL level system.

The current version of the HSK (*Hanyu Shuiping Kaoshi*) dates back to 2010, and was last revised in 2012. It consists of six levels (1-6), and was designed, in part, to correspond to the six CEFR levels. European Chinese language teachers have reported that the correspondence, in practice, is somewhat different, with HSK 6 actually matching no higher than the CEFR B2-C1 level range. Furthermore, the HSK levels are used more as a standard for academic requirements (e.g. being admitted to an undergraduate or graduate program in China) rather than real-life application (the above-mentioned "communicative proficiency").

Our conclusion is that while both leveling systems clearly have their uses, it is not possible to equally accommodate both systems in one list of grammar points. That is why the Chinese Grammar Wiki has created separate listings for CEFR levels and HSK levels. We encourage test-takers of the HSK to refer to the HSK level lists, while learners focused more on real-life communication can benefit more from the CEFR levels. This book focuses on the HSK levels.

Adjectives with "-ji le"

Just as 死了 (sǐle) can be used to intensify negative adjectives, 极了 (jíle) is a somewhat less common way to intensify both positive and negative adjectives. It is used in spoken, colloquial Chinese. 极 (jí) means "extreme" or "utmost."

Structure

This structure is technically a kind of degree complement and one of the few that you can use after the adjective and without adding a 得 (de). Remember to add the 了 (le), since it would be incorrect without it.

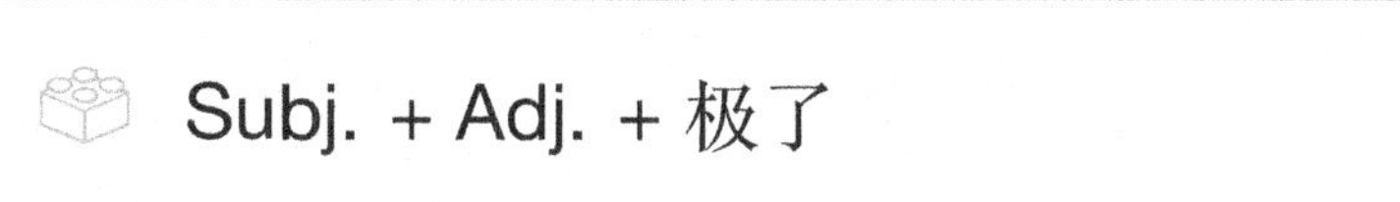

Subj. + Adj. + 极了

Examples

Some examples with a positive connotation:

- 这个主意好 极了 。

  Zhège zhǔyi hǎo jíle.

  This idea is perfect.

- 味道好 极了 ！

  Wèidào hǎo jíle!

  The taste is perfect!

- 他的英文棒 极了 。

  Tā de Yīngwén bàng jíle.

  His English is perfect.

- 婚礼热闹 极了 。

  Hūnlǐ rènao jíle.

  The wedding was very lively.

- 一点声音都没有，安静 极了 。

  Yīdiǎn shēngyīn dōu méiyǒu, ānjìng jíle.

  There is no sound at all. It's extremely quiet.

Some examples with a negative connotation:

- 昨天的派对无聊 [极了] ！
  Zuótiān de pàiduì wúliáo [jíle]!
  Yesterday's party was so boring!
- 他那么生气，我们都害怕 [极了] 。
  Tā nàme shēngqì, wǒmen dōu hàipà [jíle].
  He was so angry. We were all so scared.
- 高考那天，我紧张 [极了] 。
  Gāokǎo nà tiān, wǒ jǐnzhāng [jíle].
  I was super nervous the day I took the college entrance examination.
- 这件事让我们都尴尬 [极了] 。
  Zhè jiàn shì ràng wǒmen dōu gāngà [jíle].
  This incident made us all extremely embarrassed.
- 那个男孩讨厌 [极了] ！
  Nàge nánhái tǎoyàn [jíle]!
  That boy is super annoying!

Similar to

- Expressing “excessively” with “tai” (HSK1)
- Degree complement (HSK2)
- Expressing “really” with “zhen” (HSK2)
- Superlative “zui” (HSK2)
- Adjectives with “name” and “zheme” (HSK3), page 38
- Intensifying with “duo” (HSK3), page 46
- Special verbs with “hen” (HSK3), page 131
- Expressing “quite” with “ting” (HSK4)
- Negative adjectives with “-si le” (HSK4)
- Adjectival complement “de budeliao” (HSK5)
- Adjectival complement “de hen” (HSK5)
- Advanced degree complements (HSK5)
- Complement “-huai le” (HSK5)

Reduplication of adjectives

One of the charming features of Chinese is reduplication (repeating, or doubling up) of certain words and characters, including adjectives. Reduplication can enhance the descriptive feeling of an adjective.

One-Syllable Adjectives (AA)

If an adjective is only one syllable (one character), then reduplicating it is a no-brainer. The only tricky part about this pattern is that not all adjectives can be reduplicated in natural speech. It's mostly for adjectives that describe the physical world: colors, sizes, shapes, and other physical descriptors.

Structure

Adj. + Adj. + 的 (+ Noun)

In most Chinese textbooks and grammar books, this is known as the "AA" pattern. We'll be using this form more extensively below:

A A + 的 (+ Noun)

Note that this pattern is also identical to single-syllable reduplication of verbs[1].

Examples

- 你的脸 红红的 。
  Nǐ de liǎn hóng hóng de.
  Your face is red.
- 宝宝的眼睛 大大的 。
  Bǎobao de yǎnjīng dà dà de.
  The baby's eyes are big.
- 今晚的月亮 圆圆的 。
  Jīnwǎn de yuèliàng yuán yuán de.
  The moon is round tonight.

1. Reduplication of verbs (Grammar), page 128

- 她爸爸 高高胖胖的 。

  Tā bàba gāo gāo pàng pàng de.

  Her father is tall and fat.

- 我妹妹 瘦瘦小小的 。

  Wǒ mèimei shòu shòu xiǎo xiǎo de.

  My little sister is thin and small.

Two-Syllable Adjectives (AABB)

If the adjective has more than one character, then you should repeat each character individually (rather than the whole word). This is known as the "AABB" pattern.

Structure

In the structure below, the original two-character adjective (such as 高兴, 漂亮) is "AB," where the first character of the adjective is represented by "A," and the second by "B."

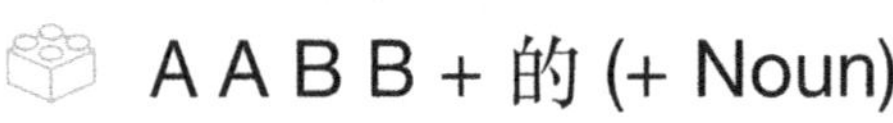

A A B B + 的 (+ Noun)

Examples

Not all two-syllable adjectives are used in AABB form, but here are some common examples of AB adjectives represented in AABB form.

- 高兴→ 高高兴兴

  gāoxìng → gāogāo-xìngxìng

  happy

- 热闹→ 热热闹闹

  rènao → rèrè-nāonāo

  noisy, boisterous

- 漂亮→ 漂漂亮亮

  piàoliang → piàopiào-liāngliāng

  pretty

- 舒服→ 舒舒服服

  shūfu → shūshū-fūfū

  comfortable

- 安静→ 安安静静

  ānjìng → ānān-jìngjìng

  quiet and still

Not all adjectives can take AABB form. Here are some examples of common adjectives that don't work in AABB form.

- ✖ 好吃→ 好好吃吃

  hǎochī → hǎohǎo-chīchī

  tasty

- ✖ 便宜→ 便便宜宜

  piányi → piánpián-yíyí

  cheap

- ✖ 麻烦→ 麻麻烦烦

  máfan → mámá-fánfán

  bothersome

Used as Adverbs (AABB)

When adjectives are used as adverbs to modify verbs, you can reduplicate the adjective using the AABB pattern.

Structure

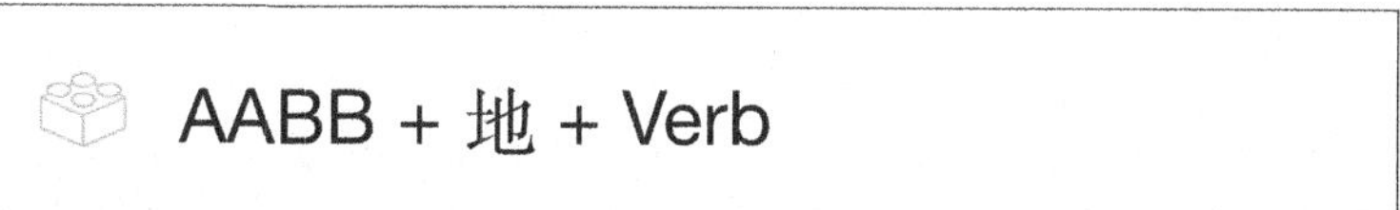

Note: The "AABB" pattern for reduplication of two-syllable adjectives contrasts with the "ABAB" pattern for reduplication of two-syllable verbs[1].

Examples

- 我们 清清楚楚 地 看到他跟一个胖胖的男人上车了。

  Wǒmen qīngqīng-chǔchǔ de kàndào tā gēn yīgè pàng pàng de nánrén shàngchē le.

  We clearly saw him get in the car with a fat man.

- 我真想 舒舒服服 地 躺在沙发上看电视。

  Wǒ zhēn xiǎng shūshū-fūfū de tǎng zài shāfā shàng kàn diànshì.

  I'd really like to comfortably lie on the couch and watch TV.

1. Reduplication of verbs (Grammar), page 128

- 你妈妈 辛辛苦苦 地 做了两个小时的饭，你怎么不吃？
  Nǐ māma xīnxīn-kǔkǔ de zuò le liǎng gè xiǎoshí de fàn, nǐ zěnme bù chī?
  Your mother labored over this meal for two hours, and you aren't going to eat it?

Used as Predicates (ABAB)

If you use an adjective as a predicate, then you're basically using the adjective like a verb, and you reduplicate it as you would a verb[1], which means ABAB form. Using an adjective in this way is roughly equivalent to using 一下 after the (non-reduplicated) adjective.

Structure

To use a reduplicated adjective as a predicate, follow this structure:

> Subj. + ABAB

or

> Subj. + AB + 一下

In the pattern above there's no verb because when an adjective serves as the predicate, it does the job of a verb. Notice also that there's no 的 after the ABAB, because 的 is used when modifying nouns.

Examples

- 妹妹快过生日了，我打算给她办一个生日派对，热闹热闹 。
  Mèimei kuài guò shēngrì le, wǒ dǎsuàn gěi tā bàn yī gè shēngrì pàiduì, rènao rènao.
  My little sister's birthday is coming and I plan to throw her a birthday party and have a blast.
- 来，喝点酒，高兴高兴 。
  Lái, hē diǎn jiǔ, gāoxìng gāoxìng.
  Come on, have a little wine and enjoy yourself.

---

1. Reduplication of verbs (Grammar), page 128

- 到这里来 凉快凉快 。
  Dào zhèlǐ lái liángkuai liángkuai .
  Come over here and cool off.
- 我想去外面走走，安静 一下 。
  Wǒ xiǎng qù wàimiàn zǒuzou, ānjìng yīxià .
  I'd like to take a walk outside, get some quiet time.
- 想不想去做个按摩，放松一下 。
  Xiǎng bu xiǎng qù zuò gè ànmó, fàngsōng yīxià .
  Would you like to go get a massage and unwind?

Similar to

- Simple "noun + adjective" sentences (HSK1)
- Reduplication of measure words (HSK2)
- Reduplication of verbs (HSK2, HSK3), page 128

Turning adjectives into adverbs

You can easily convert most Chinese adjectives into adverbs with the particle 地 (de). This usage is very similar to the suffix *-ly* in English.

Structure

In Chinese, we place the structural particle 地 (de) after the adjective to make it function as an adverb.

 Subj. + Adj. + 地 + Verb

Examples

- 你要 努力 地 学习。
  Nǐ yào nǔlì de xuéxí.
  You must study hard.
- 雨天地滑，慢慢 地 走。
  Yǔtiān dì huá, màn màn de zǒu.
  The floor is very slippery on rainy days. Walk slowly.
- 他 顺利 地 通过考试了。
  tā shùnlì de tōngguò kǎoshì le.
  He passed the exam successfully.
- 他 认真 地 对我说："我喜欢你。"
  Tā rènzhēn de duì wǒ shuō: "wǒ xǐhuan nǐ."
  In all seriousness, he said to me: "I like you."
- 他 热情 地 拥抱了我。
  Tā rèqíng de yōngbào le wǒ.
  He gave me a very warm embrace.
- 她 激动 地 对我说"谢谢"。
  Tā jīdòng de duì wǒ shuō "xièxie."
  She said "thank you" to me excitedly.

- 老师 生气 地 看着我们。
  Lǎoshī shēngqì de kàn zhe wǒmen.
  The teacher is looking at us angrily.
- 孩子们 开心 地 唱了起来。
  Háizi men kāixīn de chàng le qǐlai.
  The children started to sing happily.
- 大家都在教室里 安安静静 地 看书。
  Dàjiā dōu zài jiàoshì lǐ ānān-jìngjìng de kàn shū.
  Everybody is reading quietly in the classroom.
- 我希望你 快快乐乐 地 长大。
  Wǒ xīwàng nǐ kuàikuài-lèlè de zhǎngdà.
  I hope that you grow up happily.

Similar to

- Modifying nouns with adjective + "de" (HSK3), page 48

Expressing "again" in the past with "you"

Whenever you want to express something that has happened again, as in, "oops, I did it *again*!" in Chinese, you generally want to use 又 (yòu). (You'll want to use 再 (zài) for "again" in the future.)

Affirmative Form

Structure

Normally, 又 is used to express an action that has already happened again for (at least) the second time. It doesn't have to be in quick succession; it happened before, and now it's happened again.

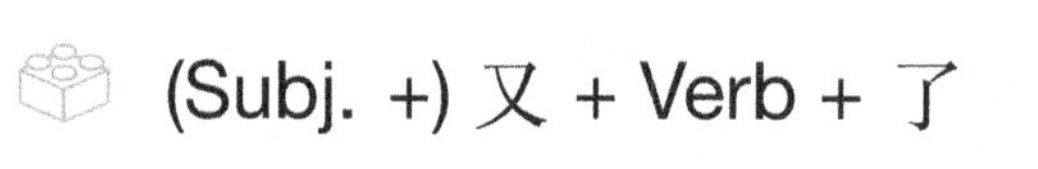

(Subj. +) 又 + Verb + 了

Examples

- 又下雨了！
  Yòu xiàyǔ le !
  It rained again!
- 你又迟到了。
  Nǐ yòu chídào le .
  You're late again.
- 宝宝又哭了。
  Bǎobao yòu kū le .
  The baby is crying again.
- 我又忘了。
  Wǒ yòu wàng le .
  I forgot again.

Negative Form

Structure

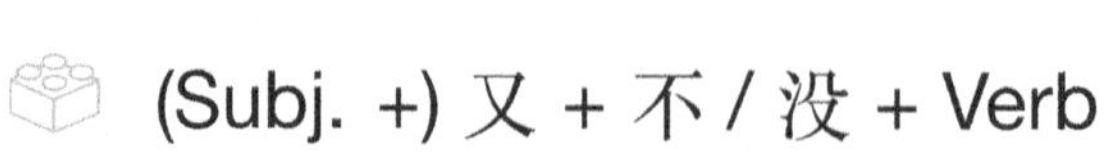

(Subj. +) 又 + 不 / 没 + Verb

Examples

- 他 又 没 来上课。
  Tā yòu méi lái shàngkè.
  He didn't come to class again.
- 你们 又 不 付钱?
  Nǐmen yòu bù fùqián?
  You're not paying again?
- 你 又 不 参加?
  Nǐ yòu bù cānjiā?
  You are not going to participate again?
- 对不起，我 又 没 带书。
  Duìbuqǐ, wǒ yòu méi dài shū.
  Sorry, I forgot to bring the book again.

Colloquial Saying 又来了

又来了 fits the above pattern, but is also a little tricky because it expresses something that is still ongoing, and has already started as the speaker is speaking. Literally it means "here it comes again," but it's more accurate to translate it as "there it is again," or "there [he] goes again." It indicates that the speaker is a bit annoyed that it happened *again*.

Other Usage

When it becomes clear that something is about to happen again, you can also use 又. It's almost as if it has already happened in your mind. In these cases, it's quite common for 又 to be immediately followed by 是 (shì), 要 (yào), 可以 (kěyǐ), or 能 (néng), and you'll notice that there's often a 了, indicating that something is about to happen.

Some examples:

- 今天 又 要 加班 了 !
  Jīntiān yòu yào jiābān le !
  We've got to work overtime again today!
- 老板请客，又 可以 吃大餐 了 !
  Lǎobǎn qǐngkè, yòu kěyǐ chī dàcān le !
  The boss is going to treat us. We can have a big meal again!

- 快过年了，我们 又 能 拿红包 了 ！
  Kuài guònián le, wǒmen yòu néng ná hóngbāo le !
  It's almost Chinese New Year. We can get our red packets [of money] again!

Similar to

- Expressing "again" in the future with "zai" (HSK2)
- Comparing "zai" and "you" (HSK3), page 229
- Emphasizing negation with "you" (HSK4)
- Advanced use of "you" (HSK5)
- Expressing "over and over again" with "zaisan" (HSK5)

Expressing "all along" with "yizhi"

一直 (yīzhí) literally means "straight." Used as an adverb, 一直 (yīzhí) can also be used to express that you have been doing something all along, have been continuously doing something since a certain time, or that something will continuously happen in the future.

Structure

This structure expresses the continuous nature of an action or a circumstance.

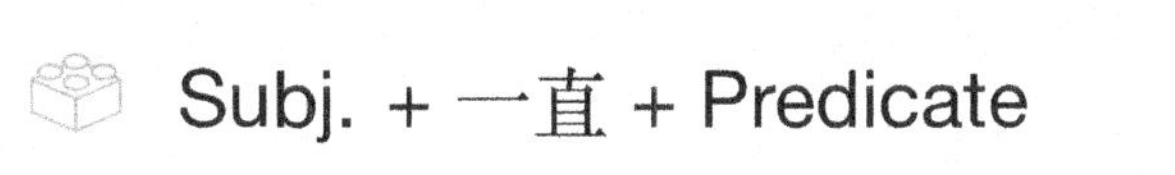

Subj. + 一直 + Predicate

Also note that although 一直 (yīzhí) means "continuously," it is frequently more natural to use the word "always" in the English translation.

Examples

- 我 一直 在学习中文。
  Wǒ yīzhí zài xuéxí Zhōngwén.
  I've been studying Chinese all along.
- 昨天晚上我 一直 在做作业。
  Zuótiān wǎnshang wǒ yīzhí zài zuò zuòyè.
  Yesterday evening I was continuously doing homework.
- 老板 一直 很忙。
  Lǎobǎn yīzhí hěn máng.
  The boss is always very busy.

  "Always" is more natural than "continuously."
- 我 一直 很喜欢你。
  Wǒ yīzhí hěn xǐhuan nǐ.
  I've always liked you a lot.
- 爸爸 一直 都不抽烟。
  Bàba yīzhí dōu bù chōuyān.
  Dad has never smoked cigarettes.
- 我男朋友 一直 在中国教英文。
  Wǒ nánpéngyou yīzhí zài Zhōngguó jiāo Yīngwén.
  My boyfriend has always been teaching English in China.

- 18 岁以后，他 一直 一个人住。
  Shíbā suì yǐhòu, tā yīzhí yīgèrén zhù.
  Since he was 18, he has always lived alone.
- 你 一直 在这家公司工作吗?
  Nǐ yīzhí zài zhè jiā gōngsī gōngzuò ma?
  Have you always worked in this company?
- 你们 一直 住在一起吗?
  Nǐmen yīzhí zhù zài yīqǐ ma?
  Have you always been living together?
- 北京的空气 一直 很不好。
  Běijīng de kōngqì yīzhí hěn bù hǎo.
  The air in Beijing has been bad for a while.

Similar to

- Expressing "always" with "zongshi" (HSK3), page 19
- Comparing "buduan" and "buting" (HSK5)
- Comparing "yizhi" and "yixiang" (HSK5)
- Expressing "since the beginning" with "yixiang" (HSK5)
- Expressing "again and again" with "yizai" (HSK6)

Expressing "always" with "zongshi"

If you are trying to describe a daily routine, a habit, or just something that consistently happens, you can use the word 总是 (zǒngshì). 总是 (zǒngshì) means "always," and like other adverbs, comes before the verb in a sentence.

总是 (zǒngshì) with Verbs

总是 (zǒngshì) is an adverb that is often translated to English as "always." It is placed before the verb that it modifies.

Structure

 Subj. + 总是 + Verb

Examples

- 他 总是 迟到。
  Tā zǒngshì chídào.
  He is always late.
- 我 总是 忘记这个词。
  Wǒ zǒngshì wàngjì zhège cí.
  I always forget this word.
- 他 总是 一个人吃饭。
  Tā zǒngshì yīgèrén chīfàn.
  He always eats alone.
- 你男朋友 总是 说脏话。
  Nǐ nánpéngyou zǒngshì shuō zānghuà.
  Your boyfriend always uses foul language.
- 我的学生 总是 问我很多有意思的问题。
  Wǒ de xuéshēng zǒngshì wèn wǒ hěn duō yǒu yìsi de wèntí.
  My students always ask me lots of interesting questions.

总是 (zǒngshì) with Adjectives

Structure

When 总是 (zǒngshì) is used together with an adjective, you will need to add a modifier in the middle, such as 很 (hěn), 特别 (tèbié), 这么 (zhème), 那么

(nàme),[1] etc.

 总是 + Adv. + Adj.

Examples

- 他 总是 很累。
  Tā zǒngshì hěn lèi.
  He is always tired.
- 你为什么 总是 很忙?
  Nǐ wèishénme zǒngshì hěn máng?
  Why are you always very busy?
- 你家 总是 很干净。
  Nǐ jiā zǒngshì hěn gānjìng.
  Your house is always very clean.
- 孩子们 总是 非常开心。
  Háizi men zǒngshì fēicháng kāixīn.
  The children are always very happy.
- 我的学生 总是 特别努力。
  Wǒ de xuéshēng zǒngshì tèbié nǔlì.
  My students are always very hard-working.

Similar to

- Expressing "all along" with "yizhi" (HSK3), page 17
- Using "always" as a complaint with "laoshi" (HSK3), page 34
- Expressing "always" with "conglai" (HSK4)
- Comparing "yizhi" and "yixiang" (HSK5)

1. Adjectives with "name" and "zheme" (Grammar), page 38

Expressing "finally" with "zhongyu"

终于 (zhōngyú) expresses that something has *finally* happened after a long wait. Usually the speaker is looking forward to what is happening at long last, and thus, 终于 (zhōngyú) typically carries a sense of joy or relief.

Structure

Unlike the English word "finally," 终于 (zhōngyú) can never be used alone. It also can't be put in front of the subject or at the end of the sentence. 终于 (zhōngyú) needs to be used with 了 to express that the action is completed.

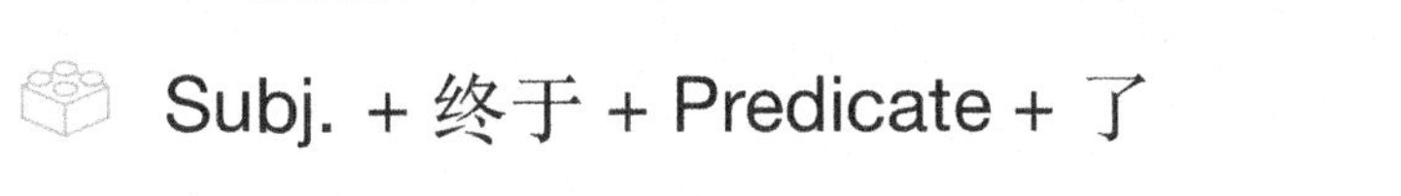

The predicate part of the pattern can be a verb or an adjective.

Examples

- 你终于到了！
  Nǐ zhōngyú dào le!
  You've finally arrived!
- 我们终于见面了！
  Wǒmen zhōngyú jiànmiàn le!
  We're finally meeting each other!
- 你们终于明白了。
  Nǐmen zhōngyú míngbai le.
  You've finally understood.
- 作业终于做完了！
  Zuòyè zhōngyú zuò wán le!
  I've finally finished my homework!
- 飞机终于起飞了！
  Fēijī zhōngyú qǐfēi le!
  The plane is finally taking off!

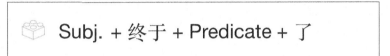

- 你们 终于 决定 了 。
  Nǐmen zhōngyú juédìng le .
  You've finally decided.
- 饭 终于 做好 了 。我快饿死了。
  Fàn zhōngyú zuò hǎo le . Wǒ kuài è sǐ le.
  Dinner is finally ready. I'm starving.
- 这个愿望 终于 实现 了 ！
  Zhège yuànwàng zhōngyú shíxiàn le !
  This dream has finally come true!
- 我们找了两个多小时，终于 找到 了 那家店。
  Wǒmen zhǎo le liǎng gè duō xiǎoshí, zhōngyú zhǎodào le nà jiā diàn.
  We'd been looking for more than two hours, and we finally found that shop.
- 这些问题 终于 解决 了 。我们应该庆祝一下。
  Zhèxiē wèntí zhōngyú jiějué le . Wǒmen yīnggāi qìngzhù yīxià.
  The problems are finally solved. We should celebrate!

Similar to

- Comparing “zongsuan” and “zhongyu” (HSK5)

Expressing "only" with "zhi"

There are a number of different ways to express "only" in Chinese, but 只 (zhǐ) is the most basic one you need to learn first. It's an adverb, so it normally comes before verbs.

Structure

The adverb 只 (zhǐ) can come directly before a verb, or before an auxiliary verb like 会 (huì) or 能 (néng).

Examples

- 我 只 有一个哥哥。
  Wǒ zhǐ yǒu yī gè gēge.
  I only have one older brother.
- 我们 只 有十块钱。
  Wǒmen zhǐ yǒu shí kuài qián.
  We only have ten RMB.
- 我们公司 只 有两个员工。
  Wǒmen gōngsī zhǐ yǒu liǎng gè yuángōng.
  Our company only has two employees.
- 你 只 爱吃肉吗?
  Nǐ zhǐ ài chī ròu ma?
  Do you only like eating meat?
- 他们 只 会说英文。
  Tāmen zhǐ huì shuō Yīngwén.
  They can only speak English.

- 我 只 能说两句中文。
  Wǒ zhǐ néng shuō liǎng jù Zhōngwén.
  I can only say two sentences in Chinese.
- 你们 只 要咖啡吗?
  Nǐmen zhǐ yào kāfēi ma?
  Do you only want coffee?
- 我老婆 只 要一个孩子。
  Wǒ lǎopo zhǐ yào yī gè háizi.
  My wife only wants one child.
- 宝宝 只 会走，不会跑。
  Bǎobao zhǐ huì zǒu, bù huì pǎo.
  The baby can only walk. He can't run.
- 我 只 想跟你在一起。
  Wǒ zhǐ xiǎng gēn nǐ zài yīqǐ.
  I only want to be with you.

Similar to

- Expressing "small quantity" with "jiu" (HSK4)

Expressing duration of inaction

Saying how long you have *not* done something is not difficult, but the word order is different from the regular pattern for expressing duration[1]. If there's a consistent keyword in this pattern, it's going to be 没 (méi), since it almost always plays a role.

Structure

Remember, this pattern differs from both simple pattern for expressing duration[1] and the pattern for ongoing duration[2].

> Subj. + (已经 +) Duration + 没 + Verb + 了

So now the duration comes right after the subject and 了 is at the end of the sentence. The verb has to be negated with 没, as the action *hasn't* happened.

Note that 已经 can be omitted.

Examples

- 他们 已经 两天 没 吃东西 了 。
  Tāmen yǐjīng liǎng tiān méi chī dōngxi le .
  They haven't eating anything for two days already.
- 我们 已经 十年 没 见 了 。
  Wǒmen yǐjīng shí nián méi jiàn le .
  We haven't seen each other for ten years already.
- 他 已经 一个星期 没 洗澡 了 。
  Tā yǐjīng yī gè xīngqī méi xǐzǎo le .
  He has already gone a whole week without showering.
- 你多长时间 没 刮胡子 了 ?
  Nǐ duō cháng shíjiān méi guā húzi le ?
  How long has it been since you last shaved?

---

1. Expressing duration with "le" (Grammar), page 120
2. Expressing ongoing duration with double "le" (Grammar), page 123

- 她半个月 没 出门 了 。
  Tā bàn gè yuè méi chūmén le .
  It's been half a month since she's left the house.
- 你们多久 没 回家 了 ？
  Nǐmen duōjiǔ méi huíjiā le ?
  How long has it been since you returned home?
- 你多久 没 休假 了 ？
  Nǐ duōjiǔ méi xiūjià le ?
  How long has it been since your last vacation?
- 买吧，你 已经 一年多 没 买新衣服 了 。
  Mǎi ba, nǐ yǐjīng yī nián duō méi mǎi xīn yīfu le .
  Just buy it. It's been more than one year since you last bought new clothes.
- 你好像很久 没 这么开心 了 。
  Nǐ hǎoxiàng hěnjiǔ méi zhème kāixīn le .
  It seems like it's been a long time since you were this happy.

In English, we may say something like, "I haven't eaten since 9:00 this morning" or "I haven't been to China since the year 2000." Note that the Chinese do not tend to say somebody hasn't done something since a *certain point in time*. Instead, you should either express it as a duration of time that one hasn't done something (as in the above examples), or you can say "the last time somebody did something was [a certain point in time]."

- 我已经十年 没 来中国 了 。
  Wǒ yǐjīng shí nián méi lái Zhōngguó le .
  It's been 10 years since I came to China last.
- 我 上次 来中国 是 2010 年。
  Wǒ shàngcì lái Zhōngguó shì èr-líng-yī-líng nián.
  The last time I came to China was 2010.

Similar to

- Expressing "already" with "dou" (HSK2)
- Expressing duration with "le" (HSK3), page 120
- Expressing ongoing duration with double "le" (HSK3), page 123

Expressing lateness with "cai"

To express that something happened later than expected, you can use 才 (cái). In English, this might be expressed with "as late as" or "not until." This form is often used with a time of some sort, like a specific time of day, age, etc. This pattern is essentially the opposite of using 就 (jiù) to express earliness.

Structure

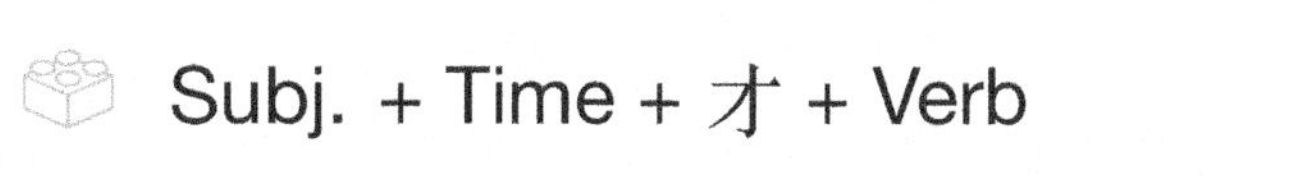

Examples

- 我昨天晚上十一点 才 到家。
  Wǒ zuótiān wǎnshang shíyī diǎn cái dào jiā.
  I didn't arrive at home until eleven o'clock last night.
- 他二十五岁 才 上大学。
  Tā èrshí-wǔ suì cái shàng dàxué.
  He didn't go to college until he was 25.
- 她四十岁 才 结婚。
  Tā sìshí suì cái jiéhūn.
  She didn't get married until she was forty.
- 我女儿昨天十二点 才 睡觉，作业太多了。
  Wǒ nǚ'ér zuótiān shí'èr diǎn cái shuìjiào, zuòyè tài duō le.
  My daughter didn't go to bed until 12 o'clock yesterday. Too much homework.
- 你九点上班，八点半 才 起床？
  Nǐ jiǔ diǎn shàngbān, bā diǎn bàn cái qǐchuáng?
  You start work at nine o'clock, but don't get up until 8:30?
- 飞机刚刚 才 起飞，晚点了两个小时。
  Fēijī gānggāng cái qǐfēi, wǎndiǎn le liǎng gè xiǎoshí.
  The airplane just took off. It was delayed for two hours.

- 电影七点半开始，可是因为堵车，我们八点 才 到。

  Diànyǐng qī diǎn bàn kāishǐ, kěshì yīnwèi dǔchē, wǒmen bā diǎn cái dào.

  The movie began at 7:30, but we didn't arrive until eight because of traffic.

You can use 才 alone with the verb to indicate the lateness when the context is clear:

- 你怎么 才 吃晚饭？已经十点了。

  Nǐ zěnme cái chī wǎnfàn? Yǐjīng shí diǎn le.

  How come you are eating dinner now? It's 10 pm.

- 你怎么 才 来？我们等了半个多小时。

  Nǐ zěnme cái lái? Wǒmen děng le bàn gè duō xiǎoshí.

  How come you came here so late? We've waited for more than half an hour.

Note that verbs following 才 should not take 了.

✘ 我昨天晚上十一点 才 到家 了 。

Wǒ zuótiān wǎnshang shíyī diǎn cái dào jiā le .

✘ 她四十岁 才 结婚 了 。

Tā sìshí suì cái jiéhūn le .

Similar to

- Expressing earliness with “jiu” (HSK2)
- Comparing “cai” and “jiu” (HSK3), page 216
- Expressing “all the way until” with “zhidao” (HSK3), page 103

Sequencing with "xian" and "zai"

The word 再 (zài) actually has a lot of uses, beyond just "again," and in this pattern it means something like "and then." 先……，再…… (xiān..., zài...) is a pattern used for sequencing events, much like "first..., then..." in English. This pattern can also include 然后 (ránhòu), meaning "and after that."

Basic Usage

In the pattern below, 先 means "first" and 再 has a meaning of "then" or "and then."

Structure

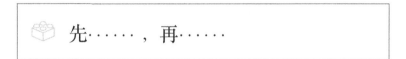

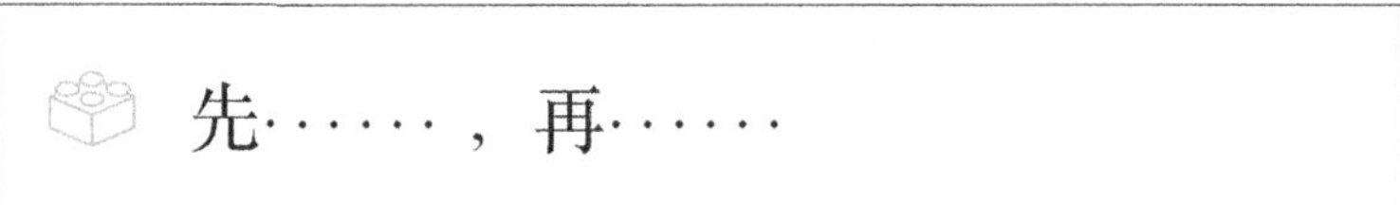

Examples

- 先 洗手 再 吃。
  Xiān xǐ shǒu zài chī.
  Wash your hands first, and then eat.
- 我喜欢 先 洗澡，再 睡觉。
  Wǒ xǐhuan xiān xǐzǎo, zài shuìjiào.
  I prefer to take a bath first and then go to bed.
- 请你 先 买票 再 进去。
  Qǐng nǐ xiān mǎi piào zài jìnqù.
  Please buy a ticket first and then enter.
- 你要 先 做作业，再 看电视。
  Nǐ yào xiān zuò zuòyè, zài kàn diànshì.
  You need to do your homework first, and then watch TV.
- 我想 先 找工作，再 搬家。
  Wǒ xiǎng xiān zhǎo gōngzuò, zài bānjiā.
  I want to find a job first, and then move.

Colloquial Usage with 再说

You may have learned that 再说 can mean "in addition." Well, the usage of 再 here is a more literal combination of 再说, fitting into the 先…… 再……

pattern.

So in this usage, 再说 doesn't really mean "in addition." Rather, it most literally means, "and then we'll talk." In other words, "let's just do this now," and then after we see the result, we can talk some more about next steps. There's a "let's see how this goes first" feeling to the expression.

Structure

Note that in the pattern below, the sentence normally ends with 再说.

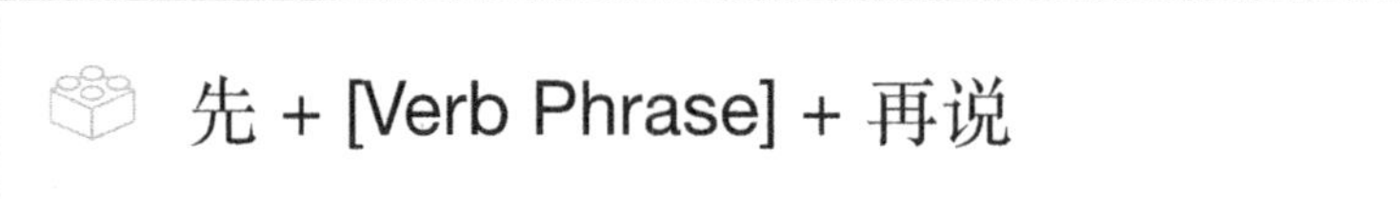

Examples

The 再说 part in the following sentences can be a little tricky to translate into English.

- 先吃饭再说。
  Xiān chīfàn zài shuō.
  Let's eat first, then we'll talk.
- 先休息一下再说。
  Xiān xiūxi yīxià zàishuō.
  Let's rest a little first, then we'll see.
- 你先看完再说。
  Nǐ xiān kàn wán zàishuō.
  Finish reading first, and then we'll see.
- 我先问一下老板再说。
  Wǒ xiān wèn yīxià lǎobǎn zàishuō.
  I'm going to ask the boss first before doing anything else.
- 你们先讨论一下再说。
  Nǐmen xiān tǎolùn yīxià zàishuō.
  You guys discuss a little first, then we'll figure out what to do next.

"and then..." with 接着

When describing a series of actions, steps, or consecutive events, your Chinese will sound more natural if you can diversify your conjunctions. 然后 (ránhòu) is most commonly used, a conjunction which means "and then." Alternatively, you can use 接着 (jiezhe), as a conjunction that means "next," or "afterwards."

A longer example to help you understand how they can all work together:

- 今天早上我起床以后 先 准备早饭，再 叫孩子们起床，接着 我们一起吃早饭，然后 我送他们去学校。
  Jīntiān zǎoshang wǒ qǐchuáng yǐhòu xiān zhǔnbèi zǎofàn, zài jiào háizi men qǐchuáng, jiēzhe wǒmen yīqǐ chī zǎofàn, ránhòu wǒ sòng tāmen qù xuéxiào.
  After I got up this morning, I first prepared breakfast, and then I woke up the kids. Next, we ate breakfast together. After that, I took them to school.

Similar to

- Expressing "again" in the future with "zai" (HSK2)
- Comparing "zai" and "you" (HSK3), page 229
- Expressing "again" in the past with "you" (HSK3), page 14
- Expressing "never again" with "zai ye bu" (HSK5)

Simultaneous tasks with "yibian"

Multitasking is everywhere in the modern world (what else are you doing while you read this?), but you if can *focus* for just a minute, you can learn a way to express simultaneous tasks in Chinese! This can be done with 一边 (yībiān).

Structure

To express that one thing is done *while* doing something else, the word 一边 (yībiān) is used.

> Subj. + 一边 + Verb (，) + 一边 + Verb

Note that you sometimes see 一边 (yībiān) shortened to 边 (biān) as well, which has a less formal feel.

Examples

- 不要 一边 吃东西，一边 说话。
  Bùyào yībiān chī dōngxi, yībiān shuōhuà.
  Don't speak while eating.
- 我常常 一边 洗澡，一边 唱歌。
  Wǒ chángcháng yībiān xǐzǎo, yībiān chànggē.
  I often sing songs while I take a shower.
- 孩子喜欢 一边 吃饭，一边 玩。
  Háizi xǐhuan yībiān chīfàn, yībiān wán.
  Children like to play while eating.
- 你喜欢 一边 听音乐，一边 做作业吗?
  Nǐ xǐhuan yībiān tīng yīnyuè, yībiān zuò zuòyè ma?
  Do you like to listen to music while doing homework?
- 我们 一边 走 一边 聊吧。
  Wǒmen yībiān zǒu yībiān liáo ba.
  Let's walk while we talk.

- 请你 一边 读 一边 写。
  Qǐng nǐ yībiān dú yībiān xiě.
  Please write as you read.
- 不要 一边 开车，一边 打电话。
  Bùyào yībiān kāichē, yībiān dǎ diànhuà.
  Don't talk on the phone while you drive.
- 老板喜欢 一边 抽烟，一边 工作。
  Lǎobǎn xǐhuan yībiān chōuyān, yībiān gōngzuò.
  The boss likes to smoke while working.
- 很多人都 一边 上班，一边 玩手机。
  Hěn duō rén dōu yībiān shàngbān, yībiān wán shǒujī.
  Many people play with their cell phones while working.
- 她常常 一边 做饭，一边 带孩子。
  Tā chángcháng yībiān zuòfàn, yībiān dài háizi.
  She often looks after the baby while cooking food.

You'll notice that the order of the two actions is sometimes different in the original Chinese and the English translations above. This is because the "main" action usually comes second in English (after the "while"), but first in Chinese. For example, "take a shower while singing" sounds strange in English, but "sing while taking a shower" doesn't.

Note that you must be actively doing both actions. That is, they have to be intentional. If you want to say something happened while another thing was happening, it would be better to use 的时候 (de shíhou).

Similar to

- Aspect particle "zhe" (HSK2, HSK3), page 86
- Expressing "when" with "de shihou" (HSK2)
- Expressing "both A and B" with "you" (HSK3), page 42
- Expressing "when" with "shi" (HSK3), page 68
- Expressing "along with···" with "suizhe" (HSK4)
- Expressing simultaneous actions with "yimian" (HSK5)

Using "always" as a complaint with "laoshi"

We have a few ways to say "always" in Chinese, and one of them is to use the word 老是 (lǎoshì). 老是 is usually used in the context of a complaint, like how your sister is "always" hogging the bathroom.

Structure

老是 is an adverb, usually translated into English as "always." It expresses that an action or a condition constantly repeats or continues and can be interchanged with the word 总是. However, 老是 also has an unsatisfied or frustrated tone.

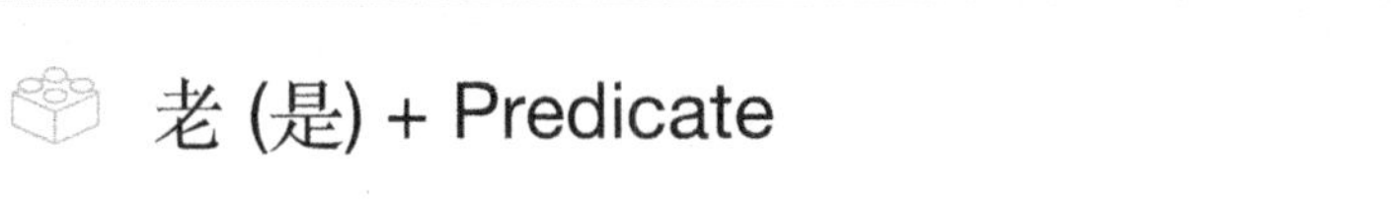

You can also use 老 instead of 老是. The predicate part of the pattern can be a verb or an adjective.

When 老是 is used together with an adjective, 老是 is usually followed by an adverb such as 不, 很, 非常, 这么, 那 etc.

Examples

- 你怎么 老是 加班?
  Nǐ zěnme lǎoshì jiābān?
  Why are you always working late?
- 那个孩子 老 说脏话。
  Nàge háizi lǎo shuō zānghuà.
  That kid always says bad words.
- 你怎么 老是 不高兴?
  Nǐ zěnme lǎoshì bù gāoxìng?
  How are you always unhappy?
- 你儿子上课的时候 老是 说话。
  Nǐ érzi shàngkè de shíhou lǎoshì shuōhuà.
  Your son talks all the time in class.
- 这个老师 老是 这么严肃。
  Zhège lǎoshī lǎoshì zhème yánsù.
  This teacher is always so serious.

- 别 老是 抱怨。
  Bié lǎoshì bàoyuàn.
  Stop complaining all the time.
- 这个机器 老是 出问题。
  Zhège jīqì lǎoshì chū wèntí.
  There is always something wrong with this machine.
- 他经常迟到，还 老是 找借口。
  Tā jīngcháng chídào, hái lǎoshì zhǎo jièkǒu.
  He's always late. And he always makes excuses.
- 奶奶 老是 忘带钥匙。
  Nǎinai lǎoshì wàng dài yàoshi.
  Grandma forgets to take her keys all the time.
- 你 老是 这么凶干吗?
  Nǐ lǎoshì zhème xiōng gànmá?
  Why are you always so mean?
- 他真讨厌，老是 跟朋友借钱。
  Tā zhēn tǎoyàn, lǎoshì gēn péngyou jièqián.
  He's such a nuisance. He's always borrowing money from his friends.

Similar to

- Expressing “always” with “zongshi” (HSK3), page 19
- Expressing “always” with “conglai” (HSK4)
- Comparing “buduan” and “buting” (HSK5)

Using "cai" for small numbers

The character 才 (cái) can be used to emphasize that a number is small, or less than expected.

Used as a Verb

Structure

In this case, 才 means "is only" or "only have."

才 + Number + [Measure Word] + Noun

In English, we often express this by using "only" or "just" to emphasize that the number is small.

Examples

- 你 才 二十岁?
  Nǐ cái èrshí suì?
  You're only twenty?
- 这个班 才 两个学生。
  Zhège bān cái liǎng gè xuéshēng.
  This class only has two students.
- 你的工资 才 两千?
  Nǐ de gōngzī cái liǎng qiān?
  Your salary is only two thousand?
  Probably RMB, per month
- 这顿饭 才 二十块，太便宜了！
  Zhè dùn fàn cái èrshí kuài. Tài piányi le!
  This meal only cost twenty kuai. It's too cheap!
- 你 才 一百斤，还要减肥?
  Nǐ cái yī bǎi jīn, hái yào jiǎnféi?
  You're only 100 jin and you still want to lose some weight?
  One "jin" = 500g

Used with a Verb

Structure

才 + Verb + Number + Measure Word + Noun

In this pattern, adding a 了 after the verb is optional.

Examples

- 她 才 来了两个月。
  Tā cái lái le liǎng gè yuè.
  She's been here for only two months.
- 这家店关门了？可是它 才 开业一个星期。
  Zhè jiā diàn guānmén le? Kěshì tā cái kāiyè yī gè xīngqī.
  This shop is out of business? But it's only been one week since it opened.
- 已经两天了，你 才 看完一页？
  Yǐjīng liǎng tiān le, nǐ cái kàn wán yī yè?
  It's been two days and you only finished reading one page?
- 我们 才 玩了一会儿，再玩一会儿吧？
  Wǒmen cái wán le yīhuìr, zài wán yīhuìr ba?
  We've only played for a short while. Can we play a little bit longer?
- 他们结婚了？他们 才 认识三个月！
  Tāmen jiéhūn le? Tāmen cái rènshi sān gè yuè!
  They got married? They've only known each other for three months!

Similar to

- Expressing lateness with “cai” (HSK3), page 27
- Expressing “small quantity” with “jiu” (HSK4)

Adjectives with "name" and "zheme"

In English, the words "that" and "so" are often used to emphasize the degree of an adjective (ex. "he is so tall" or "the food is so good"). In Chinese, 那么 (nàme) and 这么 (zhème) serve the same function.

Structure

All you have to do to use this grammar structure is put the 那么 or 这么 in front of the adjective.

 Subj. + 那么 / 这么 + Adj.

Examples

You could think of 这么 as "this" or "so," and 那么 as "that" or "so."

- 他说得 这么 快，你们听得懂吗？
  Tā shuō de zhème kuài, nǐmen tīng de dǒng ma?
  He speaks so fast. Can you guys understand?
- 我没想到这个考试 这么 难。
  Wǒ méi xiǎng dào zhège kǎoshì zhème nán.
  I didn't expect this exam would be this difficult.
- 雨 这么 大，明天再去吧。
  Yǔ zhème dà, míngtiān zài qù ba.
  The rain is so heavy. How about we go tomorrow?
- 你 那么 聪明，一定能猜到。
  Nǐ nàme cōngming, yīdìng néng cāi dào.
  You're so smart. You can definitely guess it.
- 老板 那么 忙，肯定没时间。
  Lǎobǎn nàme máng, kěndìng méi shíjiān.
  The boss is so busy. He definitely won't have time for this.
- 今天怎么 这么 冷？
  Jīntiān zěnme zhème lěng?
  Why is it so cold today?

- 你怎么 这么 没礼貌?
  Nǐ zěnme zhème méi lǐmào?
  How can you be this impolite?
- 这个外国人怎么会了解 那么 多中国历史?
  Zhège wàiguórén zěnme huì liǎojiě nàme duō Zhōngguó lìshǐ?
  How could this foreigner know that much about Chinese history?
- 中国人口 这么 多，当然会有很多社会问题。
  Zhōngguó rénkǒu zhème duō, dāngrán huì yǒu hěn duō shèhuì wèntí.
  China has such a big population. Of course there will be many social problems.
- 科技 那么 发达，什么都是有可能的。
  Kējì nàme fādá, shénme dōu shì yǒu kěnéng de.
  Science and technology is so developed. Anything is possible.

When to use which one

You might be thinking that since 这 ("this") and 那 ("that") have totally different meanings, how could they be used in an essentially interchangeable way? Well, there are some differences. 这么 is used when the subject is close by (either in space or in time), when you would say "this" or 这个. On the other hand, if the subject is far away (or in the past), you would likely use 那么.

Similar to

- Simple "noun + adjective" sentences (HSK1)
- Expressing "really" with "zhen" (HSK2)
- Superlative "zui" (HSK2)
- Adjectives with "-ji le" (HSK3), page 5
- Intensifying with "duo" (HSK3), page 46

Basic comparisons with "yiyang"

Along with 比 (bǐ) and 没有 (méiyǒu)[1], 一样 (yīyàng) is another way to make basic comparisons. However, 一样 (yīyàng) is used to express that two things are *the same* in some way.

Basic Usage

Structure

This simple structure is used for stating that two things are the same:

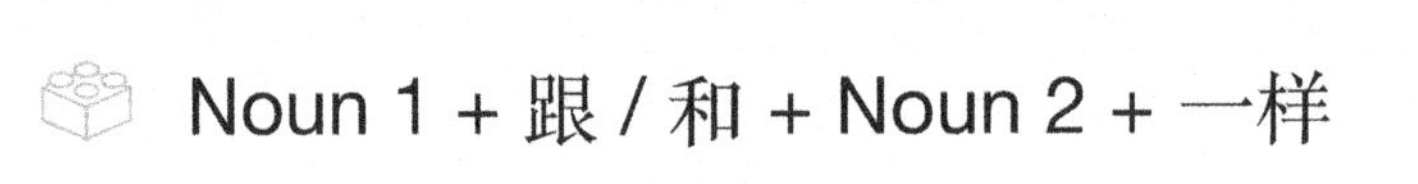

Examples

- 我 和 你 一样 。
  Wǒ hé nǐ yīyàng .
  I am the same as you.
- 他的性格 跟 他妈妈 一样 。
  Tā de xìnggé gēn tā māma yīyàng .
  He has the same personality as his mom.
- 北京的天气 和 上海不 一样 。
  Běijīng de tiānqì hé Shànghǎi bù yīyàng .
  The weather in Beijing and the weather in Shanghai are not alike.
- 这个词的意思 和 那个词 一样 吗?
  Zhège cí de yìsi hé nàge cí yīyàng ma?
  Are the meanings of this word and that word the same?
- 美国文化 跟 中国文化不 一样 。
  Měiguó wénhuà gēn Zhōngguó wénhuà bù yīyàng .
  American culture and Chinese culture are not the same.

---

1. Basic comparisons with "meiyou" (Grammar), page 109

一样 (yīyàng) with Adjectives

Structure

To add an adjective into the mix, just place it after 一样 (yīyàng):

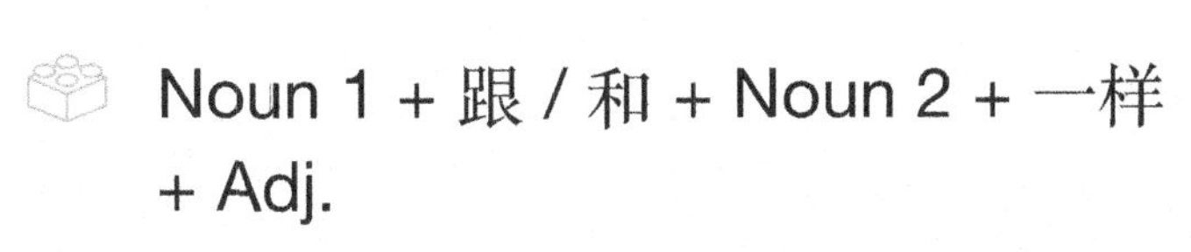

This describes Noun 1 as being as *adjective* as Noun 2.

Examples

- 你家跟我家一样大。
  Nǐ jiā gēn wǒ jiā yīyàng dà.
  Your house is just as big as mine.
- 她和她哥哥一样高。
  Tā hé tā gēge yīyàng gāo.
  She and her older brother are equally tall.
- 你的头发和我的头发一样长。
  Nǐ de tóufa hé wǒ de tóufa yīyàng cháng.
  You hair is as long as mine.
- 这里的天气跟我老家一样舒服。
  Zhèlǐ de tiānqì gēn wǒ lǎojiā yīyàng shūfu.
  The weather here is just as comfortable as my hometown's.
- 你跟老板一样忙吗?
  Nǐ gēn lǎobǎn yīyàng máng ma?
  Are you as busy as the boss is?

There is also a similar but more advanced usage of this pattern that uses 像 (xiàng).

Similar to

- Expressing “compared with” using “gen” (HSK3), page 196
- Expressing comparable degree with “you” (HSK3), page 203
- Comparing specifically with “xiang” (HSK5)

Expressing "both A and B" with "you"

When you're getting descriptive, you may find yourself wanting to use multiple adjectives at a time. The character 又 (yòu) can be used to give two qualities to something. Using the double 又 (yòu) structure is like saying that something is "both· · · and· · ·" in English.

Structure

The structure in Chinese is:

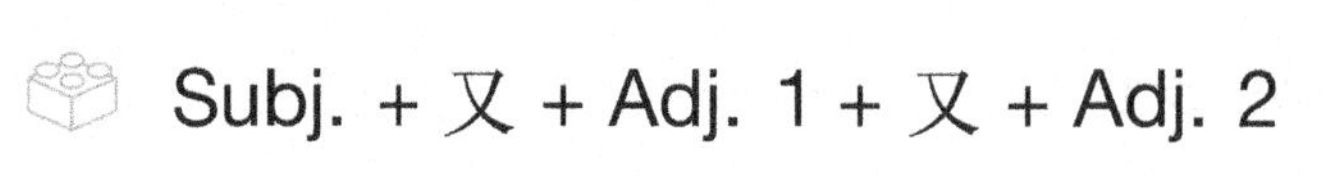

Subj. + 又 + Adj. 1 + 又 + Adj. 2

The two words shouldn't contrast in feeling. It is important to note they must both be bad or both be good.

Examples

- 她男朋友 又 高 又 帅。
  Tā nánpéngyou yòu gāo yòu shuài.
  Her boyfriend is both tall and handsome.
- 这个房子 又 大 又 亮。
  Zhège fángzi yòu dà yòu liàng.
  This house is both big and bright.
- 妈妈的头发 又 黑 又 亮。
  Māma de tóufa yòu hēi yòu liàng.
  Mom's hair is both black and shiny.
- 我姐姐 又 聪明 又 漂亮。
  Wǒ jiějie yòu cōngming yòu piàoliang.
  My older sister is both smart and beautiful.
- 中国菜 又 便宜 又 好吃。
  Zhōngguó cài yòu piányi yòu hǎochī.
  Chinese food is both cheap and good-tasting.
- 你们老板 又 年轻 又 有钱。
  Nǐmen lǎobǎn yòu niánqīng yòu yǒuqián.
  Your boss is both young and rich.

- 这里的咖啡 又 贵 又 难喝。
  Zhèlǐ de kāfēi yòu guì yòu nánhē.
  The coffee here is both expensive and bad-tasting.
- 我家小狗 又 可爱 又 听话。
  Wǒ jiā xiǎogǒu yòu kě'ài yòu tīnghuà.
  My family's dog is both cute and obedient.
- 上海的冬天 又 冷 又 湿。
  Shànghǎi de dōngtiān yòu lěng yòu shī.
  Winter here in Shanghai is both cold and humid.
- 她小时候 又 矮 又 瘦。
  Tā xiǎoshíhou yòu ǎi yòu shòu.
  She was both short and thin when she was young.

Similar to

- Simple "noun + adjective" sentences (HSK1)
- Expressing "both· · · and· · ·" with "ji…you" (HSK4)

Expressing "rather" with "bijiao"

The word 比较 (bǐjiào) can be a verb which means "to compare." But it can also be an adverb meaning "comparatively" or "rather."

Used with Adjectives

Structure

The adverb 比较 can be used to express "quite," "rather," or "relatively."

Examples

- 这个问题 比较 简单。
  Zhège wèntí bǐjiào jiǎndān.
  This question is quite easy.
- 我觉得这个价格 比较 贵。
  Wǒ juéde zhège jiàgé bǐjiào guì.
  I think this price is rather expensive.
- 我家离市中心 比较 近。
  Wǒ jiā lí shìzhōngxīn bǐjiào jìn.
  My place is relatively close to downtown.
- 大城市的工作压力 比较 大。
  Dà chéngshì de gōngzuò yālì bǐjiào dà.
  Jobs in big cities have quite a lot of pressure.
- 你上班坐地铁 比较 方便吧?
  Nǐ shàngbān zuò dìtiě bǐjiào fāngbiàn ba?
  To get to work, it's quite convenient for you to take the subway, right?

Used with Verbs

比较 can also be used with psychological verbs.

Structure

Subj. + 比较 + [Verb Phrase]

Examples

- 我 比较 讨厌男人说脏话。
  Wǒ bǐjiào tǎoyàn nánrén shuō zānghuà.
  I quite hate it when men use foul language.
- 你 比较 喜欢用 Gmail 还是 Hotmail？
  Note that for this phrase, the translation is a totally different verb.
  Nǐ bǐjiào xǐhuan yòng Gmail háishì Hotmail?
  Do you prefer to use Gmail or Hotmail?
- 我父母 比较 反对我找外国男朋友。
  Wǒ fùmǔ bǐjiào fǎnduì wǒ zhǎo wàiguó nánpéngyou.
  My parents rather object to me seeking a foreign boyfriend.
- 民众 比较 支持新的就业政策。
  Mínzhòng bǐjiào zhīchí xīn de jiùyè zhèngcè.
  The public rather supports the new employment policy.
- 老板通常 比较 关注结果，不是过程。
  Lǎobǎn tōngcháng bǐjiào guānzhù jiéguǒ, bù shì guòchéng.
  The boss usually pays more attention to results and not process.

Similar to

- Expressing "a little too" with "you dian" (HSK2)
- Moderating positive adjectives with "hai" (HSK2)
- Superlative "zui" (HSK2)
- Special verbs with "hen" (HSK3), page 131
- Expressing "quite" with "ting" (HSK4)
- Expressing "a bit too" (HSK5)
- Making judgments with "suan" (HSK5)

Intensifying with "duo"

One way to intensify a sentence is to make it an exclamation. To do this, you can use 多 (duō).

Structure

As well as asking about degree, you can also use 多 (duō) to intensify adjectives.

Examples

- 一个人 多 好！
  Yīgèrén duō hǎo!
  It's so nice being alone!
- 你女儿 多 聪明啊！
  Nǐ nǚér duō cōngming a!
  Your daughter is so smart!
- 今天天气 多 舒服！
  Jīntiān tiānqì duō shūfu!
  Today's weather is so nice!
- 你看这个地方，多 美啊！
  Nǐ kàn zhège dìfang, duō měi a!
  Look at this place, it is so beautiful!
- 学中文 多 有意思啊！
  Xué Zhōngwén duō yǒu yìsi a!
  Studying Chinese is so interesting!
- 坐地铁 多 方便！
  Zuò dìtiě duō fāngbiàn!
  How convenient it is to take the metro!
- 你看这个小狗，多 可爱！
  Nǐ kàn zhège xiǎogǒu, duō kě'ài!
  Look at this puppy! It is so cute!

- 这样做 多 麻烦！
  Zhèyàng zuò duō máfan!
  Doing it this way is so troublesome!
- 这些菜 多 好吃啊！
  Zhèxiē cài duō hǎochī a!
  These foods are so delicious!
- 你男朋友 多 帅啊！
  Nǐ nánpéngyou duō shuài a!
  Your boyfriend is so handsome!

多 (duō) can be compared to 很 (hěn) in this case. If you use 很 (hěn) instead of 多 (duō), the meaning is basically the same. However 很 (hěn) is also used to make simple "noun + adjective" sentences, which might not be exclamatory at all, whereas 多 (duō) is used only for excited exclamations.

Similar to

- Asking about degree with "duo" (HSK1, HSK2)
- Indicating a number in excess (HSK2)
- Adjectives with "name" and "zheme" (HSK3), page 38
- Doing something more with "duo" (HSK4)

Modifying nouns with adjective + "de"

One of the best ways to use the common character 的 (de) is to spice up your nouns with adjectives. By using 的 (de), we can connect sassy adjectives to otherwise boring nouns.

With a Noun

Structure

A very common way to modify nouns is to attach an adjective to them using 的 (de).

Adj. + 的 + Noun

This structure comes up extremely frequently and is an easy way to attribute features to nouns. Occasionally you will see this 的 (de) omitted, but note that if the adjective has two characters (e.g. 漂亮 (piàoliang) or 高兴 (gāoxìng)), the 的 (de) is generally required.

Examples

- 漂亮的 女孩儿
  piàoliang de nǚháir
  beautiful girl
- 辣的 菜
  là de cài
  spicy food
- 可爱的 宝宝
  kě'ài de bǎobao
  a cute baby
- 我喜欢 新鲜的 果汁。
  Wǒ xǐhuan xīnxiān de guǒzhī.
  I like fresh fruit juice.
- 他常常买 便宜的 东西。
  Tā chángcháng mǎi piányi de dōngxi.
  He often buys cheap stuff.

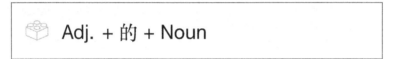

Without a Noun

Structure

In some cases, it is possible to drop the noun from the pattern, and just use the adjective + 的 (de). This is kind of like saying "the big one" or "the red one" in English. In Chinese the 的 (de) serves the same purpose as the English word "one." By using this pattern, you can avoid repeating the same noun over and over again unnecessarily. Just be sure the other person is already clear which "one" you're referring to when using this pattern!

Examples

A: 孩子喜欢吃什么东西?

Háizi xǐhuan chī shénme dōngxi?

What food do children like to eat?

B: 甜的。

Tián de.

Sweet food.

A: 你喜欢哪种女孩?

Nǐ xǐhuan nǎ zhǒng nǚhái?

What kind of girls do you like?

B: 漂亮的。

Piàoliang de.

Pretty ones.

A: 你要喝冷水还是热水?

Nǐ yào hē lěng shuǐ háishì rè shuǐ ?

Do you want to drink cold or hot water?

B: 冷的。

Lěng de.

Cold.

A: 你想找什么样的男朋友？

Nǐ xiǎng zhǎo shénmeyàng de nánpéngyou?

What kind of boyfriend do you want to find?

B: 有钱的。

Yǒuqián de.

A rich one.

A: 你不喜欢吃什么菜？

Nǐ bù xǐhuan chī shénme cài?

Which foods do you not like to eat?

B: 辣的。

Là de.

Spicy ones.

Similar to

- Expressing close possession without "de" (HSK1)
- Expressing possession with "de" (HSK1)
- Modifying nouns with phrase + "de" (HSK2)
- Turning adjectives into adverbs (HSK3), page 12

Expressing "or" in statements

In English, "or" can be used to connect words when offering or considering choices ("do you want chicken or beef?"). It can also be used as an "or" *statement* ("it doesn't matter if we eat chicken or beef"), in Chinese, this is what 或者 (huòzhě) is used for.

Structure

While 还是 (háishì) is used for "or" in questions[1], 或者 (huòzhě) is used for "or" in **statements.**

 Possibility 1 + 或者 + Possibility 2

Examples

- 我喝 咖啡 或者 茶 ，都行。
  Wǒ hē kāfēi huòzhě chá , dōu xíng.
  I drink coffee or tea. Either is OK.
- 星期六 或者 星期天 ，都可以。
  Xīngqīliù huòzhě Xīngqītiān , dōu kěyǐ.
  Saturday or Sunday are both OK.
- 今天晚上我想吃 披萨 或者 寿司 。
  Jīntiān wǎnshang wǒ xiǎng chī pīsà huòzhě shòusī .
  Tonight I would like to eat pizza or sushi.
- 周末的时候，我喜欢在家 做饭 或者 看电影 。
  Zhōumò de shíhou, wǒ xǐhuan zài jiā zuòfàn huòzhě kàn diànyǐng .
  During the weekend, I like to cook or watch movies at home.
- 你去 或者 她去 ，都可以。
  Nǐ qù huòzhě tā qù , dōu kěyǐ.
  You go or she goes, either way is fine.

---

1. Offering choices with "haishi" (Grammar), page 59

- 下班以后 我去你家 或者 你来我家 ，都可以。
  Xiàbān yǐhòu wǒ qù nǐ jiā huòzhě nǐ lái wǒ jiā , dōu kěyǐ.
  After work I will go to your house, or you can come to my house, either way is fine.
- 下个月我打算去 杭州 或者 苏州 旅行。
  Xià gè yuè wǒ dǎsuàn qù Hángzhōu huòzhě Sūzhōu lǚxíng.
  Next month I plan to go to Hangzhou or Suzhou to travel.
- 我们可以 坐飞机 或者 坐高铁 去。
  Wǒmen kěyǐ zuò fēijī huòzhě zuò gāotiě qù.
  We can go by plane or by high-speed train.
- 晚饭以后我和家人 聊天 或者 看电视 。
  Wǎnfàn yǐhòu wǒ hé jiārén liáotiān huòzhě kàn diànshì .
  After dinner I chat with or watch TV with my family.
- 你可以用 手机 或者 电脑 上网。
  Nǐ kěyǐ yòng shǒujī huòzhě diànnǎo shàngwǎng.
  You can use either a cell phone or computer to go online.

Similar to

- Comparing “haishi” and “huozhe” (HSK3), page 234
- Offering choices with “haishi” (HSK3), page 59
- Expressing “how about” with “yaobu” (HSK5)
- Providing two options with double “huozhe” (HSK5)

Expressing "then… " with "name"

English speakers often like to connect sentences together with "so..." and also try to do this in Chinese with the word 所以 (suǒyǐ). In reality, they should mostly be using 那么 (nàme).

Structure

When expressing "so…," you can use 那么 or 那 in order to begin a judgment or result from previous context. An example of this in English would be: "so, what should we do?"

Situation ，那么 + Suggestion / Decision

Examples

- 他不听，那 我应该怎么办？
  Tā bù tīng, nà wǒ yīnggāi zěnme bàn?
  He won't listen. So what should I do?
- 你说这个办法不行，那 你有别的办法吗？
  Nǐ shuō zhège bànfǎ bù xíng, nà nǐ yǒu bié de bànfǎ ma?
  You said this idea is not going to work. So do you have any other ideas?
- 大家都到了，那么 我们开始吧。
  Dàjiā dōu dào le, nàme wǒmen kāishǐ ba.
  Everybody is here, so let's begin.
- 雨停了，那 我们走吧。
  Yǔ tíng le, nà wǒmen zǒu ba.
  The rain has stopped, so let's leave.
- 你说得有道理，那么 就这么办吧。
  Nǐ shuō de yǒu dàolǐ, nàme jiù zhème bàn ba.
  What you said makes sense, so let's just do that.

- 他学过十年中文？ 那 他的中文说得很好吧？
  Tā xué guo shí nián Zhōngwén? Nà tā de Zhōngwén shuō de hěn hǎo ba?
  He's studied Chinese for ten years? So he must speak Chinese really well, then?
- 他表现不错， 那么 让他通过吧。
  Tā biǎoxiàn bùcuò, nàme ràng tā tōngguò ba.
  He performed well, so let's let him pass.
- 会议时间已经确定了， 那 你快点去安排吧。
  Huìyì shíjiān yǐjīng quèdìng le, nà nǐ kuài diǎn qù ānpái ba.
  The meeting time has been set, so please arrange it soon.
- 他们没有提前通知我们， 那么 这是他们的责任。
  Tāmen méiyǒu tíqián tōngzhī wǒmen, nàme zhè shì tāmen de zérèn.
  They didn't notify us in advance, so this is their responsibility.
- 实现这个目标应该不难， 那么 我们一起努力吧。
  Shíxiàn zhège mùbiāo yīnggāi bù nán, nàme wǒmen yīqǐ nǔlì ba.
  It shouldn't be difficult to reach this goal, so let's all really make an effort.

Similar to

- Cause and effect with “yinwei” and “suoyi” (HSK2)

Expressing "with" with "gen"

Using 跟 (gēn) to express "with" is so simple and helpful, after studying it briefly, it will always be *with* you! 跟 (gēn) is a very common word that will help complete many other sentence structures.

Structure

The preposition 跟 (gēn) is commonly used to express "with." Just remember that the "with" phrase comes *before the verb*.

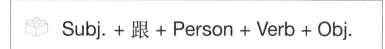

> Subj. + 跟 + Person + Verb + Obj.

The word 一起 (yīqǐ) is used a lot with 跟 (gēn), expressing the idea of "doing something *together with* somebody." It may seem kind of redundant, but it's totally normal in Chinese to use both.

Also, for most of the examples below, 跟 (gēn) is interchangeable with 和 (hé), which you may remember, also means "and," just like 跟 (gēn) does.

> Subj. + 跟 + Person + 一起 + Verb + Obj.

Certain Chinese verbs use 跟 (gēn) a lot, so be on the lookout for them (examples below)!

Examples

- 我昨天跟朋友去海滩了。
  Wǒ zuótiān gēn péngyou qù hǎitān le.
  I went to the beach with friends yesterday.
- 不要跟我说话！
  Bùyào gēn wǒ shuōhuà!
  Don't talk to me!
- 我明天要跟新客户见面。
  Wǒ míngtiān yào gēn xīn kèhù jiànmiàn.
  I'm going to meet new clients tomorrow.

- 你什么时候 跟 你女朋友 结婚 ?

  Nǐ shénme shíhou gēn nǐ nǚpéngyou jiéhūn ?

  When are you gonna marry your girlfriend?

- 你喜欢 跟 你父母 聊天 吗?

  Nǐ xǐhuan gēn nǐ fùmǔ liáotiān ma?

  Do you like to talk with your parents?

- 你想 跟 我 一起去 吗?

  Nǐ xiǎng gēn wǒ yīqǐ qù ma?

  Do you want to go with me?

- 请你们 跟 老师 一起读 。

  Qǐng nǐmen gēn lǎoshī yīqǐ dú .

  Please read together with the teacher.

- 下周谁 跟 老板 一起出差 ?

  Xià zhōu shéi gēn lǎobǎn yīqǐ chūchāi ?

  Who is going on a business trip together with the boss next week?

- 结婚以后，你想 跟 父母 一起住 吗?

  Jiéhūn yǐhòu, nǐ xiǎng gēn fùmǔ yīqǐ zhù ma?

  Do you want live together with your parents after you get married?

- 今年中秋节你会 跟 家人 一起过 吗?

  Jīnnián Zhōngqiūjié nǐ huì gēn jiārén yīqǐ guò ma?

  Are you going to spend this Mid-Autumn Festival with your family?

Note: One of the most common beginner mistakes is to fail to use 跟 (gēn) with 见面 (jiànmiàn), "to meet." It might help to think of 见面 (jiànmiàn) as "to meet *with* (somebody)," the "with" cluing you into the fact that you need a 跟 (gēn) in there. The verbs 结婚 (jiéhūn), "to marry," and 聊天 (liáotiān), "to chat" are used with 跟 (gēn) in the exact same way.

Check out the examples below:

✘ 我要 见面 你。

Wǒ yào jiànmiàn nǐ.

✔ 我要 跟 你 见面 。

Wǒ yào gēn nǐ jiànmiàn .

I want to meet with you.

✗ 我昨天 见面 他了。
Wǒ zuótiān jiànmiàn tā le.

✓ 我昨天 跟 他 见面 了。
Wǒ zuótiān gēn tā jiànmiàn le.
I met with him yesterday.

✗ 你什么时候 见面 她?
Nǐ shénme shíhou jiànmiàn tā?

✓ 你什么时候 跟 她 见面 ?
Nǐ shénme shíhou gēn tā jiànmiàn ?
When are you going to meet with her?

✗ 明天我要 见面 我男朋友的家人。
Míngtiān wǒ yào jiànmiàn wǒ nánpéngyou de jiārén.

✓ 明天我要 跟 我男朋友的家人 见面 。
Míngtiān wǒ yào gēn wǒ nánpéngyou de jiārén jiànmiàn .
Tomorrow I am going to meet my boyfriend's family.

✗ 你有没有 见面 过 Obama?
Nǐ yǒu méiyǒu jiànmiàn guo Obama?

✓ 你有没有 跟 Obama 见过面 ?
Nǐ yǒu méiyǒu gēn Obama jiàn guo miàn ?
Have you ever met Obama?

Later on you'll learn more about why this is the case, but for now just memorize the correct pattern.

Where 和 (hé) and 跟 (gēn) Differ

We mentioned earlier that 跟 (gēn) is essentially interchangeable with 和 (hé). There's at least one common usage where this is not the case, though:

✗ 和 我读。
Hé wǒ dú.

✓ 跟 我读。
Gēn wǒ dú.
Read after me.

The reason is that although 跟 (gēn) and 和 (hé) can both mean "and" or "with," the word 跟 (gēn) also has a sense of "to follow" embedded in it. There's a before/after aspect.

The following sentences are both correct, because they're simultaneous rather than before/after:

- ✔ 和我一起读。
  Hé wǒ yīqǐ dú.
- ✔ 跟我一起读。
  Gēn wǒ yīqǐ dú.
  Read with me.

Because of this slight difference between 跟 (gēn) and 和 (hé), it's recommended to start out using 跟 (gēn) to mean "with."

Similar to

- Expressing "together" with "yiqi" (HSK2)
- Verbs preceded by "gei" (HSK2)
- Expressing "towards" with "xiang" (HSK3), page 105
- Comparing "gen" and "dui" (HSK5)

Offering choices with "haishi"

还是 (háishì) is used in Chinese to provide options in a **question**. This is equivalent to one of our uses of "or" in English.

Simplest Form

Structure

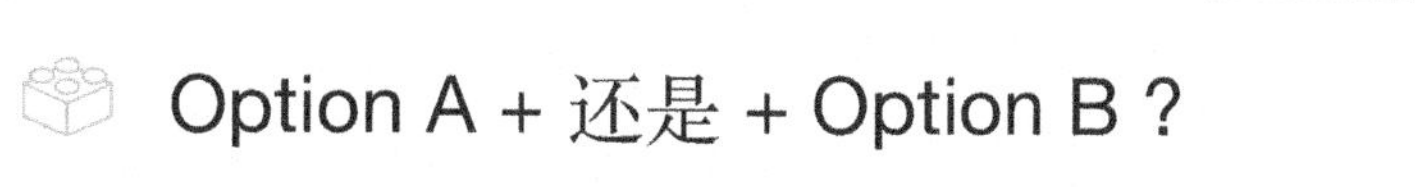

Option A + 还是 + Option B ?

When you're asked a question of this form, there are two ways you're expected to answer: either Option A or Option B. (Pick one, but not both.) It's not that no other answers are possible, it's that usually when you're asked a question this way, the person asking expects you to just choose one. For example, if asked if you'd like to drink coffee or tea, most people are going to choose one or the other, not ask for both. 还是 (háishì) is used to ask people to make that choice between the two.

Examples

- 我 还是 他 ?
  Wǒ háishì tā?
  Me or him?
- 一个 还是 两个 ?
  Yī gè háishì liǎng gè ?
  One or two?
- 辣的 还是 不辣的 ?
  Là de háishì bù là de ?
  Spicy or non-spicy?
- 冰的 还是 热的 ?
  Bīng de háishì rè de ?
  Cold or hot?
- 上海 还是 北京 ?
  Shànghǎi háishì Běijīng?
  Shanghai or Beijing?

The eternal China expat question! Choose wisely...

Full Sentence Form

Structure

You can take the structure above, add a subject and a verb, and create all kinds of questions with the following structure:

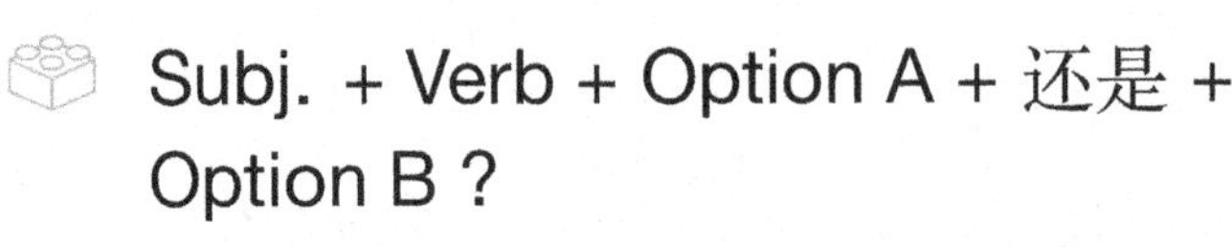

Examples

- 这是 水 还是 酒 ?
  Zhè shì shuǐ háishì jiǔ ?
  Is this water or alcohol?
- 他是 美国人 还是 英国人 ?
  Tā shì Měiguó rén háishì Yīngguó rén ?
  Is he American or British?
- 你喜欢 我 还是 我的钱 ?
  Nǐ xǐhuan wǒ háishì wǒ de qián ?
  Do you like me or my money?
- 你要喝 茶 还是 咖啡 ?
  Nǐ yào hē chá háishì kāfēi ?
  Do you want to drink tea or coffee?
- 你们想吃 中国菜 还是 法国菜 ?
  Nǐmen xiǎng chī Zhōngguó cài háishì Fǎguó cài ?
  Do you want to eat Chinese food or French food?

Please note that 还是 (háishì) is for offering options in a **question**. It should not be used for "or" in statements[1].

Similar to

- Affirmative-negative question (HSK2)
- Comparing "haishi" and "huozhe" (HSK3), page 234

1. Expressing "or" in statements (Grammar), page 51

- Expressing "or" in statements (HSK3), page 51
- Reviewing options with "ba" (HSK4)

Before a specific time with "yiqian"

As well as talking about the past in general[1], you can use 以前 (yǐqián) to talk about things that happened *before* a specific time.

Structure

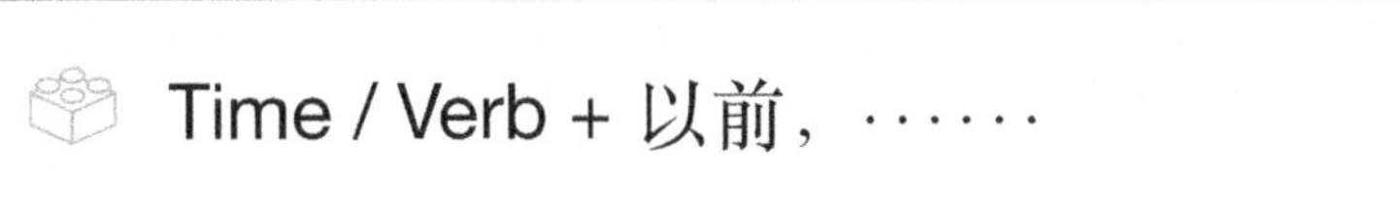

Time / Verb + 以前，……

The time can be a specific time, or an action (technically, "*when* the action was done").

Examples

- 吃饭 以前 ，你洗手了吗?
  Chīfàn yǐqián, nǐ xǐ shǒu le ma?
  Did you wash your hands before eating?
- 睡觉 以前 ，不要吃东西。
  Shuìjiào yǐqián, bùyào chī dōngxi.
  Don't eat anything before you go to sleep.
- 两年 以前 ，你认识他吗?
  Liǎng nián yǐqián, nǐ rènshi tā ma?
  Did you know him two years ago?
- 星期五 以前 ，你要做完这些工作。
  Xīngqīwǔ yǐqián, nǐ yào zuò wán zhèxiē gōngzuò.
  You need to finish this work before Friday.
- 上大学 以前 ，你来过上海吗?
  Shàng dàxué yǐqián, nǐ lái guo shànghǎi ma?
  Before you went to college, did you ever come to Shanghai?
- 结婚 以前 ，你应该先买房子。
  Jiéhūn yǐqián, nǐ yīnggāi xiān mǎi fángzi.
  Before getting married, you should first buy a house.

1. Expressing "before" in general with "yiqian" (Grammar), page 64

- 二十年 以前 ，这里是一个公园。
  Èrshí nián yǐqián, zhèlǐ shì yī gè gōngyuán.
  Twenty years ago, this was a park.
- 几个月 以前 ，他们分手了。
  Jǐ gè yuè yǐqián, tāmen fēnshǒu le.
  They broke up a few months ago.
- 毕业 以前 ，我要找到工作。
  Bìyè yǐqián, wǒ yào zhǎodào gōngzuò.
  I need to find a job before graduation.
- 当总统 以前 ，Obama 没有白头发。
  Dāng zǒngtǒng yǐqián, Obama méiyǒu bái tóufa.
  Before he became the president, Obama didn't have white hair.

Note that this use of 以前 (yǐqián) can also be shortened to 前 (qián).

Similar to

- Structure of times (advanced) (HSK1, HSK3), page 79
- Structure of times (basic) (HSK1, HSK3), page 83
- Expressing “when” with “de shihou” (HSK2)
- Expressing “before” in general with “yiqian” (HSK3), page 64
- Expressing “when” with “shi” (HSK3), page 68
- Expressing “once” with “cengjing” (HSK5)

Expressing "before" in general with "yiqian"

To talk about things that previously occurred, you can use the word 以前 (yǐqián). You can use this structure to talk about actions that happened at some unspecified time in the past.

Structure

One way to use 以前 (yǐqián) is to start the sentence with it. This is like starting off a sentence in English with "before..." or "in the past..."

以前 + Subj. + Verb + Obj.

You can also move 以前 (yǐqián) to right after the subject, and it's also correct.

Subj. + 以前 + Verb + Obj.

Examples

- 以前 我不会说中文。
  Yǐqián wǒ bù huì shuō Zhōngwén.
  Before, I could not speak Chinese.
- 你 以前 住在哪儿?
  Nǐ yǐqián zhù zài nǎr?
  Before, where did you live?
- 以前 我不认识他。
  Yǐqián wǒ bù rènshi tā.
  Before, I didn't know him.
- 以前 他是我们的客户吗?
  Yǐqián tā shì wǒmen de kèhù ma?
  Was he our client before?

- 以前 他是一个服务员，现在是老板。
  Yǐqián tā shì yī gè fúwùyuán, xiànzài shì lǎobǎn.
  Before, he was a waiter. Now, he is a boss.
- 我父母 以前 都是老师。
  Wǒ fùmǔ yǐqián dōu shì lǎoshī.
  Before, both of my parents were teachers.
- 爸爸 以前 很喜欢抽烟。
  Bàba yǐqián hěn xǐhuan chōuyān.
  Before, dad really liked smoking.
- 姐姐 以前 有一个很有钱的男朋友。
  Jiějie yǐqián yǒu yī gè hěn yǒuqián de nánpéngyou.
  My older sister had a very rich boyfriend before.
- 他们 以前 没有钱，可是很快乐。
  Tāmen yǐqián méiyǒu qián, kěshì hěn kuàilè.
  They didn't have much money before, but they were happy.
- 我男朋友 以前 在美国工作，现在在中国工作。
  Wǒ nánpéngyou yǐqián zài Měiguó gōngzuò, xiànzài zài Zhōngguó gōngzuò.
  Before, my boyfriend worked in the USA. Now, he works in China.

Similar to

- Before a specific time with "yiqian" (HSK1, HSK3), page 62
- Expressing "once" with "cengjing" (HSK5)

Expressing "just now" with "gangcai"

In order to say that something "just now" occurred, use the time noun 刚才 (gāngcái). It can be placed in front of the verb or the subject of a statement.

Structure

This grammar structure is pretty straightforward. Similar to the English "just now," you can put 刚才 (gāngcái) right before the verb in a sentence. It can also come before or after the subject.

Examples

- 你刚才说什么了?
  Nǐ gāngcái shuō shénme le?
  What did you just say?
- 刚才谁来了?
  Gāngcái shéi lái le?
  Who came just now?
- 刚才你去哪儿了?
  Gāngcái nǐ qù nǎr le?
  Where did you go just now?
- 刚才我去洗手间了。
  Gāngcái wǒ qù xǐshǒujiān le.
  I just went to the restroom.
- 老板刚才生气了。
  Lǎobǎn gāngcái shēngqì le.
  The boss just got angry.
- 你们刚才在看什么?
  Nǐmen gāngcái zài kàn shénme?
  What were you looking at just now?

- 不好意思，我 刚才 出去 了。
  Bù hǎoyìsi, wǒ gāngcái chūqù le.
  I'm sorry, I just now stepped out.
- 宝宝 刚才 哭 了。
  Bǎobao gāngcái kū le.
  The baby just cried.
- 他们 刚才 去 开会 了。
  Tāmen gāngcái qù kāihuì le.
  They just went to a meeting.
- 刚才 有人 找 你。
  Gāngcái yǒu rén zhǎo nǐ.
  Just now, there was someone looking for you.

Note that for all of those cases, we're talking about something that happened *just now*, as in, within the past 5 minutes or so. If you're talking about something that "just happened" yesterday or last week, don't use 刚才 (gāngcái), use 刚 (gāng).

Similar to

- Comparing "gang" and "gangcai" (HSK3, HSK4), page 221
- Expressing "just" with "gang" (HSK4)

Expressing "when" with "shi"

By now you should now how to express "when" using 的时候 (de shíhou). But there's also a slightly shorter, more formal way to do it: simply use 时 (shí) all by itself. (No 的!)

Structure

Time + 时，Subj. ……

As time words can appear before or after the subject, you can also place the "Time + 时" phrase after the subject.

Examples

- 考试 时 不要说话。
  Kǎoshì shí bùyào shuōhuà.
  Don't talk when you're taking a test.
- 我面试 时 经常会问这个问题。
  Wǒ miànshì shí jīngcháng huì wèn zhège wèntí.
  I often ask this question during job interviews.
- 会议结束 时 老板才来。
  Huìyì jiéshù shí lǎobǎn cái lái.
  The boss didn't show up until the meeting was over.
- 我生气 时 不想说话。
  Wǒ shēngqì shí bù xiǎng shuōhuà.
  I don't want to talk when I'm angry.
- 他们大学毕业 时 就分手了。
  Tāmen dàxué bìyè shí jiù fēnshǒu le.
  They broke up when they graduated from college.
- 飞机起飞 时 ，他关了手机和电脑。
  Fēijī qǐfēi shí, tā guān le shǒujī hé diànnǎo.
  When the plane took off, he turned off his cell phone and computer.

- 他太太提出离婚 时 ，他很惊讶。
  Tā tàitai tíchū líhūn shí, tā hěn jīngyà.
  He was very surprised when his wife asked for a divorce.
- 他去世 时 ，他的孩子都不在身边。
  Tā qùshì shí, tā de háizi dōu bù zài shēnbiān.
  His children weren't with him when he passed away.
- 我们公司成立 时 只有三个人。
  Wǒmen gōngsī chénglì shí zhǐyǒu sān gè rén.
  There were only three people when this company was founded.
- 跟别人说话 时 不要玩手机。
  Gēn biérén shuōhuà shí bùyào wán shǒujī.
  Don't play with your cell phone when you're talking with other people.

There are also two great examples of this pattern in the poem below:

你

一会儿看我

一会儿看云

你看我时很远

你看云时很近

Similar to

- Expressing "when" with "de shihou" (HSK2)

In the future in general with "yihou"

Similar to talking about things in the past, talking about things in the future is very straight forward. You can use the simple but useful 以后 (yǐhòu), which also means "later."

Structure

To talk about things happening at some unspecified time in the future, you can use 以后 (yǐhòu). The structure is:

> 以后 + Subj. + Verb + Obj.

You can also move 以后 (yǐhòu) to right after the subject, and it's also correct.

> Subj. + 以后 + Verb + Obj.

This can be used to talk about actions in the future, or to talk about events that happened *after other events* in a story.

Examples

In the examples below, the translation "in the future" is used, because using "later" for 以后 (yǐhòu) either sounds weird, or makes it sound like it's going to happen really soon (just a little later), rather than at some indefinite point in the future, which is what is meant.

- 以后 你们会想我吗?
  Yǐhòu nǐmen huì xiǎng wǒ ma?
  In the future, will you miss me?
- 以后 你想来中国吗?
  Yǐhòu nǐ xiǎng lái Zhōngguó ma?
  In the future, do you want to come to China?
- 我 以后 不喝酒了。
  Wǒ yǐhòu bù hējiǔ le.
  I will not drink alcohol in the future.

- 我们 以后 不在这里工作了。
  Wǒmen yǐhòu bù zài zhèlǐ gōngzuò le.
  We will not work here in the future.
- 你儿子 以后 想做什么?
  Nǐ érzi yǐhòu xiǎng zuò shénme?
  In the future, what does your son want to do?
- 以后 你们想去哪儿工作?
  Yǐhòu nǐmen xiǎng qù nǎr gōngzuò?
  In the future, where would you like to work?
- 以后 我们会有一些新的同事。
  Yǐhòu wǒmen huì yǒu yīxiē xīn de tóngshì.
  We will have some new co-workers in the future.
- 以后 你可以住在这里。
  Yǐhòu nǐ kěyǐ zhù zài zhèlǐ.
  In the future, you can live here.
- 他们 以后 会结婚吗?
  Tāmen yǐhòu huì jiéhūn ma?
  Will they get married in the future?
- 你 以后 不要跟他见面了。
  Nǐ yǐhòu bùyào gēn tā jiànmiàn le.
  In the future, stop seeing him.

Similar to

- After a specific time with "yihou" (HSK1)
- Expressing "when" with "de shihou" (HSK2)
- Expressing "before" in general with "yiqian" (HSK3), page 64
- Expressing "when" with "shi" (HSK3), page 68
- Sequencing past events with "houlai" (HSK3), page 72
- Comparing "yihou" "ranhou" "houlai" (HSK5)
- Comparing "yihou" and "zhihou" (HSK5)
- Expressing future with "jiang" (HSK5)

Sequencing past events with “houlai”

The word 后来 (hòulái) is used to sequence past events in the same way that “afterward” is in English. Something very important to note is that 后来 can only be used with two events **that have already occurred**.

Structure

[Past Event 1] , 后来, [Past Event 2]

Examples

Here are some examples of this pattern in action:

- 他说他会来，后来 又说不来了。
  Tā shuō tā huì lái, hòulái yòu shuō bù lái le.
  He said he would come, but later he said that he's not coming.
- 他们上周吵架了，后来 和好了。
  Tāmen shàng zhōu chǎojià le, hòulái hé hǎo le.
  They had a fight last week, and they made up afterwards.
- 他以前是厨师，后来 当了老板。
  Tā yǐqián shì chúshī, hòulái dāng le lǎobǎn.
  He used to be a chef. Afterwards, he became the owner.
- 我昨晚走得早，不知道 后来 发生了什么。
  Wǒ zuówǎn zǒu de zǎo, bù zhīdào hòulái fāshēng le shénme.
  I left early yesterday evening, so I don't know what happened afterwards.
- 开始我父母不同意，后来 他们同意了。
  Kāishǐ wǒ fùmǔ bù tóngyì, hòulái tāmen tóngyì le.
  My parents disapproved in the beginning, but they approved later.
- 空调我上个月修好了，后来 又坏了。
  Kōngtiáo wǒ shàng gè yuè xiū hǎo le, hòulái yòu huài le.
  I fixed the air conditioner last month, but it broke again afterwards.

- 他们在一起差不多三年，后来分手了。

  Tāmen zài yīqǐ chàbuduō sān nián, hòulái fēnshǒu le.

  They had been together for about three years. But they broke up afterwards.

- 她以前是兼职老师，后来做了全职。

  Tā yǐqián shì jiānzhí lǎoshī, hòulái zuò le quánzhí.

  She used to be a part-time teacher. Afterwards, she became full-time.

- 我的大学老师辞职了，后来去上海做生意了。

  Wǒ de dàxué lǎoshī cízhí le, hòulái qù Shànghǎi zuò shēngyi le.

  My college professor quit his job. Afterwards, he went to Shanghai to do business.

- 北京以前叫北平，后来改成了北京。

  Běijīng yǐqián jiào Běipíng, hòulái gǎi chéng le Běijīng.

  Beijing used to be called Beiping. Later, the name was changed to Beijing.

Similar to

- In the future in general with "yihou" (HSK3), page 70
- Comparing "yihou" "ranhou" "houlai" (HSK5)
- Expressing "ever since" with "yilai" (HSK5)

Approximating with sequential numbers

Expressing approximate numbers in Chinese is quite simple, and this article introduces one of the most basic ways to do so.

Structure

An easy way to express approximate numbers is to use two sequential numbers in a row.

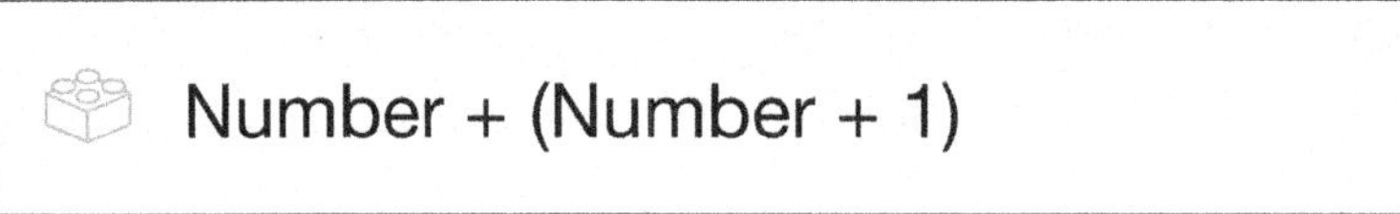

This is similar to saying "x or y" or "about x" in English.

Examples

- 一两 天
  yī liǎng tiān
  one or two days
- 三四 个人
  sān sì gè rén
  three or four people
- 老板昨天喝了 七八 瓶胡萝卜汁。
  Lǎobǎn zuótiān hē le qī bā píng húluóbo zhī.
  The boss drank 7 or 8 bottles of carrot juice yesterday.
- 这个词我们学过 两三 次了。
  Zhège cí wǒmen xué guo liǎng sān cì le.
  We've studied this word two or three times now.
- 我等了你 三四 个小时。
  Wǒ děng le nǐ sān sì gè xiǎoshí.
  I waited for you for three or four hours.
- 他们 七八 年没见面了。
  Tāmen qī bā nián méi jiànmiàn le.
  They haven't seen each other for seven or eight years.

- 要做完这个工作需要 一两 个月。
  Yào zuò wán zhège gōngzuò xūyào yī liǎng gè yuè.
  To complete this work, you need one to two months.
- 他们家的孩子 五六 岁了吧。
  Tāmen jiā de háizi wǔ liù suì le ba.
  Their child is about five or six years old.
- 这件衣服只要 七八十 块钱。
  Zhè jiàn yīfu zhǐ yào qī bā shí kuài qián.
  This clothing only costs seventy to eighty kuai.
- 这几本书花了我 两三百 。
  Zhè jǐ běn shū huā le wǒ liǎng sān bǎi .
  These few books cost me two or three hundred kuai.

Similar to

- Counting money (HSK1)
- Structure of numbers (HSK1)
- Indicating a number in excess (HSK2)
- Measure words for counting (HSK2)
- Big numbers in Chinese (HSK3), page 76

Big numbers in Chinese

The manner in which large numbers are broken down in Chinese is a little different from English. Unlike in English, where large numbers are broken down by the number of *thousands* they have, Chinese forms numbers between 10,000 and 100,000,000 based off of how many *tens* of thousands they have (with another set of rules for numbers 100,000,000 onwards that will be explained later). While the structure can be difficult to grasp for some learners, there are some easy ways to remember how to form these big numbers.

Different Units

Mandarin has two units that English doesn't have (or at least, it has unique words for these units, whereas English describes them with combinations of other units). These are:

- 万 (wàn): ten thousand
- 亿 (yì): hundred million

Ten Thousand - 万 (wàn)

万 (wàn) comes up the most often and is the largest stumbling block for most people learning Mandarin numbers. In English, numbers are usually broken up into chunks of three digits. Because of 万 (wàn), it's easier to break numbers up into groups of four in Mandarin. In English, we split "twelve thousand" numerically into "12,000" (chunks of three digits). Split it the Chinese way, "1,2000," and the Chinese reading "一万两千" (one *wan* and two "thousand" = yīwàn liǎngqiān) makes more sense.

One way to remember how to write out numbers 10,000 through 99,999 in Chinese characters is that in Chinese, the comma is (mentally) moved one digit to the left. For example, 11,000 could be thought of in tens of thousands as "1,1000," with 万 (wàn) replacing the comma, and then what's left written as 一千 (yīqiān): 一万一千 (yīwàn yīqiān).

Typical split	Chinese split	Characters	Pinyin
10,000	1,0000	一万	yīwàn
12,000	1,2000	一万二	yīwàn èr
13,200	1,3200	一万三千两百	yīwàn sānqiān liǎngbǎi
56,700	5,6700	五万六千七百	wǔwàn liùqiān qībǎi

One Hundred Million - 亿 (yì)

After 99,999,999, there is yet another new numerical unit, 亿 (yì), which is used to express "hundred million." A number like 1,101,110,000 would be written out as "十一亿一百一十一万 (shíyī yì yībǎi yīshí-yī wàn)." Again, an easier way to translate between the two methods is to write the number out in English, move the comma one digit to the left, and then insert the appropriate characters in their respective places, replacing the commas.

Mandarin Number Structure

Numerals	Characters	Pinyin	English
1,000,000,000	十亿	shí yì	Billion
100,000,000	亿	yì	Hundred million
10,000,000	千万	qiān wàn	Ten million
1,000,000	百万	bǎi wàn	Million
100,000	十万	shí wàn	Hundred thousand
10,000	万	wàn	Ten thousand
1,000	千	qiān	Thousand
100	百	bǎi	Hundred
10	十	shí	Ten
1	一	yī	One

A Shortcut

One more simple way to remember how to correctly write out large numbers is to pick one or two numbers and just memorize them. One million, for example, is 一百万 (yībǎi wàn). If you can memorize that, then going to 一千万 (yīqiān wàn) is way easier and faster, since you don't have to count all those zeroes.

The recommended shortcuts are:

- 一百万

  frequently a useful number to know

  yībǎi wàn

  1 million

- 十四亿
  shísì yì
  1.4 billion

  this just happens to be the population of China

Examples

- 五 [万] 两千一百五十二
  wǔ [wàn] liǎngqiān yībǎi wǔshí-èr
  52,152
- 二百九十一 [万] 四千六百八十
  èrbǎi jiǔshí-yī [wàn] sìqiān liùbǎi bāshí
  2,914,680
- 七百八十九 [万] 零二百九十八
  qībǎi bāshí-jiǔ [wàn] líng èrbǎi jiǔshí-bā
  7,890,298
- 两千七百二十一 [万] 四千八百九十六
  liǎngqiān qībǎi èrshí-yī [wàn] sìqiān bābǎi jiǔshí-liù
  27,214,896
- 五千三百七十九 [万] 八千两百五十
  wǔqiān sānbǎi qīshí-jiǔ [wàn] bāqiān liǎngbǎi wǔshí
  53,798,250
- 四 [亿] 一千四百二十九 [万] 四千一百八十二
  sì [yì] yīqiān sìbǎi èrshí-jiǔ [wàn] sìqiān yībǎi bāshí-èr
  414,294,182
- 十三 [亿] 两千六百八十 [万]
  shísān [yì] liǎngqiān liùbǎi bāshí [wàn]
  1,326,800,000
- 两百五十一 [亿] 五千八百三十六 [万] 七千二百
  liǎngbǎi wǔshí-yī [yì] wǔqiān bābǎi sānshí-liù [wàn] qīqiān èrbǎi
  25,158,367,200

Structure of times (advanced)

If you already know the basics of how to tell time in Chinese[1], you may want to get a little more specific or sophisticated, using words like 分 (fēn) and 刻 (kè).

Minutes Past the Hour

Minutes are marked with 分 (fēn) (short for 分钟 (fēnzhōng)). The way to include them in the time depends on whether they're minutes *past* or *to* the hour.

Minutes *past* the hour are expressed after 点 (diǎn) in the same way as half and quarter hours.

Minutes Less Than 10

Structure

In Chinese, when the minute is under 10, the word 零 (líng) is often used after 点 (diǎn). For example, 2:07 would be said as "两点零七分" (liǎng diǎn líng qī fēn). However, note that when speaking, it is very common for most Chinese people take out the "分 (fēn)" at the end of the time.

Examples

- 两点零九分
  liǎng diǎn líng jiǔ fēn
  2:09
- 三点零八分
  sān diǎn líng bā fēn
  3:08
- 五点零三分
  wǔ diǎn líng sān fēn
  5:03

---

1. Structure of times (basic) (Grammar), page 83

- 七 点 零 一 分
  qī diǎn líng yī fēn
  7:01
- 八 点 零 五 分
  bā diǎn líng wǔ fēn
  8:05

Minutes Greater Than 10

There's nothing tricky about this, since there's no 零 (líng). Just remember that in casual speech, the 分 (fēn) at the end is sometimes dropped.

Structure

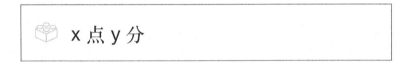

Examples

- 一 点 四十 分
  yī diǎn sìshí fēn
  1:40
- 两 点 十 分
  liǎng diǎn shí fēn
  2:10
- 三 点 二十 分
  sān diǎn èrshí fēn
  3:20
- 七 点 十五 分
  qī diǎn shíwǔ fēn
  7:15
- 九 点 五十 分
  jiǔ diǎn wǔshí fēn
  9:50

Quarter Hours

In Chinese, quarter hours are only expressed on the 1st quarter x:15, and the third quarter x:45. Like half hours, they also come after the word 点 (diǎn). We use the word 刻 (kè) to express “quarter hour.”

Structure

Examples

- 九 点 一 刻
  jiǔ diǎn yī kè
  9:15
- 十二 点 一 刻
  shí'èr diǎn yī kè
  12:15
- 六 点 三 刻
  liù diǎn sān kè
  6:45

You can totally just use 十五分 (shíwǔ fēn) for “15 minutes (past)” or 四十五分 (sìshí-wǔ fēn) for “45 minutes (past)” if you're lazy, though. It also works!

Minutes to the Hour

When expressing how many minutes it will be till the next full hour, you put 差 (chā) in front of the time expression.

Structure

Minutes *to* the hour use this structure:

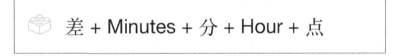

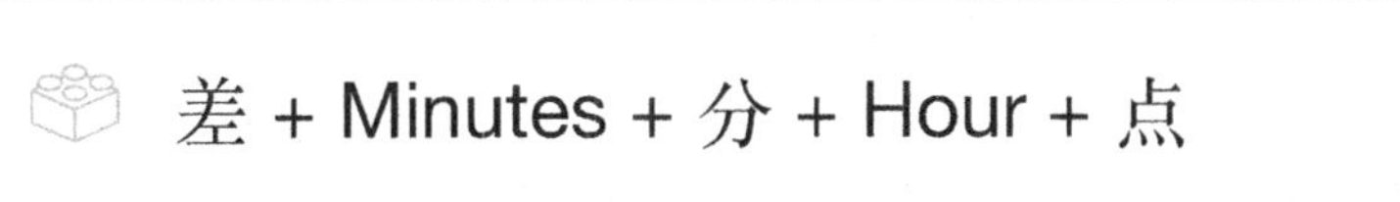

or

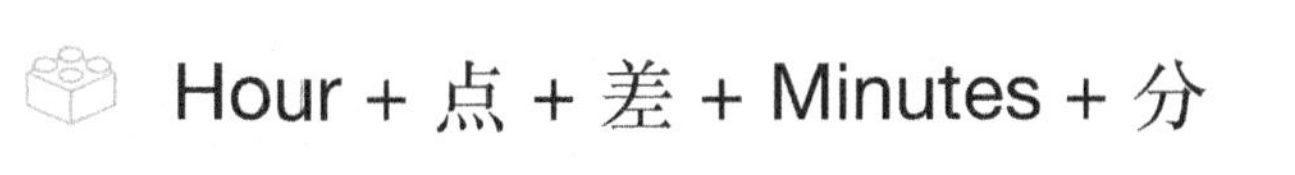

Examples

- 差 五分三 点
  chā wǔ fēn sān diǎn
  five minutes til 3 o'clock
- 十二 点 差 三分
  shí'èr diǎn chā sān fēn
  three minutes til 12 o'clock
- 差 五分八 点 半
  chā wǔ fēn bā diǎn bàn
  five minutes til 8:30
- 十 点 差 两分
  shí diǎn chā liǎng fēn
  two minutes til 10:00

HSK Notes

Only the basic 分 (fēn) usage is tested on HSK1. The others are not tested until HSK3.

Similar to

- Structure of times (basic) (HSK1, HSK3), page 83

Structure of times (basic)

Time in Chinese, just like in English, is expressed by stating the hour first, and then the minute (big to small).

On the Hour

The time of day in Chinese is formed with a number 1 to 12 (一 (yī) to 十二 (shí'èr)) followed by 点 (diǎn). This 点 (diǎn) is equivalent to *o'clock* in English. In China, people generally use a twelve-hour clock, preceded by 上午 (shàngwǔ) for "a.m." or 下午 (xiàwǔ) for "p.m." when necessary.

Structure

 (Date and/or time of day +) x 点

Sometimes people use the longer 点钟 (diǎnzhōng) instead of just 点 (diǎn), but you're fine using the short form.

Examples

If you want to include more specific information, start with the day or date, followed by the general time of day, with the exact clock time last. (This is the big-to-small pattern.) This is how Chinese gets around the need for "a.m." or "p.m.": use 上午 (shàngwǔ) for times in the morning, and 下午 (xiàwǔ) for times in the afternoon.

- 九 点
  jiǔ diǎn
  9 o'clock
- 上午七 点
  shàngwǔ qī diǎn
  7 o'clock a.m.
- 下午四 点
  xiàwǔ sì diǎn
  4 o'clock p.m.
- 中午十二 点
  zhōngwǔ shí'èr diǎn
  12 o'clock noon

- 明天晚上七 点
  míngtiān wǎnshang qī diǎn
  7 o'clock p.m. tomorrow evening
- 9 月 9 号早上六 点
  jiǔ yuè jiǔ hào zǎoshang liù diǎn
  September 9th, 6 o'clock a.m.
- 星期三上午九 点
  Xīngqīsān shàngwǔ jiǔ diǎn
  Wednesday at 9 o'clock a.m.

Note that **two o'clock is 两点** (liǎng diǎn), not 二点 (èr diǎn). (For more information on when to use 两 (liǎng) vs. 二 (èr), see our article on comparing "er" and "liang").

"*Twelve* o'clock," however, is still 十二点 (shí'èr diǎn).

Half Hours

Half hours are added after 点 (diǎn) and are indicated with 半 (bàn).

Structure

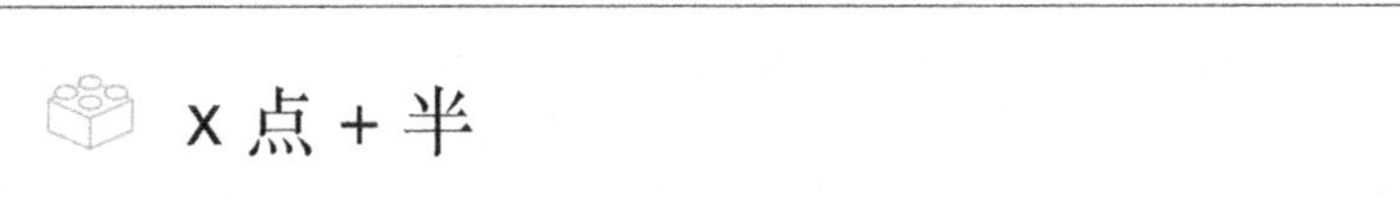

Examples

- 五 点半
  wǔ diǎn bàn
  5:30
- 下午两 点半
  xiàwǔ liǎng diǎn bàn
  2:30 p.m.
- 星期天上午十 点半
  Xīngqītiān shàngwǔ shí diǎn bàn
  Sunday at 10:30 a.m.
- 昨天晚上七 点半
  zuótiān wǎnshang qī diǎn bàn
  7:30 yesterday evening

- 今天下午四 点半
  jīntiān xiàwǔ sì diǎn bàn
  4:30 p.m. this afternoon.

As a beginner, that should be all you need. If you've mastered all of these structures and want to get a little more advanced, see structure of times (advanced)[1].

HSK Notes

Simple times with 点 (diǎn) is on HSK1, but the usage above with 半 (bàn) is not. It is not tested until HSK3.

Similar to

- Before a specific time with "yiqian" (HSK1, HSK3), page 62
- Structure of dates (HSK1)
- Structure of numbers (HSK1)
- Structure of times (advanced) (HSK1, HSK3), page 79

1. Structure of times (advanced) (Grammar), page 79

Aspect particle "zhe"

The particle 着 (zhe) is one way of indicating the *continuous aspect* in Mandarin Chinese (another common way is using the adverb 在 in front of verbs). You may have heard that the Chinese particle 着 added onto the end of verbs is similar to the use of *-ing* in English. This isn't particularly helpful, however, because the use of 着 in Chinese is not nearly so commonly used, and can also be quite idiomatic.

Basic Usage

The main idea here is that the action won't just happen and stop immediately; it will continue for a while.

Structure

Examples

This basic pattern is often used with commands involving certain verbs where the action persists for a while.

- 我读，你听 着 。
  Wǒ dú, nǐ tīng zhe .
  I'll read, and you listen.
- 我们做，你们看 着 。
  Wǒmen zuò, nǐmen kàn zhe .
  We will do it, and you all watch.
- 你们坐 着 ，我马上回来。
  Nǐmen zuò zhe , wǒ mǎshàng huílái.
  Sit for a while. I'll be right back.
- 我出去一下，你帮我看 着 行李。
  Wǒ chūqù yīxià, nǐ bāng wǒ kān zhe xíngli.
  I'll go out for a second, and you watch the luggage for me.

Used for Manner or State in which an Action is Performed

This pattern is used when you want to use one verb to describe how *another* action is performed.

Structure

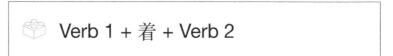

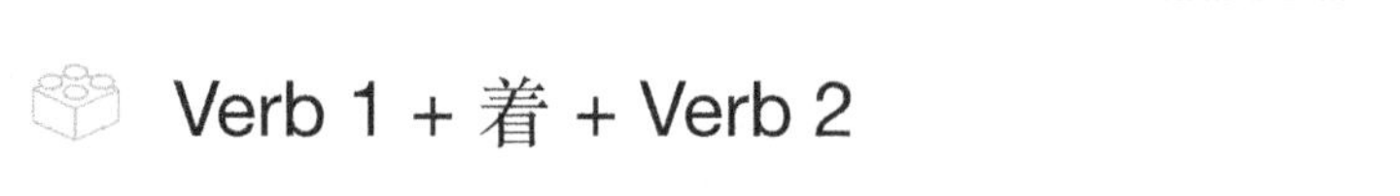

Note that the **first verb** (followed by 着) describes the **state**; the second verb is the action verb. In this case, the "-ing" translation can be useful for the state.

Examples

- 她喜欢站 着 吃饭。
  Tā xǐhuan zhàn zhe chīfàn.
  She likes to eat standing up.
  "standing + eat = eating while standing"
- 他笑 着 说 "对不起"。
  Tā xiào zhe shuō "duìbuqǐ".
  Smiling, he said, "I'm sorry."
  "smiling + say = saying "I'm sorry" while smiling"
- 孩子抱 着 爸爸哭了起来。
  Háizi bào zhe bàba kū le qǐlái.
  Hugging his daddy, the child started to cry.
  "hugging + cry = crying while hugging

Note: If you want to make a sentence where both verbs are action verbs (neither is truly a state), then you don't want this pattern; you want 一边……, 一边…… (yībiān..., yībiān...)[1].

Used for Continuous State

While it's true that the "full progressive pattern" can make use of 着, this is not a pattern you're going to want to use all the time.

Usage Examples

The verbs most commonly used with 着 are the ones below:

- 开 (kāi) alone can mean "to open" or "to turn on." Adding 着 allows one to express that something "is open" or "is on."

---

1. Simultaneous tasks with "yibian" (Grammar), page 32

- 关 (guān) alone can mean "to close" or "to turn off." Adding 着 allows one to express that something "is closed" or "is off."
- 穿 (chuān) alone means "to wear." Adding 着 allows one to express that one "is wearing" something (on one's person).
- 戴 (dài) alone means "to wear" (an accessory). Adding 着 allows one to express that one "is wearing" a hat, jewelry, or accessory (on one's person).
- 躺 (tǎng) alone means "to lie on one's back." Adding 着 allows one to express that someone "is lying down."

Sentence Examples

✔ 公司的门开 着 ，可是没人在。
Gōngsī de mén kāi zhe, kěshì méi rén zài.
The office door is open but no one is in there.
"Being open" is a state, so using 着 is natural.)

✘ 公司的门 在 开，可是没人在。
Gōngsī de mén zài kāi, kěshì méi rén zài.
"Being open" is not an action, so don't use 在.)

✔ 她穿 着 一条小黑裙。
Tā chuān zhe yī tiáo xiǎo hēi qún.
She's wearing a little black dress.
"Be wearing" is a state, so using 着 is natural.)

✘ 她 在 穿一条小黑裙。
Tā zài chuān yī tiáo xiǎo hēi qún.
"Be wearing" is not an action, so don't use 在.)

✔ 躺 着 最舒服。
Tǎng zhe zuì shūfu.
It's most comfortable just lying down.
"Lying down" is a state, so using 着 is natural.)

✘ 在 躺最舒服。
Zài tǎng zuì shūfu.
"Lying here" is not strictly an action, so don't use 在.)

Colloquial Sayings

Certain verbs tend to take 着 more frequently than others, and what the 着 exactly is *doing* might not be apparent at all. It's best to think of these usages as set phrases.

Examples

- 听 着 ！
  Tīng zhe!
  "to listen and keep listening"

- 别客气，拿 着 吧。
  Bié kèqi, ná zhe ba.
  "to take and keep it"

- 你们等 着 ！
  Nǐmen děng zhe!
  "to wait and keeping waiting"

Verb + 着 + 玩 "For Fun"

There's also one colloquial usage of 着 that's often chosen for special treatment by Chinese textbooks, so we'll cover it here as well:

Subj. + 是 + Verb + 着 + 玩 + 的

This pattern may look like that "doing an action in a particular state" pattern already covered above, but in practice it doesn't really work that way. It just means "[Verb] for fun" or "[Verb] as a joke."

Examples of Verb + 着 + 玩

- 你不要生气，我是说 着 玩的。
  Nǐ bùyào shēngqì, wǒ shì shuō zhe wán de!
  Don't be mad. I was just joking.

- 我听不懂英文歌，只是听 着 玩的。
  Wǒ tīng bu dǒng Yīngwén gē, zhǐshì tīng zhe wán de.
  I don't understand English songs. I just listen to them for fun.

Similar to

- Expressing actions in progress with "zai" (HSK1)
- Alternative existential sentences (HSK3), page 181
- Simultaneous tasks with "yibian" (HSK3), page 32
- Using "zhe" when "verbing away" (HSK4)

Change of state with “le”

Also known as: 了 2, change-of-state 了, sentence 了 and modal 了.

了 (le) has many uses. You probably first learned 了 (le) as a particle that tells you an action is completed, which is also known as “了 1.” However, this article is not about that use of 了 (le); instead, it is about indicating a *change of state* (了 2). In other words, there is now a new situation, or there is about to be a new situation. This whole “change of state” idea can take numerous forms, and this page includes some helpful examples.

Used with Adjectives

When an adjective indicates a change to the subject, 了 (le) is placed at the end of the sentence to indicate a change of state.

Structure

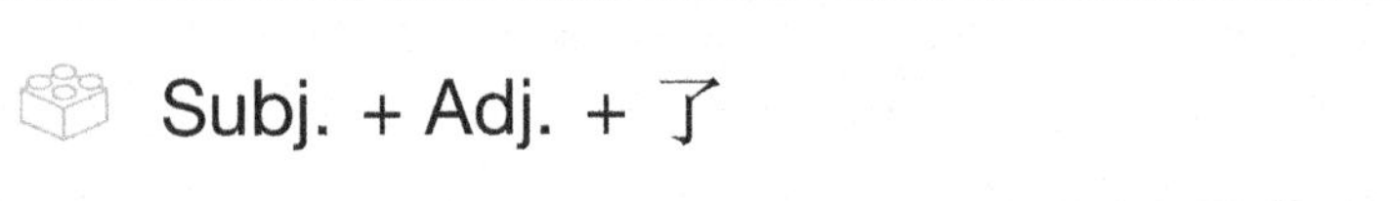

Subj. + Adj. + 了

Examples

- 我饿了。
  Wǒ è le.
  I'm hungry.
- 孩子们都累了。
  Háizi men dōu lèi le.
  The kids are all tired.
- 妈妈老了。
  Māma lǎo le.
  Mom has gotten old.
  We aren't used to thinking of her as old, but she is now.
- 你胖了。
  Nǐ pàng le.
  You've gotten fat.
  You used to not be fat.
- 你是不是生气了？
  Nǐ shì bu shì shēngqì le?
  Are you mad?

Used with Verbs

When following a verb or verb phrase, the 了 (le) indicates a change in an overall situation. For these sentences, sometimes you can translate this 了 (le) as "now."

Structure

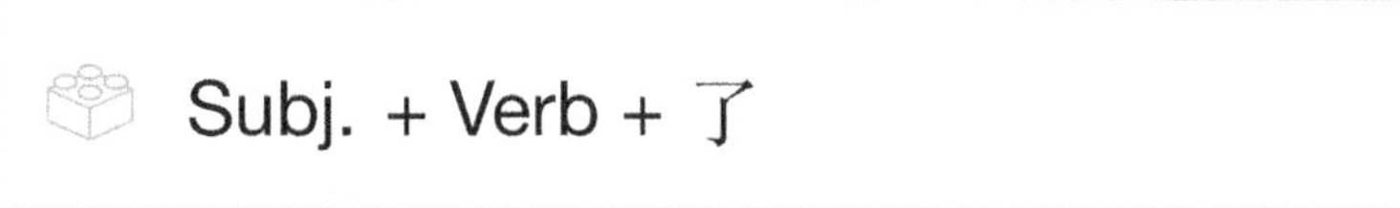

Subj. + Verb + 了

Examples

- 下雨 了 。 *It wasn't raining, but now it is.*
  Xià yǔ le.
  It's raining.
- 宝宝会说话 了 。 *He couldn't before.*
  Bǎobao huì shuōhuà le.
  The baby can speak now.
- 他当经理 了 。 *He wasn't a manager before.*
  Tā dāng jīnglǐ le.
  He became a manager.
- 你有女朋友 了 ? *He didn't have one before.*
  Nǐ yǒu nǚpéngyou le?
  You have a girlfriend now?
- 我男朋友找到新工作 了 。 *A big change for sure.*
  Wǒ nánpéngyou zhǎodào xīn gōngzuò le.
  My boyfriend has found a new job.

Change of Situation in the Negative

When you take the same "change of situation" pattern and put a 不 (bù) before the verb, you're indicating that something already decided has changed. What had once been green-lit is now getting a red light. What was once "on" is now "off." The "change of situation" indicated by 了 (le) is still the same, although the change is often simply mental: it's a change of plans, or a change of intent.

Structure

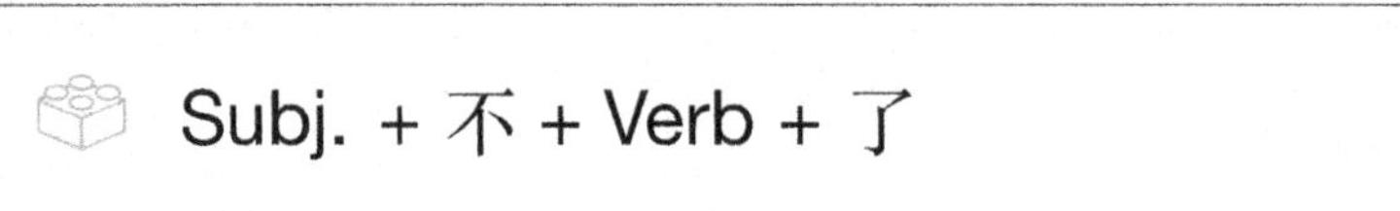
Subj. + 不 + Verb + 了

Examples

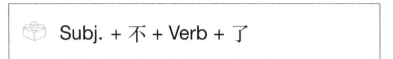

- 我不买了。 *I had previously decided to buy it.*
  Wǒ bù mǎi le.
  I'm not buying it now.
- 我不回家吃晚饭了。 *I had previously decided to go home for dinner.*
  Wǒ bù huí jiā chī wǎnfàn le.
  I'm not going to go home for dinner tonight.
- 我不去看电影了。 *I had said I was going.*
  Wǒ bù qù kàn diànyǐng le.
  I decided not to go to the movies.
- 我不结婚了。 *I had previously planned to get married.*
  Wǒ bù jiéhūn le.
  I'm not getting married.

This pattern is somewhat similar to expressing "not anymore" with "le".

Too General?

The whole "change of state" concept might seem very general, and it is. It's vague, and it also takes some getting used to. You should expect it to take a while to get used to this use of 了 (le).

Because it's a little vague and confusing, most learners find it useful to break this "change of state" 了 (le) down into more specific usages, such as using it to mean "now", "already", or "not anymore". Although these are all "flavors" of the "change of state" 了 (le), identifying them as specific cases can make it much easier to get used to using 了 (le) in this way.

Questions with "ne"

The particle 呢 (ne) can be used to ask reciprocal questions, also known as "bounce back" questions. 呢 (ne) can also be used to form simple questions asking "what about...?" or "how about...?"

General Questions with 呢 (ne)

Structure

And it's as simple as that. Say what you want to ask about, then stick 呢 (ne) on the end. A very common way to use this is to return a question after being asked it. The classic example is this exchange:

A: 你好吗?

Nǐ hǎo ma?

B: 我很好。你 呢 ?

Wǒ hěn hǎo. Nǐ ne?

A: 我也很好。

Wǒ yě hěn hǎo.

Examples

More 呢 (ne) examples (each of these can be translated as a "what about" question):

- 这个很好，那个 呢 ?

  Zhège hěn hǎo, nàge ne?

  This one is good. What about that one?

- 这个用中文怎么说? 那个 呢 ?

  Zhège yòng Zhōngwén zěnme shuō? Nàge ne?

  How do I say this in Chinese? And that?

- 我在家，你 呢 ?

  Wǒ zài jiā. Nǐ ne?

  I'm at home. What about you?

- 你爸爸是上海人，你妈妈 呢 ？
  Nǐ bàba shì Shànghǎi rén, nǐ māma ne ?
  Your father is Shanghainese. And your mom?
- 你哥哥有工作，弟弟 呢 ？
  Nǐ gēge yǒu gōngzuò. Dìdi ne ?
  Your big brother has a job. What about your little brother?
- 北京下雨了。上海 呢 ？
  Běijīng xiàyǔ le. Shànghǎi ne ?
  It's raining in Beijing. How about in Shanghai?
- 我现在要出去。你 呢 ？
  Wǒ xiànzài yào chūqù. Nǐ ne ?
  I'm going to go out now. How about you?
- 我知道你会说中文。你老公 呢 ？
  Wǒ zhīdào nǐ huì shuō Zhōngwén. Nǐ lǎogōng ne ?
  I know you can speak Chinese. What about your husband?
- 这个周末我想去酒吧。你们 呢 ？
  Zhège zhōumò wǒ xiǎng qù jiǔbā. Nǐmen ne ?
  I want to go to a bar this weekend. What about you all?
- 今天晚上没空？明天晚上 呢 ？
  Jīntiān wǎnshang méi kòng? Míngtiān wǎnshang ne ?
  You don't have time tonight? What about tomorrow evening?

Asking "Where" with 呢 (ne)

You'll occasionally hear someone seemingly using 呢 (ne) out of the blue. When this happens, they're usually asking *where* someone or something is, and they expect that you know what they're talking about and know where that person or thing is.

Structure

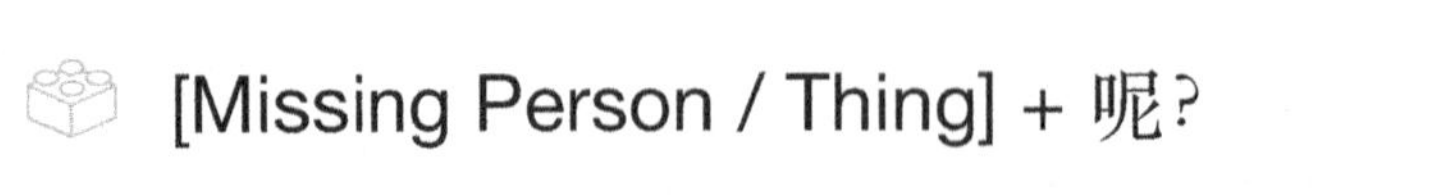

Examples

This one is simple, so just a few examples are needed:

- 钱 呢 ?
  Qián ne ?
  Where's the money?
- 你妈妈 呢 ?
  Nǐ māma ne ?
  Where's your mom?
- 我的手机 呢 ?
  Wǒ de shǒujī ne ?
  Where's my cell phone?

Similar to

- Sentence-final interjection “a” (HSK1)
- Yes-no questions with “ma” (HSK1)
- Modal particle “ne” (HSK2)
- Tag questions with “ma” (HSK2)
- Advanced yes-no questions with “ma” (HSK4)
- Softening the tone of questions with “ne” (HSK5)

Structural particle "de"

The structural particle "de" has three written forms in modern Chinese, each with its own uses:

- 的 (de), most often used for modifying nouns
- 得 (de), most often used with complements
- 地 (de), most often used with adverbial phrases

There is also a modal particle 的 (de), not covered in this grammar point.

的 (de) Before Nouns

Before nouns, 的 (de) is used to mark **possession** or **modification**. One way to think about 的 (de) is that it works like apostrophe-"s" in English. Think of this one as the "possessive *de*" or "noun-modifying *de*."

- 小李 的 房子
  Xiǎo Lǐ de fángzi
  Xiao Li's house

This comparison works very well for possession, as it shows how English and Chinese handle possession in a similar way. Just remember that Chinese uses this "possession" far more widely than English. Modifying, describing qualities, and assigning attributes are all handled in the same way as possession, by using 的 (de).

Another way to use 的 (de) is as an attributive. It's just a way of connecting adjectives or other words with a noun. It gives us more information about the noun, and the 的 (de) makes it clear that the extra information is connected to the noun. Here's an example:

- 红色 的 自行车
  hóngsè de zìxíngchē
  red bicycle

Here 的 (de) is used to modify "bicycle" with the color "red." It attributes the color "red" to the "bicycle."

Structure

Although certainly not complete for all uses, this simple structure should help as a general guideline:

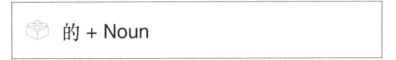

Examples

- 我 的 手机
  wǒ de shǒujī
  my cell phone
- 我们 的 老师
  wǒmen de lǎoshī
  our teacher
- 漂亮 的 衣服
  piàoliang de yīfu
  beautiful clothes
- 热闹 的 酒吧
  rènao de jiǔbā
  a boisterous bar
- 我女朋友 的 公司
  wǒ nǚpéngyou de gōngsī
  my girlfriend's company

For you nerdier learners, 的 (de) is known to the Chinese as 白勺的 (bái-sháo de) as it's composed of the characters 白 (bái) and 勺 (sháo).

得 (de) After Verbs

This *de* is probably the trickiest to crack for English speakers as it has no obvious equivalent in English. 得 (de) is used to construct various kinds of complements and is usually associated with verbs. You can think of it as the "complement *de*."

Structure

Although certainly not complete for all uses, this simple structure should help:

Examples

- 做 得 很好
  zuò de hěn hǎo
  do very well

- 说 得 太快
  shuō de tài kuài
  speak too fast
- 玩 得 很开心
  wán de hěn kāixīn
  play very happily
- 开 得 很快
  kāi de hěn kuài
  drive very fast
- 住 得 很舒服
  zhù de hěn shūfu
  live very comfortably

For you nerdier learners, 得 (de) is known as 双人得 (shuāngrén de), as the character component 彳 is often referred to as 双人 (shuāngrén), or the "double person" component.

Not an Adverb?

You might be wondering how the examples using 得 (de) above are different from adverbs. That's actually a really good question, but it's one that you should defer until later in your studies. Complements are a bit tricky, and you'll be learning a lot more about them at the intermediate level, so be patient!

地 (de) Before Verbs

地 (de) is used to turn adjectives into adverbs, and can be thought of as equivalent to the suffix *-ly* in English. You could call it the "adverb *de*" or "adverbial *de*," since it precedes verbs like adverbs do.

Structure

Although not complete for all uses, this simple structure should help:

Note that it's the "adjective + 地 (de)" structure that makes the adjective into an "adverb phrase" (called an adverbial). If it's a straight-up adverb you're using (instead of an adjective), then you don't need 地 (de) at all.

This pattern is also the least common of the three; you'll be using 的 (de) and 得 (de) a lot more in everyday communication than this one.

Examples

- 生气 地 说
  shēngqì de shuō
  angrily say
- 开心 地 笑
  kāixīn de xiào
  happily laugh
- 慢慢 地 走
  mànmàn de zǒu
  slowly walk
- 伤心 地 哭
  shāngxīn de kū
  sadly cry
- 认真 地 听
  rènzhēn de tīng
  carefully listen

Again, you don't have to know this, but this 地 (de) is known in Chinese as 土也地 (tǔ-yě de), as it's composed of the 土 (tǔ) component on the left with a 也 (yě) on the right.

Using All Three "de"s

This example is naturally going to be a little more difficult than the ones above, since we're cramming all three usages into one sentence, but you may find this useful.

- 今天 的 作业你做 得 不好，因为你没认真 地 听课。
  Jīntiān de zuòyè nǐ zuò de bù hǎo, yīnwèi nǐ méi rènzhēn de tīngkè.
  You didn't do today's homework well because you didn't listen attentively in class.

Similar to

- Turning adjectives into adverbs (HSK3), page 12

Expressing “about” with “guanyu”

关于 (guānyú) means “about.” It can be used in a few ways, often marking a topic of a statement or modifying a noun.

Used for Topic-Marking

Structure

As an adverb/adverbial clause, it can only be placed at the beginning of the sentence.

Examples

- 关于 中国历史，我知道的不多。
  Guānyú Zhōngguó lìshǐ, wǒ zhīdào de bù duō.
  As for Chinese history, I don't know a lot.
- 关于 这次考试，我还有几个问题要问。
  Guānyú zhè cì kǎoshì, wǒ hái yǒu jǐ gè wèntí yào wèn.
  As for this exam, I still have a few questions that I need to ask.
- 关于 这个问题，你们还是问他吧。
  Guānyú zhège wèntí, nǐmen háishì wèn tā ba.
  As for this question, you'd better ask him.
- 关于 你的建议，老板还在考虑。
  Guānyú nǐ de jiànyì, lǎobǎn hái zài kǎolǜ.
  As for your suggestion, the boss is still thinking it over.
- 关于 调查结果，我们也不太清楚。
  Guānyú diàochá jiéguǒ, wǒmen yě bù tài qīngchu.
  As for the result of that investigation, we don't know much either.

Used as Part of a Modifier

As an attributive modifier, 关于 (guānyú) is placed before the noun phrase (rather than after, as in English), and you should always add a 的.

Structure

关于······的 + Noun

Examples

- 网上有很多 关于 这件事情的评论。

  Wǎngshang yǒu hěn duō guānyú zhè jiàn shìqing de pínglùn.

  There are lots of comments about this matter online.

- 他写过很多 关于 男女平等的文章。

  Tā xiě guo hěn duō guānyú nánnǚ píngděng de wénzhāng.

  He wrote many articles about gender equality.

- 汉语有很多 关于 饮食的成语。

  Hànyǔ yǒu hěn duō guānyú yǐnshí de chéngyǔ.

  There are lots of idioms about food in Chinese.

- 我昨天看了一部 关于 动物保护的纪录片。

  Wǒ zuótiān kàn le yī bù guānyú dòngwù bǎohù de jìlùpiàn.

  I saw a documentary about animal protection yesterday.

- 这是一份 关于 中国奢侈品市场的报告。

  Zhè shì yī fèn guānyú Zhōngguó shēchǐpǐn shìchǎng de bàogào.

  This is a report about the Chinese luxury market.

The Unspoken "About"

The word "about" often follows verbs in English, such as "talk about" or "ask about." In Chinese, however, this "about" meaning is built into the verb and no additional "about" word is needed, much like we don't say "discuss about" in English.

A few examples:

- 我们聊聊你的新工作吧。

  Wǒmen liáoliao nǐ de xīn gōngzuò ba.

  Let's talk about your new job.

- 今天开会要说说公司下个月的培训。

  Jīntiān kāihuì yào shuōshuo gōngsī xià gè yuè de péixùn.

  Today, we need to hold a meeting about the company training next month.

Similar to

- Expressing “related to…” with “you guan de” (HSK5)

Expressing "all the way until" with "zhidao"

直到 (zhídào) is for describing a time frame that began in the past and continued until a point closer to the present. It is like the English phrase, "all the way until." It can be used in an affirmative or negative form, expressing that something has taken a while or is late. The word 才 (cái) often teams up with 直到, and serves to emphasize the lateness aspect[1].

Affirmative Form

In the positive form, which uses 才, it may be more natural in English to express the idea as "not until... did" something happen.

Structure

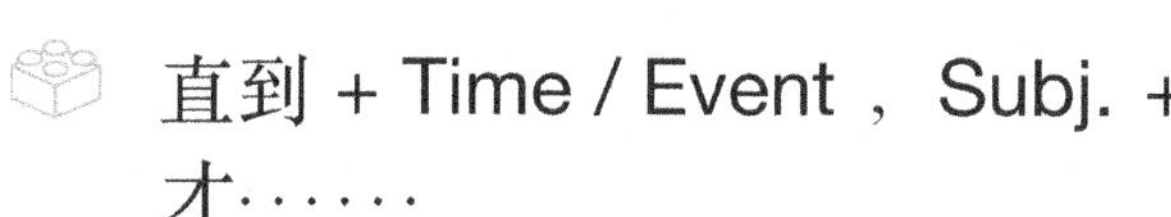

直到 + Time / Event ， Subj. + 才……

This subject can also be placed before 直到.

Examples

- 直到 十二点半，我 才 做完作业。
  Zhídào shí'èr diǎn bàn, wǒ cái zuò wán zuòyè.
  It wasn't until twelve thirty in the morning that I finished my homework.
- 直到 半个月以后，我的感冒 才 好。
  Zhídào bàn gè yuè yǐhòu, wǒ de gǎnmào cái hǎo.
  It took me half a month to recover from the cold.
- 她 直到 十八岁 才 见到亲生父母。
  Tā zhídào shíbā suì cái jiàndào qīnshēng fùmǔ.
  It wasn't until she was eighteen that she met her biological parents.
- 我 直到 大学毕业 才 开始独立生活。
  Wǒ zhídào dàxué bìyè cái kāishǐ dúlì shēnghuó.
  It wasn't until I graduated from college that I started living independently.

1. Expressing lateness with "cai" (Grammar), page 27

- 直到 去了北京，他 才 知道一个人在大城市多辛苦。
  Zhídào qù le Běijīng, tā cái zhīdào yīgèrén zài dà chéngshì duō xīnkǔ.
  It wasn't until he went to Beijing that he understood how hard it is to be alone in a big city.

Negative Form

Structure

直到 + Time / Event ， Subj. + 都 + 不 / 没……

Examples

- 直到 他搬到上海，我们 都没 见过。
  Zhídào tā bān dào Shànghǎi, wǒmen dōu méi jiàn guo.
  We didn't meet until he moved to Shanghai.
- 他们是同学，但是 直到 毕业， 都没 说过话。
  Tāmen shì tóngxué, dànshì zhídào bìyè, dōu méi shuō guo huà.
  They were classmates, but they had never spoken until they graduated.
- 直到 电影结束，他 都没 来。
  Zhídào diànyǐng jiéshù, tā dōu méi lái.
  He didn't show up until the movie was over.
- 直到 我弟弟上大学，他 都不 会洗衣服。
  Zhídào wǒ dìdi shàng dàxué, tā dōu bù huì xǐ yīfu.
  My younger brother didn't know how to wash clothes until he went to college.
- 我认识他一年多了， 直到 现在，我 都不 知道他的全名。
  Wǒ rènshi tā yī nián duō le, zhídào xiànzài, wǒ dōu bù zhīdào tā de quánmíng.
  I've known him for over a year, but even now I still don't know his full name.

Similar to

- Expressing lateness with “cai” (HSK3), page 27
- Expressing “until” with “dao” (HSK4)

Expressing "towards" with "xiang"

向 (xiàng) is a preposition that means "towards" and is used often with certain verbs. These usages need to be learned together with 向.

Used as "Towards"

Structure

When used as a preposition, 向 indicates an action that is performed towards a reference point but doesn't have any actual motion towards that point.

 向 + Direction / Person + Verb

Examples

- 向 东走。
  Xiàng dōng zǒu.
  Walk to the east.
- 向 前看。
  Xiàng qián kàn.
  Look forward.
- 向 左转。
  Xiàng zuǒ zhuǎn.
  Turn to the left.
- 老师正 向 我们走来。
  Lǎoshī zhèng xiàng wǒmen zǒu lái.
  The teacher is currently walking towards us.
- 火车已经开了，她还在 向 我招手。
  Huǒchē yǐjīng kāi le, tā hái zài xiàng wǒ zhāoshǒu.
  The train already departed. She kept waving at me.
- 你必须 向 他道歉！
  Nǐ bìxū xiàng tā dàoqiàn!
  You must apologize to him!

- 这件事你应该 向 老板汇报一下。

  Zhè jiàn shì nǐ yīnggāi xiàng lǎobǎn huìbào yīxià.

  You should report this matter to the boss!

Used as "From"

Whereas in English we would say "learn from someone," in Chinese this would be expressed as "learn toward someone," as in the following example (and famous propaganda slogan):

- 向 雷锋同志学习！

  Xiàng Léi Fēng tóngzhì xuéxí!

  Learn from Comrade Lei Feng!

More examples:

- 我不喜欢 向 朋友借钱。

  Wǒ bù xǐhuan xiàng péngyou jiè qián.

  I don't like to borrow money from friends.

- 你会 向 陌生人求助吗?

  Nǐ huì xiàng mòshēngrén qiúzhù ma?

  Would you ask strangers for help?

- 我们都没经验，是来 向 你请教的。

  Wǒmen dōu méi jīngyàn, shì lái xiàng nǐ qǐngjiào de.

  None of us has experience. We're here to ask you for advice.

Similar to

- Expressing "toward" with "wang" (HSK2)
- Using "dui" with verbs (HSK2)
- Verbs followed by "gei" (HSK2)

Appearance with "kanqilai"

One of the most common ways to express how something "looks" is to use 看起来 (kànqǐlái). This is what we would use if we wanted to express something like "he looks tired."

Used for Judgement

This pattern is most commonly followed by an adjectival phrase. This can include regular adverbs of degree like 很, or negative adverbs like 不.

Structure

Examples

- 蛋糕 看起来 很好吃。
  Dàngāo kànqǐlái hěn hǎochī.
  The cake looks really tasty.
- 这家餐厅 看起来 不错。
  Zhè jiā cāntīng kànqǐlái bùcuò.
  This restaurant looks good.
- 你男朋友 看起来 很成熟。
  Nǐ nánpéngyou kànqǐlái hěn chéngshú.
  Your boyfriend looks very mature.
- 老板 看起来 有点不高兴。
  Lǎobǎn kànqǐlái yǒudiǎn bù gāoxìng.
  The boss looks a little unhappy.
- 你们 看起来 差不多高。
  Nǐmen kànqǐlái chàbuduō gāo.
  You look to be about the same height.

Used for Analogy

If you want to state *what* something looks *like*, you'll also need to follow 看起来 with 像 (xiàng), and then the noun phrase.

Structure

Subj. + 看起来 + 像 + Noun Phrase

Examples

- 你妈妈真年轻！看起来 像 你姐姐。
  Nǐ māma zhēn niánqīng! Kànqǐlái xiàng nǐ jiějie.
  Your mother is so young! She looks like your older sister.
- 我 看起来 像 不 像 大老板?
  Wǒ kànqǐlái xiàng bu xiàng dà lǎobǎn.
  Do I look like a big boss?
- 你们俩 看起来 像 情侣。
  Nǐmen liǎ kànqǐlái xiàng qínglǚ.
  You two look like a couple.
- 他们 看起来 不 像 有钱人。
  Tāmen kànqǐlái bù xiàng yǒuqián rén.
  They don't look like rich people.
- 那个喝醉的男人 看起来 像 你老公。
  Nà gè hēzuì de nánrén kànqǐlái xiàng nǐ lǎogōng.
  That drunk guy looks like your husband.

Similar to

- Advanced uses of direction complement "-qilai" (HSK4)
- Assessing situations with "kanlai" (HSK4)
- Direction complement "-qilai" (HSK4)
- Expressing "it seems" with "haoxiang" (HSK4)
- Expressing "as if" with "sihu" (HSK6)

Basic comparisons with "meiyou"

In Chinese, there is another way to make comparisons. You can use 没有 (méiyǒu) to express that something is "not as" *adjective* as something else. (Yes, that's the same 没有 (méiyǒu) that means "not have," used here in a different way.)

Basic Usage

As well as with 比 (bǐ), you can also use 没有 (méiyǒu) to make basic comparisons. You could think of 没有 (méiyǒu) as the opposite of 比 (bǐ) - it works in the same way, but rather than expressing "more... than..." it expresses "not as... as...":

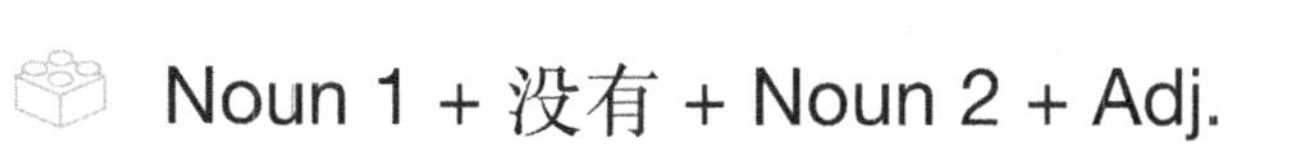

In this structure, the noun that's placed first is *less* "adjective" than the second noun, making 没有 (méiyǒu) the *opposite* of 比 (bǐ) for comparison purposes. So in the sentence:

- 小张 没有 小李高。
  Xiǎo Zhāng méiyǒu Xiǎo Lǐ gāo.
  Xiao Zhang is not as tall as Xiao Li.

小李 (Xiǎo Lǐ) is taller. The same situation could be described as:

- 小李 没有 小张矮。
  Xiǎo Lǐ méiyǒu Xiǎo Zhāng ǎi.
  Xiao Li is not as short as Xiao Zhang.

Examples

- 这个地方 没有 上海好玩。
  Zhège dìfang méiyǒu Shànghǎi hǎowán.
  This place is not as fun as Shanghai.
- 火车 没有 飞机快。
  Huǒchē méiyǒu fēijī kuài.
  Trains are not as fast as airplanes.

- 他 没有 他弟弟聪明。
  Tā méiyǒu tā dìdi cōngming.
  He's not as smart as his younger brother.
- Clinton 没有 Obama 帅。
  Clinton méiyǒu Obama shuài.
  Clinton is not as handsome as Obama.
- 马云 没有 Bill Gates 有钱。
  Mǎyún méiyǒu Bill Gates yǒuqián.
  Jack Ma is not as rich as Bill Gates.
- 你们公司 没有 我们公司大。
  Nǐmen gōngsī méiyǒu wǒmen gōngsī dà.
  Your company is not as big as ours.
- 拼音 没有 汉字难。
  Pīnyīn méiyǒu Hànzì nán.
  Pinyin is not as difficult as Chinese characters.
- 坐公交车 没有 坐地铁方便。
  Zuò gōngjiāochē méiyǒu zuò dìtiě fāngbiàn.
  Taking the bus is not as convenient as taking the metro.
- 小米手机 没有 iPhone 贵。
  Xiǎomǐ shǒujī méiyǒu iPhone guì.
  The Xiaomi phone is not as expensive as the iPhone.
- 爸爸做的菜 没有 妈妈做的菜好吃。
  Bàba zuò de cài méiyǒu māma zuò de cài hǎochī.
  The food dad cooks is not as tasty as the food mom cooks.

Similar to

- Comparing "bu" and "mei" (HSK1)
- Negation of "you" with "mei" (HSK1)
- Basic comparisons with "bi" (HSK2)
- Basic comparisons with "yiyang" (HSK3), page 40
- Expressing "compared with" using "gen" (HSK3), page 196
- Expressing comparable degree with "you" (HSK3), page 203

Causative verbs

Causative verbs are used to cause or influence people to do things. In English, these are verbs like "make," "let," "have," and "get," when used in a sentence like "get Billy to eat a live worm."

The most common causative verbs in Chinese are:

- 让 (ràng)
- 叫 (jiào)
- 请 (qǐng)
- 使 (shǐ)

Structure

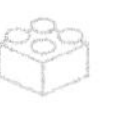

Subj. + [Causative Verb] + Person + Predicate

The predicate part of the pattern can be a verb or an adjective.

使 (shǐ) and 让 (ràng), when used as causative verbs, basically mean the same thing ("to make"), but 使 (shǐ) is used in more formal or written Chinese, while 让 (ràng) is used more in spoken Chinese.

"Make" vs. "Let"

It's worth noting that 让 is the most common causative verb in spoken Mandarin and is often translated into English as either "make" or "let." It may seem strange to speakers of English that these two very different words are the same word in Chinese. "Make" is kind of like forcing, and "let" is kind of like allowing, right? But in Chinese, the context generally makes clear how willing the object of the causative verb is. It's just something that takes time for learners to get used to.

Examples

- 你为什么不 让 我去?
  Nǐ wèishénme bù ràng wǒ qù?
  Why won't you let me go?

- 这部电影 让 人很感动。
  Zhè bù diànyǐng ràng rén hěn gǎndòng.
  This movie really moves people.
- 那个老人 让 我想到了我爷爷。
  Nàge lǎorén ràng wǒ xiǎng dào le wǒ yéye.
  That old man made me think of my grandpa.
- 他不听话，你 叫 我怎么办?
  Tā bù tīnghuà, nǐ jiào wǒ zěnmebàn?
  He won't listen. What would you have me do?
- 他偷偷约别的女孩，你 叫 我怎么想?
  Tā tōutōu yuē bié de nǚhái, nǐ jiào wǒ zěnme xiǎng?
  He secretly asked other girls out. Tell me what I'm supposed to think.
- 你儿子在学校的表现 叫 老师很头疼。
  Nǐ érzi zài xuéxiào de biǎoxiàn jiào lǎoshī hěn tóuténg.
  Your son's behavior at school gives the teacher quite a headache.
- 我想 请 你帮我一个忙。
  Wǒ xiǎng qǐng nǐ bāng wǒ yī gè máng.
  I want to ask you to do me a favor.
- 能不能 请 你明天照顾一下我的狗?
  Néng bu néng qǐng nǐ míngtiān zhàogù yīxià wǒ de gǒu?
  Can I ask you to look after my dog tomorrow?
- 他的演讲 使 听众们非常激动。
  Tā de yǎnjiǎng shǐ tīngzhòng men fēicháng jīdòng.
  His speech made the audience very excited.
- 经济危机 使 很多公司倒闭了，也 使 很多人失去了工作。
  Jīngjì wēijī shǐ hěn duō gōngsī dǎobì le, yě shǐ hěn duō rén shīqù le gōngzuò.
  The financial crisis caused lot of companies to go out of business and also caused many people to lose their jobs.

Obviously, not every causative verb maps perfectly to an English causative verb. You can see from these examples than in some cases the natural English translation doesn't even need a causative verb.

Similar to

- Polite requests with “qing” (HSK1)
- Using the verb “jiao” (HSK1)

Expressing "through" with "jingguo"

When 经过 (jīngguò) is used as a verb, it means "to pass by." 经过 can be also used as a preposition to describe what experiences or times one went "through."

Used as a Verb

As a verb, 经过 means "to pass by" or "to pass through." It's for saying things like, "I passed through downtown" or "I passed by the shop."

Examples

- 我每天上班都 经过 这里。
  Wǒ měi tiān shàngbān dōu jīngguò zhèlǐ.
  I pass by this place every day on the way to work.
- 我坐火车回老家常常 经过 这个城市。
  Wǒ zuò huǒchē huí lǎojiā chángcháng jīngguò zhège chéngshì.
  I usually pass by this city when I take the train back to my hometown.
- 你 经过 我家门口的时候叫我一下。
  Nǐ jīngguò wǒ jiā ménkǒu de shíhou jiào wǒ yīxià.
  Call me when you pass by my door.
- 她 经过 这个咖啡店的时候就会想到他。
  Tā jīngguò zhège kāfēidiàn de shíhou jiù huì xiǎngdào tā.
  She thinks about him when she walks past this cafe.

Used as a Preposition

As a preposition, 经过 means something like "through" (or "after going through"), and is used to emphasize the process of an experience.

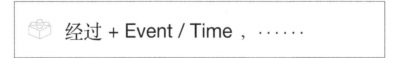

Structure

Examples

- 经过 自己的 努力 ，她考上了北京大学。
  Jīngguò zìjǐ de nǔlì , tā kǎoshàng le Běijīng Dàxué.
  Through her own hard work, she was admitted into Peking University.

- 经过 两个月的 准备 ，他顺利地通过了这次面试。
  Jīngguò liǎng gè yuè de zhǔnbèi , tā shùnlì de tōngguò le zhè cì miànshì.
  After two months of preparation, he successfully passed the job interview.
- 经过 这几年的 发展 ，这个城市发生了很大变化。
  Jīngguò zhè jǐ nián de fāzhǎn , zhège chéngshì fāshēng le hěn dà biànhuà.
  After the last few years of development, this city has changed a lot.
- 经过 一个星期的 调查 ，警察认为他没有罪。
  Jīngguò yī gè xīngqī de diàochá , jǐngchá rènwéi tā méiyǒu zuì.
  After one week of investigation, the police believe that he's not guilty.

Similar to

- Expressing “through” with “tongguo” (HSK4)

Expressing "should" with "yinggai"

应该 (yīnggāi) translates to the English word "should," and is an essential word to know for your conversaitonal Chinese. You *should* definitely get comfortable using 应该 (yīnggāi) right away!

Basic Usage

Structure

The auxiliary verb 应该 (yīnggāi) is the most common way to express "should" in Chinese. The structure is:

Subj. + 应该 + Verb + Obj.

Examples

- 在中国，你 应该 喝白酒。
  Zài Zhōngguó, nǐ yīnggāi hē báijiǔ.
  In China, you should drink baijiu.
- 我 应该 给你多少钱？
  Wǒ yīnggāi gěi nǐ duōshao qián?
  How much money should I give you?
- 感冒的时候 应该 喝热水。
  Gǎnmào de shíhou yīnggāi hē rè shuǐ.
  You should drink hot water when you have a cold.
- 明天你 应该 八点半来公司。
  Míngtiān nǐ yīnggāi bādiǎn bàn lái gōngsī.
  You should come to the office tomorrow at 8:30.
- 他太累了，应该 回家休息。
  Tā tài lèi le, yīnggāi huíjiā xiūxi.
  He's too tired. He should go home and rest.

Negate 应该 (yīnggāi) with 不 (bù)

Structure

Add the negative adverb 不 (bù) before 应该 (yīnggāi) to negate it.

 Subj. + 不 + 应该 + Verb + Obj.

Examples

- 你 不应该 告诉他。
  Nǐ bù yīnggāi gàosu tā.
  You should not tell him.
- 他 不应该 打人。
  Tā bù yīnggāi dǎ rén.
  He should not hit people.
- 我们 不应该 迟到。
  Wǒmen bù yīnggāi chídào.
  We shouldn't be late.
- 你们 不应该 笑她。
  Nǐmen bù yīnggāi xiào tā.
  You shouldn't laugh at her.
- 你们 不应该 拿别人的东西。
  Nǐmen bù yīnggāi ná biérén de dōngxi.
  You should not take other people's stuff.

Similar to

- Expressing "would like to" with "xiang" (HSK1)
- Wanting to do something with "yao" (HSK2)
- Expressing "had better" with "haishi" (HSK4)
- Expressing "had better" with "zuihao" (HSK4)
- Expressing "must" with "dei" (HSK4)

Expressing "difficult" with "nan"

难 (nán) is an adjective that means "difficult." When something is "hard to do" (as in difficult), the word 难 (nán) can be used before the verb.

难 (nán) with General Verbs

Just as 好 (hǎo) can be used to indicate that it's easy to do something, 难 (nán) can be attached to verbs (with a few special exceptions), to indicate that something is *hard to do*.

Structure

The structure is:

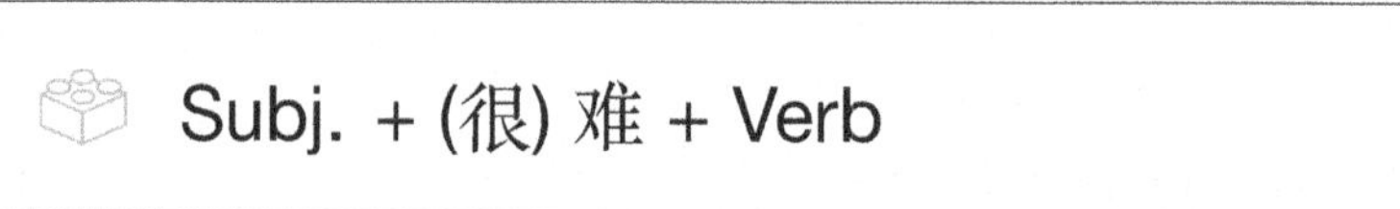

Examples

- 这句话很 难懂 。
  Zhè jù huà hěn nán dǒng.
  This sentence is hard to understand.
- 汉语很 难学 。
  Hànyǔ hěn nán xué.
  Mandarin is hard to learn.
- 中国菜很 难做 。
  Zhōngguó cài hěn nán zuò.
  Chinese food is hard to make.
- 这个东西现在很 难买 。
  Zhège dōngxi xiànzài hěn nán mǎi.
  This thing is really difficult to purchase now.
- 这个汉字很 难写 。
  Zhège Hànzì hěn nán xiě.
  This character is very difficult to write.

难 (nán) with Sense Verbs

难 (nán) can also be attached to "sense verbs" (e.g. look, taste, smell, etc.) to indicate that something offers a "bad sensory experience."

Structure

The structure is:

Subj. + (很) 难 + [Sense Verb]

Examples

- 你做的菜很 难吃 。
  Nǐ zuò de cài hěn nánchī.
  The dishes you cook taste bad.
- 这里的咖啡很 难喝 。
  Zhè lǐ de kāfēi hěn nánhē.
  The coffee here tastes bad.
- 这首歌很 难听 。
  Zhè shǒu gē hěn nántīng.
  This song is terrible (hard to listen to).
- 这种花很 难闻 。
  Zhè zhǒng huā hěn nánwén.
  This kind of flower smells bad.
- 这件衣服很 难看 吗?
  Zhè jiàn yīfu hěn nánkàn ma?
  Is this article of clothing ugly?

Warning! If you're trying to say that a particular dish is "difficult to eat," don't use 难吃 (nánchī)! The word 难吃 (nánchī) *only* means "bad-tasting" and *not* "difficult to eat."

Similar to

- Using "hao" to mean "easy" (HSK2)
- Expressing "hard to avoid" with "nanmian" (HSK5)
- Expressing difficulty with "hao (bu) rongyi" (HSK5)

Expressing duration with "le"

Whether you need to express how long you lived somewhere, how long you studied astrophysics, or how long you worked as a mime, you'll need to use 了 (le) to express that time duration.

Basic Usage

Structure

Saying *how long* you did something *for* in Chinese can seem tricky, as there is no preposition as in English. Instead it's all about word order:

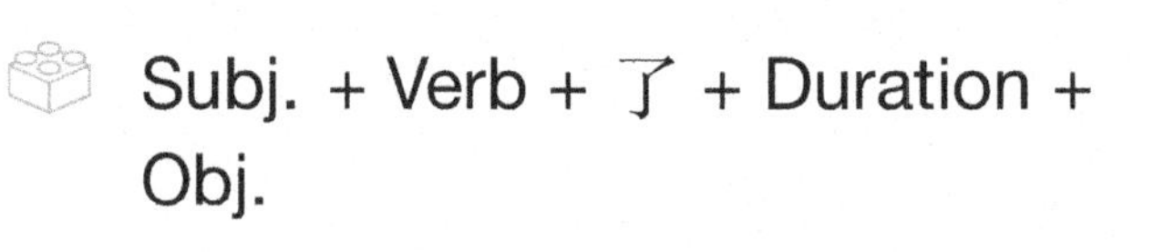

So 了 (le) is placed after the verb (to indicate that the action is completed), followed by the duration. This is how you talk about the duration of completed actions.

Examples

- 他学了 一年 中文。
  Tā xué le yī nián Zhōngwén.
  He studied Chinese for a year.
- 我看了 一个晚上 书。
  Wǒ kàn le yī gè wǎnshang shū.
  I read books all evening.
- 他做了 八年 经理。
  Tā zuò le bā nián jīnglǐ.
  He worked as a manager for eight years.

Also note that 的 can be used in this pattern, which must be placed between the duration and the object.

Subj. + Verb + 了 + Duration + 的 + Obj.

Some examples:

- 我们坐了 十五个小时 的 飞机。
  Wǒmen zuò le shíwǔ gè xiǎoshí de fēijī.
  We took a fifteen hour flight.
- 奶奶看了 一天 的 电视。
  Nǎinai kàn le yī tiān de diànshì.
  Grandma watched TV all day.
- 妈妈洗了 一上午 的 衣服。
  Māma xǐ le yī shàngwǔ de yīfu.
  Mom washed clothes all morning.

To Express "Definitely Concluded"

Structure

Note that the previous pattern can be used to express the duration of completed actions *which are no longer in progress*, although strictly speaking, it's not entirely clear if the actions are still ongoing or not. To indicate that the actions are definitely concluded (not ongoing), a time word may be inserted into the sentence to indicate that you're talking about an event in the past:

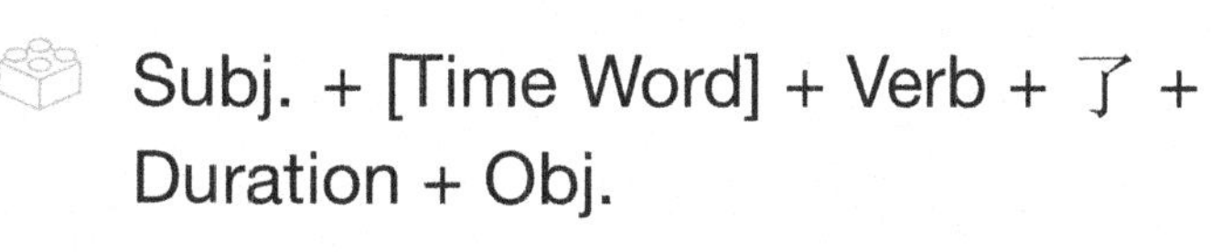

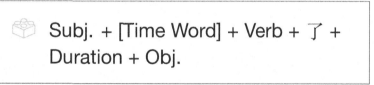

Subj. + [Time Word] + Verb + 了 + Duration + Obj.

Examples

- 孩子们周六写了 一天 的 作业。
  Háizi men zhōuliù xiě le yī tiān de zuòyè.
  The kids did their homework all day Saturday.
- 我刚才打了 半个小时 电话。
  Wǒ gāngcái dǎ le bàn gè xiǎoshí diànhuà.
  I was on the phone for half an hour.
- 我昨天玩了 一晚上 游戏。
  Wǒ zuótiān wán le yī wǎnshang yóuxì.
  Yesterday, I played games all evening.

- 他昨天开了 一天 的 车。
  Tā zuótiān kāi le yī tiān chē.
  He drove all day yesterday.
- 老板今天开了 一下午 的 会。
  Lǎobǎn kāi le yī xiàwǔ de huì.
  The boss had meetings all afternoon today.

To indicate that the action is *definitely still in progress*, use a slightly different pattern[1].

Similar to

- Expressing duration of inaction (HSK3), page 25
- Expressing ongoing duration with double "le" (HSK3), page 123

1. Expressing ongoing duration with double "le" (Grammar), page 123

Expressing ongoing duration with double "le"

The 了 (le) particle is used in many different ways. In this article, we will explore how to use the double 了 (le) to express the duration of an activity that is ongoing.

Ongoing Duration with Simple Verbs

Expressing *how long* you did something in the past[1] is one thing, but what if the action is still ongoing?

A clarifying example (in English) is appropriate:

- I lived in Shanghai for 5 years. (concluded, not ongoing)
- I have lived in Shanghai for 5 years. (mostly likely ongoing)
- I have been living in Shanghai for 5 years. (definitely ongoing)

This article is about expressing the third situation above, the one which is *definitely ongoing*.

Structure

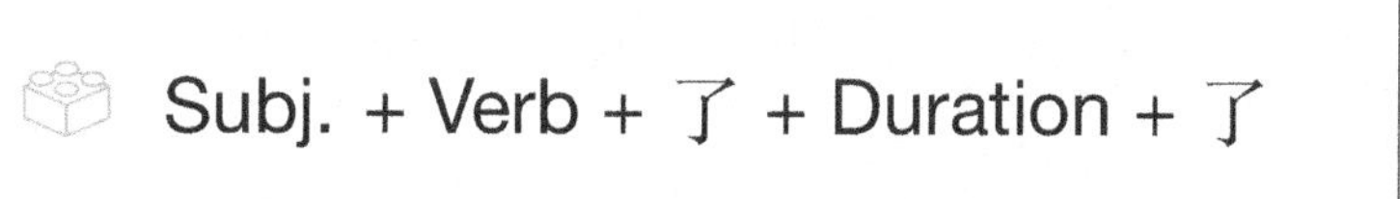

The first 了 (le) is placed after the verb (to indicate that the action is completed), followed by the duration, followed by an additional 了 (le) which tells us that the action has not concluded and is ongoing. You can think of the second 了 (le) as communicating the meaning of "up until now."

Examples

- 你睡了一天了。
  Nǐ shuì le yī tiān le.
  You have been sleeping for the whole day.
- 他在北京住了两年了。
  Tā zài Běijīng zhù le liǎng nián le.
  He has been living in Beijing for two years.

1. Expressing duration with "le" (Grammar), page 120

- 这个会，他们开 了 两个小时 了 。
  Zhège huì, tāmen kāi le liǎng gè xiǎoshí le.
  They've been holding this meeting for the past two hours.
- 我在这儿等 了 半个小时 了 。
  Wǒ zài zhèr děng le bàn gè xiǎoshí le.
  I have been waiting here for half an hour.
- 他们在酒吧待 了 一个晚上 了 。
  Tāmen zài jiǔbā dāi le yī gè wǎnshang le.
  They have been staying at the bar for the whole evening.

When the Verb Takes an Object

Structure

Note that in the examples above, the verbs have no objects. When the verb has an object, the verb is often repeated:

> Subj. + Verb + Obj. + Verb + 了 + Duration + 了

Examples

- 我学中文学 了 一年 了 。
  Wǒ xué Zhōngwén xué le yī nián le.
  I have been learning Chinese for a year.
- 他打电话打 了 一个多小时 了 。
  Tā dǎ diànhuà dǎ le yī gè duō xiǎoshí le.
  He has been on the phone for more than an hour.
- 老板打游戏打 了 一个上午 了 。
  Lǎobǎn dǎ yóuxì dǎ le yī gè shàngwǔ le.
  The boss has been playing video games all morning.
- 你洗澡洗 了 差不多一个小时 了 。
  Nǐ xǐzǎo xǐ le chàbuduō yī gè xiǎoshí le.
  You have been showering for almost an hour.

- 妈妈看电视看 了 一晚上 了 。
  Māma kàn diànshì kàn le yī wǎnshang le.
  Mom has been watching TV all evening.

Similar to

- Expressing duration of inaction (HSK3), page 25
- Expressing duration with “le” (HSK3), page 120

Inability with "mei banfa"

If you are trying to express that something is impossible, you can use the phrase 没办法 (méi bànfǎ). 没办法 (méi bànfǎ) essentially means "there is no way," and while it works just fine by itself, it can also come before verbs.

Structure

One easy way to express inability is to place the phrase 没办法 (méi bànfǎ) before the verb.

Subj. + 没办法 + Verb + Obj.

Examples

- 今天太忙了，中午 没办法 出去吃饭。
  Jīntiān tài máng le, zhōngwǔ méi bànfǎ chūqù chīfàn.
  It's too busy today. There's no way to go out for lunch.
- 他没带手机，没办法 给我打电话。
  Tā méi dài shǒujī, méi bànfǎ gěi wǒ dǎ diànhuà.
  He didn't bring his phone, so he has no way to give me a call.
- 没有水，我们 没办法 洗衣服。
  Méiyǒu shuǐ, wǒmen méi bànfǎ xǐ yīfu.
  There's no water. There's no way for us to wash clothes.
- 这里太吵了，我 没办法 工作。
  Zhèlǐ tài chǎo le, wǒ méi bànfǎ gōngzuò.
  It's too noisy here. I can't work.
- 他不开门，所以她 没办法 进去。
  Tā bù kāimén, suǒyǐ tā méi bànfǎ jìnqù.
  He didn't open the door, so she has no way to enter.
- 你不会说中文，没办法 在我们公司工作。
  Nǐ bù huì shuō Zhōngwén, méi bànfǎ zài wǒmen gōngsī gōngzuò.
  You can't speak Chinese, so there is no way for you to work for our company.

- 事情太多了，我今天 没办法 做完。
  Shìqing tài duō le, wǒ jīntiān méi bànfǎ zuò wán.
  There's too much to do. I have no way to finish today.
- 老板不同意，我 没办法 帮你。
  Lǎobǎn bù tóngyì , wǒ méi bànfǎ bāng nǐ.
  The boss didn't agree, so I have no way to help you.
- 这里没有 wifi，我 没办法 上网。
  Zhèlǐ méiyǒu wifi，wǒ méi bànfǎ shàngwǎng.
  There is no wifi here, so I have no way of going online.
- 他很笨，我 没办法 跟他一起工作。
  Tā hěn bèn, wǒ méi bànfǎ gēn tā yīqǐ gōngzuò.
  He's really dumb. There is no way I can work with him.

Similar to

- Negation of “you” with “mei” (HSK1)

Reduplication of verbs

One of the fun things about Chinese is that when speaking, you can repeat a verb to express "a little bit" or "briefly." This is called reduplication. It creates a casual tone, and a sense that whatever the action is, it's not going to take long.

Reduplication with the AA Pattern

Structure

In Chinese, verbs can be reduplicated to indicate that they happen briefly or "a little bit."

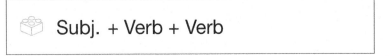

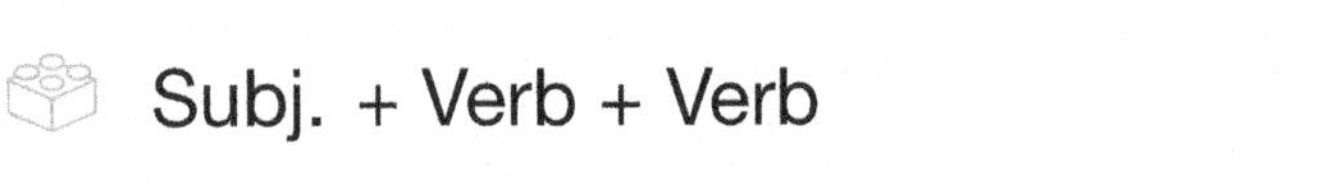

Chinese grammar books frequently refer to the reduplication of a single-character word as a "AA" pattern. Note that for this pattern, the second verb's tone changes to the neutral tone.

Examples

- 你 看看 。
  Nǐ kànkan.
  Take a little look.
- 我 试试 。
  Wǒ shìshi.
  I'll give it a try.
- 说说 你的想法。
  Shuōshuo nǐ de xiǎngfǎ.
  Talk a little bit about your ideas.
- 出去 玩玩 吧！
  Chūqù wánwan ba!
  Go out and have fun!
- 我想出去 走走 。
  Wǒ xiǎng chūqù zǒuzou.
  I want to go out and walk for a bit.

Reduplication with 一 (yī)

Structure

Another way to reduplicate verbs is to insert 一 (yī), in the following structure:

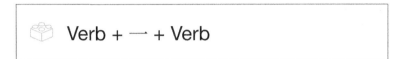

Verb + 一 + Verb

Examples

- 别生气了，笑一笑！
  Bié shēngqì le, xiào yī xiào!
  Don't be mad, gimme a smile!
- 你去问一问他们厕所在哪里。
  Nǐ qù wèn yī wèn tāmen cèsuǒ zài nǎlǐ.
  Go and ask them where the bathroom is.
- 我可以用一用你的电脑吗？
  Wǒ kěyǐ yòng yī yòng nǐ de diànnǎo ma?
  Can I use your computer for a little bit?
- 你现在有时间吗？我们聊一聊吧。
  Nǐ xiànzài yǒu shíjiān ma? Wǒmen liáo yī liáo ba.
  Do you have a second? Let's chat for a bit.
- 你想尝一尝我做的菜吗？
  Nǐ xiǎng cháng yī cháng wǒ zuò de cài ma?
  Do you want to taste the food that I cooked?

Using this kind of structure lightens the mood and seriousness of the question. It also adds variety to sentence structure. Because these phrases are used colloquially, there is not set rule to which verbs this can be applied to. There are some verbs that are often reduplicated and some verbs that sound weird when reduplicated. With practice and exposure, you will learn which ones are often used.

ABAB Reduplication with Two-Syllable Verbs

In the examples above, all verbs are only one syllable. Those verbs get reduplicated a lot, so those examples are quite useful. Occasionally, though, two-syllable verbs get reduplicated as well. When this happens, it's important to use the "ABAB" pattern for verbs (meaning the entire word is repeated), and not the "AABB" pattern you use for adjectives[1] (where each character is repeated individually).

Examples

- 考虑考虑

  kǎolǜ kǎolǜ

  think it over

- 讨论讨论

  tǎolùn tǎolùn

  discuss it

- 商量商量

  shāngliang shāngliang

  talk it over

- 打听打听

  dǎting dǎting

  inquire about it

Similar to

- Softening speech with "ba" (HSK1)
- Reduplication of measure words (HSK2)
- Verbing briefly with "yixia" (HSK2)
- Reduplication of adjectives (HSK3), page 7

1. Reduplication of adjectives (Grammar), page 7

Special verbs with "hen"

Using 很 (hěn) to intensify verbs that express thoughts or feeling is really easy.

Structure

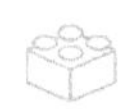 Subj. + 很 + [Certain Verbs]

Certain "psychological verbs" related to feelings or emotional sates can be modified with 很 (hěn) to increase their intensity. This is similar to using "really" or "very much" in English. Remember that this only applies to psychological verbs, such as:

- 想 (xiǎng) to think; to want; to miss
- 喜欢 (xǐhuan) to like
- 小心 (xiǎoxīn) to be careful
- 怕 (pà) to fear; to be afraid of
- 了解 (liǎojiě) to know a lot about
- 讨厌 (tǎoyàn) to hate
- 担心 (dānxīn) to worry about
- 希望 (xīwàng) to hope

Examples

- 我很想你。
  Wǒ hěn xiǎng nǐ.
  I really miss you.
- 他很喜欢你。
  Tā hěn xǐhuan nǐ.
  He really likes you.
- 你应该很小心。
  Nǐ yīnggāi hěn xiǎoxīn.
  You should be very careful.

- 我很怕晚上一个人在家。
  Wǒ hěn pà wǎnshang yīgèrén zài jiā.
  I fear staying home alone at night.
- 你应该很了解自己的孩子。
  Nǐ yīnggāi hěn liǎojiě zìjǐ de háizi.
  You should know a lot about your child.
- 外国人很讨厌中国的公共厕所。
  Wàiguó rén hěn tǎoyàn Zhōngguó de gōnggòng cèsuǒ.
  Foreigners really hate public toilets in China.
- 你两天没回家，妈妈很担心你。
  Nǐ liǎng tiān méi huíjiā, māma hěn dānxīn nǐ.
  You haven't gone home in two days. Mom is really worried about you.
- 父母都很希望我能上一个好大学。
  Fùmǔ dōu hěn xīwàng wǒ néng shàng yī gè hǎo dàxué.
  Both of my parents really hope that I can go to a good college.

Did you ever notice that some Chinese people with less-than-perfect English will use the phrase "very like?" Now you know why!

Similar to

- Expressing "excessively" with "tai" (HSK1)
- Simple "noun + adjective" sentences (HSK1)
- Adjectives with "-ji le" (HSK3), page 5

Direction complement

Also known as: 趋向补语 (qūxiàng bǔyǔ), directional complement and complement of direction.

A direction complement is a complement used to describe the direction of a verb. Verbs often already have some inherent movement implied, but by adding a direction complement, it becomes clearer where, exactly, that action is going.

Simple Direction Complement

The most basic (and common) form of direction complement is formed by a verb and 来 or 去.

Structure

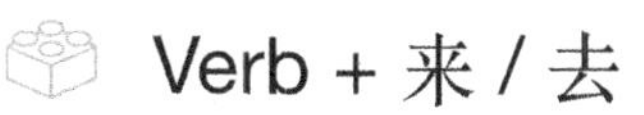

The most important thing to consider with direction complements is **the position of the speaker**. If the action moves towards the speaker or comes closer in any way, use 来. If the action moves away from the speaker or becomes more distant in any way, use 去.

Verb	+ Complement	Explanation
下	下来 xiàlái	The movement is down towards the speaker: "come down"
下	下去 xiàqù	The movement is down away from the speaker: "go down"
上	上来 shànglái	The movement is up towards the speaker: "come up"
上	上去 shàngqù	The movement is up and away from the speaker: "go up"
出	出来 chūlái	The movement is out and towards the speaker: "come out"
出	出去 chūqù	The movement is out and away from the speaker: "go out"
进	进来 jìnlái	The movement is in and towards the speaker: "come in"

进	进去 jìnqù	The movement is in and away from the speaker: "go in"
回	回来 huílái	The movement is towards the speaker: "come back"
回	回去 huíqù	The movement is away from the speaker: "go back"

You might be wondering how the directional distinction between 来 and 去 works when you're talking about yourself moving. You can't move away from or towards yourself, so should it be 来 or 去? The answer is to look at the context of the movement you're talking about. Are you telling someone you'll see them tomorrow? Similar to English, in Chinese you'd say something like "I'll come and see you tomorrow."

Examples

You can use these simple compounds in a huge variety of situations. Here are some example dialogs to provide a little more context:

A: 我在楼上，你 上来 。

Wǒ zài lóushàng, nǐ shànglái.

I'm on the upper floor. Come up to me.

B: 你在楼上等我一下。我一会儿就 上去 。

Nǐ zài lóushàng děng wǒ yīxià. Wǒ yīhuìr jiù shàngqù.

Please wait a moment on the upper floor. I'll come up in a few minutes.

A: 出来 玩吧，我们在酒吧等你。

Chūlái wán ba, wǒmen zài jiǔbā děng nǐ.

Come and hang out with us. We'll be waiting in the bar.

B: 我妈不让我 出去 。

Wǒ mā bù ràng wǒ chūqù.

My mother won't let me go out.

A: 这是我家，进来 吧，随便坐。

Zhè shì wǒ jiā, jìnlái ba, suíbiàn zuò.

This is my house. Please come inside. Feel free to take a seat.

B: 那是你的卧室吗？我能 进去 吗？

Nà shì nǐ de wòshì ma? Wǒ néng jìnqù ma?

Is that your bedroom? Can I go in?

A: 你下班了吗？几点 回来 吃饭？

Nǐ xiàbān le ma? Jǐ diǎn huílái chīfàn?

Are you off work now? When are you coming back for dinner?

B: 我今天不 回去 吃饭。

Wǒ jīntiān bù huíqù chīfàn.

I'm not going back home for dinner today.

Compound Direction Complements

Direction complements can be more complex than just 来 or 去.

Forming Compound Direction Complements

You can form compound direction complements in the following way:

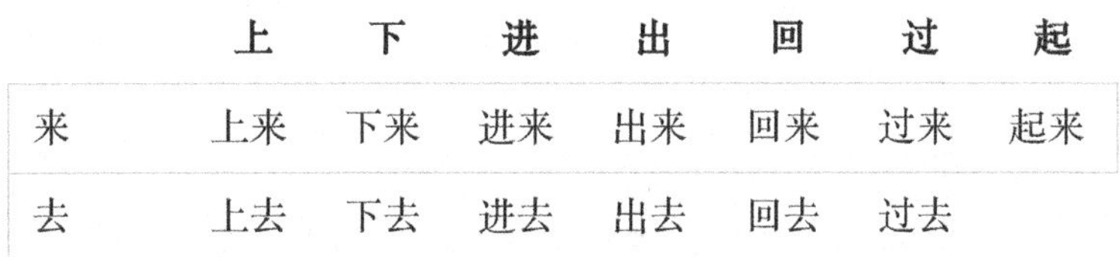

	上	下	进	出	回	过	起
来	上来	下来	进来	出来	回来	过来	起来
去	上去	下去	进去	出去	回去	过去	

These compounds can then be used in much the same way as 来 and 去. Attach them to verbs to give detail about the direction of the action.

Structure

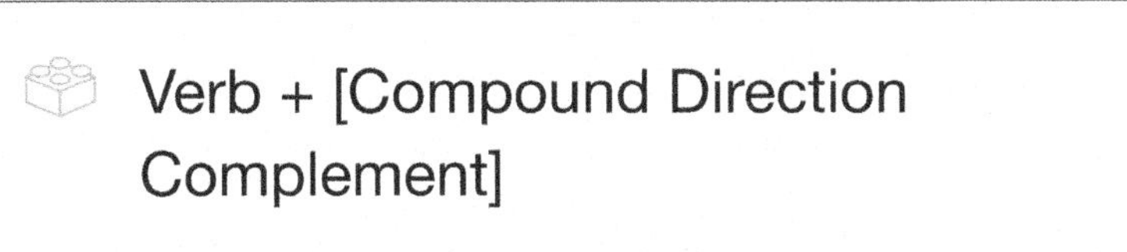

Examples

- 请站 起来 。

  Qǐng zhàn qǐlái.

  Please stand up.

- 不要让它跑 出去 。

  Bùyào ràng tā pǎo chūqù.

  Don't let it run out.

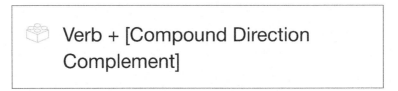

- 从我家走 过来 要半个小时。
  Cóng wǒ jiā zǒu guòlái yào bàn gè xiǎoshí.
  It took me half an hour to walk here from my place.
- 你包里的东西都拿 出来 了吗?
  Nǐ bāo lǐ de dōngxi dōu ná chūlái le ma?
  Did you take all your stuff out of your bag?

Direction Complements with Objects

Direction complements are not only used to describe the movement of people. Moving objects can also be described with direction complements. Again, the direction of the movement relative to the speaker (or at least to the context of the conversation) is important when deciding what complement to use.

The verbs that commonly appear in this construction include 拿, 送, and 带.

Structure

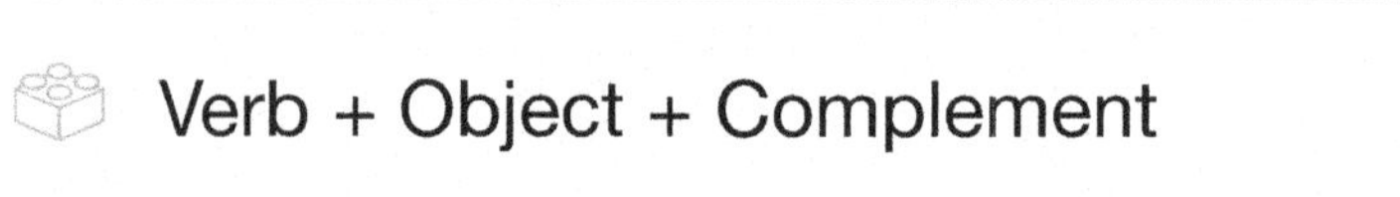

Examples

Some examples:

- 服务员，请再拿 几个碗 来 。
  Fúwùyuán, qǐng zài ná jǐ gè wǎn lái.
  Waiter, please bring a few more bowls.
- 快点送 孩子 去 吧，别迟到了。
  Kuàidiǎn sòng háizi qù ba, bié chídào le.
  Hurry up, send the kids off. Don't be late.
- 师傅，送 两桶水 来 。
  Shīfu, sòng liǎng tǒng shuǐ lái.
  Shifu, please deliver two buckets of water.
- 可以带 朋友 过来 吗?
  Kěyǐ dài péngyou guòlái ma?
  Can I bring some friends over?

- 他们带了 一些礼物 回去 。

  Tāmen dài le yīxiē lǐwù huíqù.

  They took some presents back with them.

Common Mistakes

Although 回来 and 回去 can be compound complements, they can each also just be the verb 回 with a simple direction complement. Many Chinese learners make the following mistakes:

✗ 回来中国

huílai Zhōngguó

✓ 回中国来

huí Zhōngguó lái

come back to China

✗ 回去美国

huíqu Měiguó

✓ 回美国去

huí Měiguó qù

go back to the USA

You can't say 回来中国 because 回 is the verb, 来 is the complement, and 中国 is the object. You can't put both a complement and an object after a single verb, but it's OK to put just a 来 or 去 after the object. In spoken language, if the context is clear, people often omit 来 or 去 and only say 回美国 or 回中国.

Direction Complements with 把

Direction complements work very well in 把 sentences, as they can be used to describe the disposal of an object (what happened to it in the end). Because of this, it's very common to see direction complements and 把 appearing together.

Structure

Subj. + 把 + Obj. + Verb + [Direction Complement]

Examples

- 把 书 拿出来 。
  Bǎ shū ná chūlái.
  Take out your book.
- 把 手 举起来 。
  Bǎ shǒu jǔ qǐlái.
  Raise your hands.
- 帮我 把 这个箱子 搬过去 。
  Bāng wǒ bǎ zhège xiāngzi bān guòqù.
  Help me move this suitcase over there.

See also: 把 sentences

Converting to Potential Complement

Adding 得 to directional complements makes the phrase an affirmative potential complement. Adding 不 makes the phrase a negative potential complement.

Direction Complement	Aff. Potential Complement	Neg. Potential Complement
回去	回 得 去	回 不 去
过来	过 得 来	过 不 来
站起来	站 得 起来	站 不 起来
走上去	走 得 上去	走 不 上去
开进去	开 得 进去	开 不 进去
拿出来	拿 得 出来	拿 不 出来

Additional Meanings

A lot of direction complements, particularly compound direction complements, have additional idiomatic meanings beyond literally describing the direction of an action. The most common of these are:

- 起来 (-qǐlái)

- 出来 (-chūlái)
- 下去[1] (-xiàqù)

Similar to

- Directional verbs “lai” and “qu” (HSK1)
- Result complement “-xiaqu” (HSK3), page 144
- Using “bei” sentences (HSK3), page 175
- Advanced uses of direction complement “-qilai” (HSK4)
- Direction complement “-qilai” (HSK4)
- Advanced uses of “ba” (HSK5)

1. Result complement “-xiaqu” (Grammar), page 144

Potential complement

Verbs can take potential complements to indicate whether or not an action is possible. Potential complements contain a 得 (de) or a 不 (bu) immediate after the verb being modified, and are quite common in everyday spoken Mandarin.

Affirmative Form

Structurally, potential complements are closely related to both result complements and direction complements[1], so it helps to be familiar with those first. The most important and commonly used potential complements are derived from other complements such as the following:

- Verb + 见 e.g. 看见, 听见 (result complements)
- Verb + 懂 e.g. 看懂, 听懂 (result complements)
- Verb + 完 e.g. 吃完, 做完, 用完, 花完 (result complements)
- Verb + Adj. e.g. 看清楚, 听明白, 洗干净 (result complements)
- Verb + 到 e.g. 找到, 买到, 收到 (result complements)
- Verb + Direction e.g. 上来, 下去, 进去, 起来, 走过去, 爬上去 (direction complements[1])

These forms will be our starting point for forming potential complements.

Structure

Subj. + Verb + 得 + Complement

Examples

- 你没戴眼镜，看 得 清楚 吗?
  Nǐ méi dài yǎnjìng, kàn de qīngchu ma?
  You didn't wear glasses. Can you see clearly?
- 他这么粗心，做 得 好 吗?
  Tā zhème cūxīn, zuò de hǎo ma?
  He'a so careless. Can he do it well?

1. Direction complement (Grammar), page 133

- 你这么聪明，肯定学 得 会 。
  Nǐ zhème cōngming, kěndìng xué de huì .
  You're so smart. You can definitely learn this.
- 早上五点出发，孩子们起 得 来 吗？
  Zǎoshang wǔdiǎn chūfā, háizi men qǐ de lái ma?
  We're leaving at five a.m.. Will the kids be able to get up?
- 这么高的山，你爬 得 上去 吗？
  Zhème gāo de shān, nǐ pá de shàngqù ma?
  The mountain is so high. Can you climb to the top?

Negative Form

The only difference between the affirmative and negative forms is swapping a 得 for a 不.

Structure

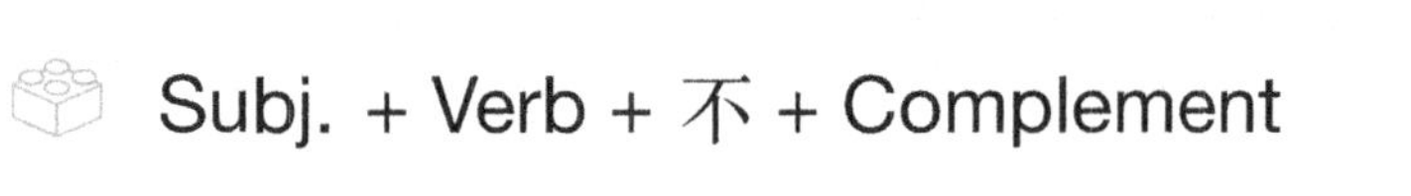
Subj. + Verb + 不 + Complement

Examples

- 你的声音太小了，我们听 不 见 。
  Nǐ de shēngyīn tài xiǎo le, wǒmen tīng bu jiàn .
  Your voice is too soft. We can't hear you.
- 这里太暗了，我看 不 清楚 。
  Zhèlǐ tài àn le, wǒ kàn bu qīngchu .
  It's too dim here. I can't see clearly.
- 这个自行车太破了，谁都修 不 好 。
  Zhège zìxíngchē tài pò le, shéi dōu xiū bu hǎo .
  This bike is so beaten up. Nobody can fix it.
- 她的腿受伤了，站 不 起来 了。
  Tā de tuǐ shòushāng le, zhàn bu qǐlái le.
  Her leg is injured. She can't stand.

- 包太小了，手机放 不 进去 。
  Bāo tài xiǎo le, shǒujī fàng bu jìnqù .
  The bag is too small. I can't fit the cell phone in it.

Potential Complement with Objects

Objects in sentences with potential complements can occur either after the complement or at the beginning of a sentence.

A few examples:

- 你听 得 懂 上海话吗?
  Nǐ tīng de dǒng Shànghǎi-huà ma?
  Can you understand Shanghai dialect?
- 她这么小，看 得 懂 这本书吗?
  Tā zhème xiǎo, kàn de dǒng zhè běn shū ma?
  She's so young. Can she really understand this book?
- 我怕我做 不 好 这份工作。
  Wǒ pà wǒ zuò bu hǎo zhè fèn gōngzuò.
  I'm afraid that I can't do this job well.
- 这种手机现在买 不 到 了。
  Zhè zhǒng shǒujī xiànzài mǎi bu dào le.
  You can't buy this type of cell phone now.
- 这本书我一个星期肯定看 得 完 。
  Zhè běn shū wǒ yī gè xīngqī kěndìng kàn de wán .
  I can definitely finish reading this book within one week.

Advanced Potential Complements

There are actually quite a few potential complements out there, and this article touches on some of the simplest and most common ones. Be aware that there are many more, but they all follow the same basic pattern outlined here. You can also refer to our article on advanced potential complements.

Similar to

- Potential complement "-bu dong" for not understanding (HSK2)
- Direction complement (HSK3, HSK4), page 133
- Advanced potential complements (HSK5)

- Advanced result complements (HSK5)
- Using “zhao” as complement (HSK5)

Result complement "-xiaqu"

下去 (xiàqù) can be used as a result complement to talk about things *continuing* or *carrying on*. Think of it as a figurative way of "keeping the ball rolling" (downhill).

Affirmative Form

Structure-wise, this pattern is the same as other result complements.

Structure

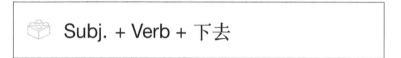

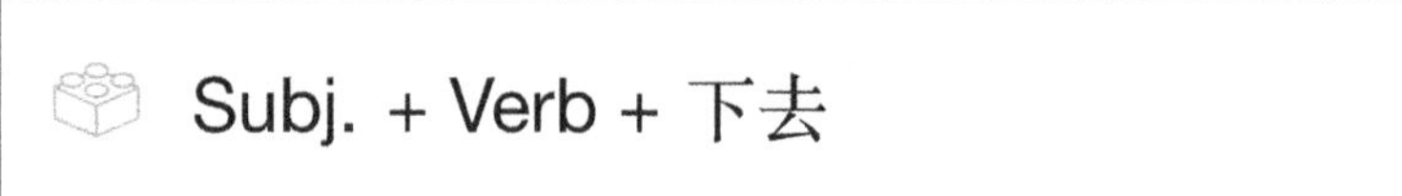

Examples

- 说 下去 。
  Shuō xiàqù.
  Keep talking.
- 这本书你一定要认真地 看 下去 。
  Zhè běn shū nǐ yīdìng yào rènzhēn de kàn xiàqù.
  You must keep reading this book carefully.
- 这样做很有意义，你应该 做 下去 。
  Zhèyàng zuò hěn yǒu yìyì, nǐ yīnggāi zuò xiàqù.
  It's very meaningful to do this. You should keep doing it.
- 他走了，因为他没脸 待 下去 了。
  Tā zǒu le, yīnwèi tā méiliǎn dāi xiàqù le.
  He left because he felt shame if he stayed.
- 你不能这样 生活 下去 了。
  Nǐ bù néng zhèyàng shēnghuó xiàqù le.
  You can't keep living like this.

Negative Form

Strictly speaking, simply adding 不 in front of the main verb is all it takes to create the negative form. But it's actually more common to use this negative potential complement[1] form. So it's not just "not go on" (doing something), but actually "*can't* go on" (doing something).

Structure

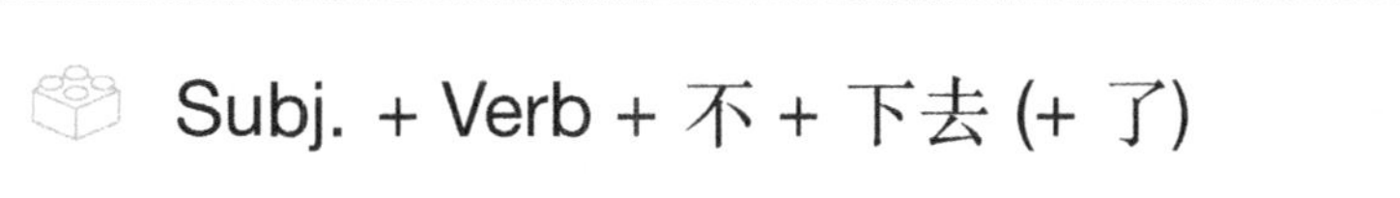

Subj. + Verb + 不 + 下去 (+ 了)

Note that 了 is often used when it's negated.

Examples

- 这个故事太无聊了，我听 不下去 了 。
  Zhège gùshi tài wúliáo le, wǒ tīng bu xiàqù le .
  This story is too boring, I can't keep listening.
- 这个电影太暴力了，我看 不下去 了 。
  Zhège diànyǐng tài bàolì le, wǒ kàn bu xiàqù le .
  This movie is too violent. I can't keep watching it.
- 你说话太恶心了，我吃 不下去 了 。
  Nǐ shuōhuà tài ěxīn le, wǒ chī bu xiàqù le .
  The way you talk is so disgusting. I can't continue eating my food.
- 这个宾馆太脏了，我待 不下去 了 。
  Zhège bīnguǎn tài zāng le, wǒ dāi bu xiàqù le .
  This hotel is too dirty. I can't stay here any longer.
- 我跟他过 不下去 了 ，我要离婚。
  Wǒ gēn tā guò bu xiàqù le , wǒ yào líhūn.
  I can't go on like this with him. I want a divorce.

Used with 再

When the adverb 再 comes before the verb, there's an implication that if "things keep going on this way," then something bad is going to happen.

A few examples:

---

1. Potential complement (Grammar), page 140

- 你 再 赌 下去 会 输光的。

  Nǐ zài dǔ xiàqù huì shūguāng de.

  If you keep gambling, you're going to lose all your money.

- 你 再 喝 下去 就 醉了。

  Nǐ zài hē xiàqù jiù zuì le.

  If you keep drinking you're going to get drunk.

Similar to

- Advanced uses of direction complement "-qilai" (HSK4)
- Direction complement "-qilai" (HSK4)
- Advanced result complements (HSK5)

Result complements

Result complements come immediately after verbs to indicate that an action has led to a certain result and make that result clear to the listener. Often the complement is simply an adjective like 好 (hǎo) or a single syllable like 完 (wán).

Using Adjectives

好 (hǎo) implies that something is done to *completion* or done *well*. Forming a result complement with 好 has a very similar meaning to forming one with 完. It expresses that the action has been completed successfully.

错 (cuò) is used to express that an action has been performed incorrectly in some way, resulting in a mistake (错). This pattern covers what is often expressed with the adverb "incorrectly" in English.

Other adjectives commonly used as result complements include: 晚 (wǎn), 饱 (bǎo), 坏 (huài), 清楚 (qīngchu), 干净 (gānjìng), 破 (pò).

Structure

For the basic structure, you'll almost always see a 了 after the complement:

Subj. + Verb + Adj. + 了 (+ Obj.)

To negate a result complement, use 没 instead of 不:

Subj. + 没 + Verb + Adj. (+ Obj.)

Examples

- 你吃好了吗?
  Nǐ chī hǎo le ma?
  Are you done eating?
- 对不起，我记错了时间。
  Duìbuqǐ, wǒ jì cuò le shíjiān.
  Sorry, I misremembered the time.

- 你来 晚 了 ，我们已经关门 了 。
  Nǐ lái wǎn le , wǒmen yǐjīng guānmén le .
  You came too late. We're already closed.
- 他玩 坏 了 哥哥的玩具。
  Tā wán huài le gēge de wánjù.
  He broke his older brother's toy.
- 我 没 吃 饱 。
  Wǒ méi chī bǎo .
  I didn't get full.
- 他还 没 想 好 。
  Tā hái méi xiǎng hǎo .
  He hasn't thought it through yet.
- 我们 没 听 清楚 ，请再说一遍。
  Wǒmen méi tīng qīngchu , qǐng zài shuō yī biàn.
  We didn't hear it clearly. Please say it again.

When using result complements, it's very common to make the object a topic. This means the object is moved to the beginning of the sentence and the subject is often omitted.

Some examples:

- 这个字 写 错 了。
  Zhège zì xiě cuò le.
  You wrote this character wrong.
- 杯子 摔 坏 了。
  Bēizi shuāi huài le.
  The cup is broken.
- 房间 打扫 干净 了吗?
  Fángjiān dǎsǎo gānjìng le ma?
  Is your room all cleaned up?

Using One-Syllable Verbs

Besides adjectives, there are a few single-syllable verbs which can also be used as result complements. Some examples include 到 (dào), 见 (jiàn), 懂 (dǒng), 会 (huì), 走 (zǒu), 掉 (diào). There really aren't a lot of these, which is part of the reason why these are usually seen as one verb instead of a verb-complement structure.

Structure

For the basic structure, you'll often see a 了 after the complement:

> Subj. + Verb + [One-syllable Verb] + 了 (+ Obj.)

Examples

- 你们都 听懂 了吗?
  Nǐmen dōu tīng dǒng le ma?
  Do you all understand?
- 我看了，但是没 看懂 。
  Wǒ kàn le, dànshì méi kàn dǒng .
  I read it, but I didn't really understand it.
- 你 踩到 了我的脚。
  Nǐ cǎi dào le wǒ de jiǎo.
  You're stepping on my foot.
- 我不小心 撞到 了墙。
  Wǒ bù xiǎoxīn zhuàng dào le qiáng.
  I hit the wall by accident.
- 我女儿 学会 了数数。
  Wǒ nǚ'ér xué huì le shǔ shù.
  My daughter has learned how to count.
- 我爸爸还没 学会 用智能手机。
  Wǒ bàba hái méi xué huì yòng zhìnéng shǒujī.
  My father hasn't learned how to use a smartphone yet.
- 老师 拿走 了我的 iPad 。
  Lǎoshī ná zǒu le wǒ de iPad.
  The teacher took away my iPad.

- 小偷 偷走 了我的钱包。
  Xiǎotōu tōu zǒu le wǒ de qiánbāo.
  The thief stole my wallet.
- 他不小心 推倒 了一个老人。
  Tā bù xiǎoxīn tuī dǎo le yī gè lǎorén.
  He pushed over an old person by accident.
- 你 撞倒 了我的自行车。
  Nǐ zhuàng dǎo le wǒ de zìxíngchē.
  You knocked over my bike.
- 谁 扔掉 了我的袜子?
  Shéi rēng diào le wǒ de wàzi?
  Who threw away my socks?
- 我 卖掉 了我的旧手机。
  Wǒ mài diào le wǒ de jiù shǒujī.
  I sold my old cell phone.

Compared with Potential Complements

Result Complement	Aff. Potential Complement	Neg. Potential Complement
做完	做 得 完	做 不 完
听懂	听 得 懂	听 不 懂
看清楚	看 得 清楚	看 不 清楚
洗干净	洗 得 干净	洗 不 干净

Used in 把 Sentences

Although we have avoided 把 sentences in this article for the sake of simplicity, you may have noticed that sentences which feature result complements often also use 把. This is because 把 sentences and result complements work particularly well together, as they both deal with the result of an action or the "disposal" of an object. Apart from result complements involving perception and psychological verbs, most result compounds work nicely in 把 sentences.

- 我 把 杯子 摔坏 了。
  Wǒ bǎ bēizi shuāi huài le .
  I broke the glass.
- 他 把 我的电脑 修好 了。
  Tā bǎ wǒ de diànnǎo xiū hǎo le .
  He fixed my computer.
- 小偷 把 我的钱包 偷走 了。
  Xiǎotōu bǎ wǒ de qiánbāo tōu zǒu le .
  The thief made off with my wallet.
- 我们 把 房间 打扫干净 了。
  Wǒmen bǎ fángjiān dǎsǎo gānjìng le .
  We've cleaned the room.

Similar to

- Result complement "-wan" for finishing (HSK2)
- Using "bei" sentences (HSK3), page 175
- Expressing "mistakenly think that" with "yiwei" (HSK4)
- Expressing not knowing how to do something using "hao" (HSK4)
- Adjectival complement "de hen" (HSK5)

Expressing "as long as" with "zhiyao"

只要……就……(zhǐyào… jiù…) means "as long as… then…." In other words, *whenever* A happens, B (always) results.

Structure

Use this structure to express that "as long as" [something happens], "then" [something else will happen]. In logic, this is referred to as a "sufficient condition," meaning that it may not be the *only way* to bring about the these specific consequences, but it is *one reliable way*.

只要 + Condition，就 + Result

Examples

- 只要 你真的喜欢，我 就 给你买。
  Zhǐyào nǐ zhēnde xǐhuan, wǒ jiù gěi nǐ mǎi.
  As long as you really like it, I will buy it for you.
- 只要 你努力学习，就 会有进步。
  Zhǐyào nǐ nǔlì xuéxí, jiù huì yǒu jìnbù.
  As long as you study hard, you'll make progress.
- 只要 有你在，我 就 放心了。
  Zhǐyào yǒu nǐ zài, wǒ jiù fàngxīn le.
  As long as you are here, I won't be worried.
- 只要 下雨，她 就 会心情不好。
  Zhǐyào xiàyǔ, tā jiù huì xīnqíng bù hǎo.
  Whenever it rains, she will be in a bad mood.
- 只要 看到妈妈，宝宝 就 不哭了。
  Zhǐyào kàn dào māma, bǎobao jiù bù kū le.
  As long as she sees her mother, the baby will stop crying.
- 只要 你完成了工作，就 可以不用加班。
  Zhǐyào nǐ wánchéng le gōngzuò, jiù kěyǐ bùyòng jiābān.
  As long as you have finished your work, there is no need to do overtime.

- 只要 你妈妈同意你去北京，我 就 没有意见。
  Zhǐyào nǐ māma tóngyì nǐ qù Běijīng, wǒ jiù méiyǒu yìjiàn.
  As long as your mother agrees with you going to Beijing, I have no issue with it.
- 只要 不堵车，我们 就 能准时到。
  Zhǐyào bù dǔchē, wǒmen jiù néng zhǔnshí dào.
  As long as traffic isn't bad, we can get there on time.
- 只要 你不生气，我 就 告诉你。
  Zhǐyào nǐ bù shēngqì, wǒ jiù gàosu nǐ.
  As long as you won't get mad, I'll tell you.
- 只要 你的要求是合理的，我们 就 可以考虑。
  Zhǐyào nǐ de yāoqiú shì hélǐ de, wǒmen jiù kěyǐ kǎolǜ.
  As long as your requirements are reasonable, we can consider them.

Similar to

- Expressing "only if" with "zhiyou" (HSK3), page 154
- Expressing "as long as" with "fanshi" (HSK6)

Expressing "only if" with "zhiyou"

只有 (zhǐyǒu) means "only if," and is used with 才 (cái) to emphasize that *only one* course of action will bring about the desired outcome.

Structure

只有 + Essential Condition + 才 + Desired Outcome

Note that 才 is often followed by 能, but not always.

Examples

- 只有 努力 才 能做好工作。
  Zhǐyǒu nǔlì cái néng zuò hǎo gōngzuò.
  Only if you work hard is it possible to do a good job.
- 只有 多吃饭 才 能长高。
  Zhǐyǒu duō chīfàn cái néng zhǎng gāo.
  Only if you eat more will you be able to grow tall.
- 只有 多说，你的中文 才 会提高。
  Zhǐyǒu duō shuō, nǐ de Zhōngwén cái huì tígāo.
  Only if you speak more will your Chinese improve.
- 只有 大家一起做 才 能成功。
  Zhǐyǒu dàjiā yīqǐ zuò cái néng chénggōng.
  Only if everyone works together can we succeed.
- 只有 写完你的作业 才 能看电视。
  Zhǐyǒu xiě wán nǐ de zuòyè cái néng kàn diànshì.
  Only if you finish your homework can you watch TV.
- 只有 妈妈在我们 才 能出去玩。
  Zhǐyǒu māma zài wǒmen cái néng chūqù wán.
  Only if Mom is here can we go out and play.

- 只有 每天跑步，你的身体 才 会健康。
  Zhǐyǒu měi tiān pǎobù, nǐ de shēntǐ cái huì jiànkāng.
  Only if you go running every day can you have a healthy body.
- 只有 老板同意这个建议，我们 才 能做。
  Zhǐyǒu lǎobǎn tóngyì zhège jiànyì, wǒmen cái néng zuò.
  We can only do this if the boss agrees with the suggestion.
- 只有 你吃过了，你 才 能说好不好吃。
  Zhǐyǒu nǐ chī guò le, nǐ cái néng shuō hǎo bù hǎochī.
  You can only tell if it's good or not if you have eaten it before.
- 只有 学习了拼音，你 才 能更好地学汉字。
  Zhǐyǒu xuéxí le pīnyīn, nǐ cái néng gèng hǎo de xué hànzì.
  Only if you have learned pinyin can you learn Chinese characters better.

Similar to

- Expressing "as long as" with "zhiyao" (HSK3, HSK4), page 152
- Expressing "if" with "ruguo… dehua" (HSK3), page 208
- Expressing "if… then…" with "ruguo… jiu…" (HSK3), page 210
- Expressing "once…then…" with "yidan…jiu…" (HSK5)

Using "youde" to mean "some"

To refer to just *certain* members of group, you can use 有的 (yǒude). This usage is normally translated as "some" in English. It is often used multiple times in one sentence to refer to different groups.

Structure

All you need to do is put 有的 (yǒude) before the nouns there are "some of" in the sentence. If there is already some context, you can omit the subject, and the 有的 (yǒude) can just mean "some" instead of "some of something."

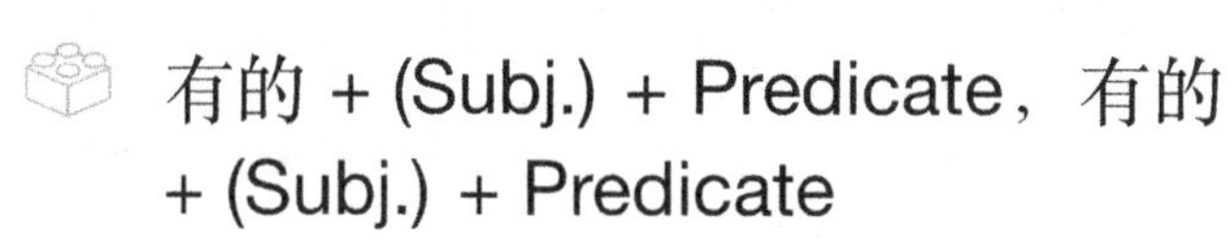

Also, you aren't limited to just two 有的 (yǒude) in the sentence. You can have multiple groups doing different things, and just precede them with a 有的 (yǒude) each time.

Examples

- 外国人 有的 很有钱，有的 没钱。
  Wàiguó rén yǒude hěn yǒuqián, yǒude méi qián.
  Some foreigners are rich, but some aren't.
- 我们公司有一些电脑，有的 是新的，有的 是旧的。
  Wǒmen gōngsī yǒu yīxiē diànnǎo, yǒude shì xīn de, yǒude shì jiù de.
  Our company has some computers. Some are new, and some are old.
- 他写了很多书，有的 卖得很好，有的 卖得不好。
  Tā xiě le hěn duō shū, yǒude mài de hěn hǎo, yǒude mài de bù hǎo.
  He has written a lot of books. Some sell well, but some don't.
- 中国菜 有的 好吃，有的 不好吃。
  Zhōngguó cài yǒude hāochī, yǒude bù hāochī.
  Some Chinese foods are tasty, while some aren't.
- 这家店的衣服 有的 贵，有的 便宜。
  Zhè jiā diàn de yīfu yǒude guì, yǒude piányi.
  In this shop, some of the clothes are expensive and some are cheap.

- 他有很多房子，有的 在国内，有的 在国外。
  Tā yǒu hěn duō fángzi, yǒude zài guónèi, yǒude zài guówài.
  He has a lot of houses, some of them are within the country and some are abroad.
- 晚上六点以后，有的 人下班了，有的 人在加班。
  Wǎnshang liùdiǎn yǐhòu, yǒude rén xiàbān le, yǒude rén zài jiābān.
  After six o'clock some people are off work, while some are still working.
- 我的大学老师 有的 很年轻，有的 很老。
  Wǒ de dàxué lǎoshī yǒude hěn niánqīng, yǒude hěn lǎo.
  Some of my college teachers are young, some are old.
- 酒吧里，有的 人在喝酒，有的 人在跳舞，还 有的 人在聊天。
  Jiǔbā lǐ, yǒude rén zài hējiǔ, yǒude rén zài tiàowǔ, hái yǒude rén zài liáotiān.
  In the bar, some people are drinking, some are dancing, and some are chatting.
- 因为工作，我认识了很多人，有的 是大学老师，有的 是 CEO。
  Yīnwèi gōngzuò, wǒ rènshi le hěn duō rén, yǒude shì dàxué lǎoshī, yǒude shì CEO.
  I know a lot of people because of my work. Some are college teachers and some are CEOs.

Similar to

- Expressing “some” with “yixie” (HSK1)
- Using “ji” to mean “several” (HSK2)

Expressing "half" with "ban"

The Chinese word 半 (bàn) means "half." That's simple enough, but what can get slightly tricky is the rules for how it combines with measure words.

Basic Usage

Used Alone

Structure

You'll need to use a measure word (Measure Word) in this structure.

Examples

The measure words are also indicated below.

- 半 个 小时
  bàn gè xiǎoshí
  half an hour
- 半 个 月
  bàn gè yuè
  half a month
- 半 碗 米饭
  bàn wǎn mǐfàn
  half a bowl of rice
- 半 瓶 酒
  bàn píng jiǔ
  half a bottle of liquor
- 半 份 炒面
  bàn fèn chǎomiàn
  half a serving of chow mein

With a Number

When it's more than just a half, then 半 (bàn) comes after the measure word instead of before. It's the difference between "half an hour" and "an hour and a half."

- 半 个 小时
  bàn gè xiǎoshí
  half an hour
- 一 个 半 小时
  yī gè bàn xiǎoshí
  an hour and a half

The order is actually basically the same as what we do in English (we just don't have so many pesky measure words to keep track of in English!).

Structure

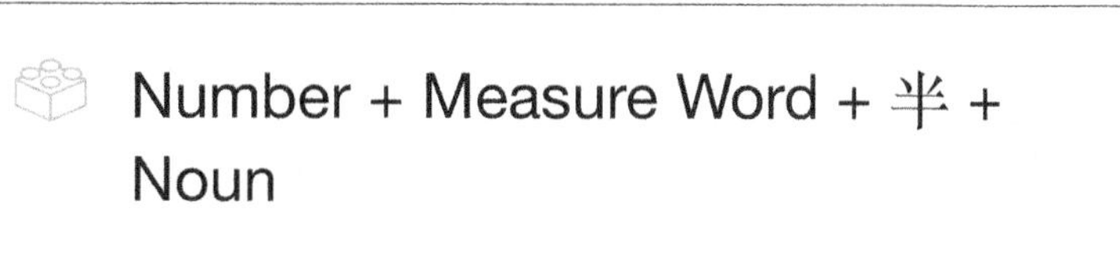
Number + Measure Word + 半 + Noun

Examples

- 三 个 半 小时
  sān gè bàn xiǎoshí
  three and a half hours
- 两 个 半 月
  liǎng gè bàn yuè
  two and a half months
- 一 斤 半 水果
  yī jīn bàn shuǐguǒ
  one and a half jin of fruit

One "jin" = 500g

- 一 瓶 半 白酒
  yī píng bàn báijiǔ
  one and a half bottles of wine
- 四 块 半 巧克力
  sì kuài bàn qiǎokèlì
  four and a half pieces of chocolate

Notable Exceptions

There are some words that act as their own measure words, notably the time words 天 (tiān), meaning "day," and 年 (nián), meaning "year."

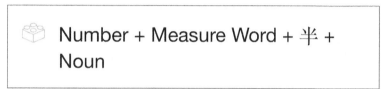

Used Alone

Structure

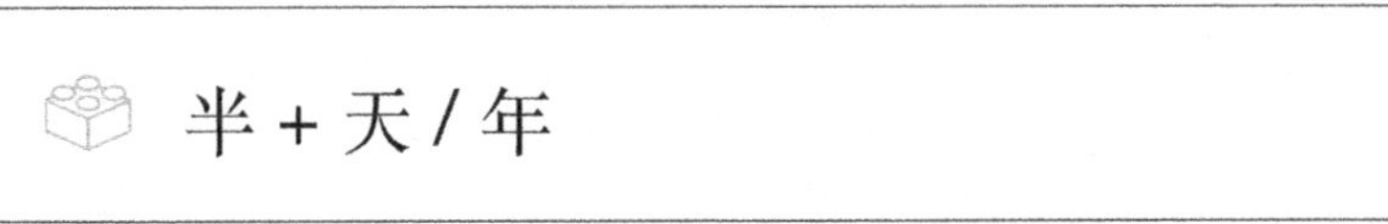

Examples

半 天
bàn tiān
half a day
半 年
bàn nián
half a year

Note that you do *not* need to use 个 (gè) here; in fact, it's *wrong* to do so:

× 半 个 天
bàn gè tiān
half a day
× 半 个 年
bàn gè nián
half a year

With a Number

天 (tiān) and 年 (nián) aren't the *only* words that take this alternate pattern, but they're the two key ones you need to learn first.

Structure

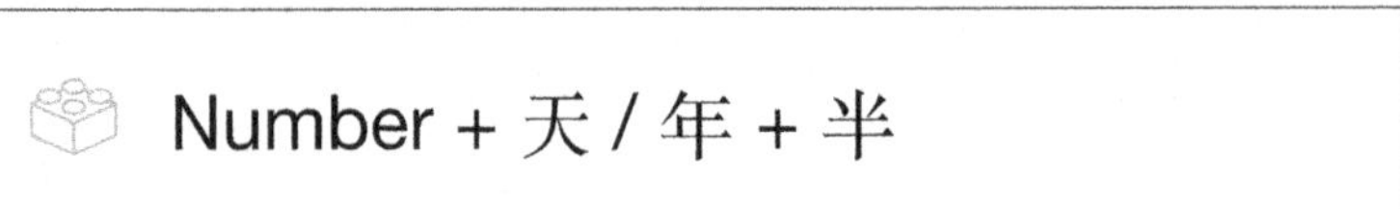

Examples

- 两 天 半
  liǎng tiān bàn
  two and a half days

- 一 年 半
  yī nián bàn
  a year and a half
- 三 天 半
  sān tiān bàn
  three and a half days
- 四 年 半
  sì nián bàn
  four and a half years

Expressing "not even one"

In English we might want to say something like "I have absolutely no money, not even one penny." Expressing that "not even one" can take one of several forms, all of which are common in everyday Chinese.

Basic Pattern

Structure

This structure is usually used for emphasizing how little of something there is. The measure word in the middle of the sentence and the noun should be compatible with the verb at the end.

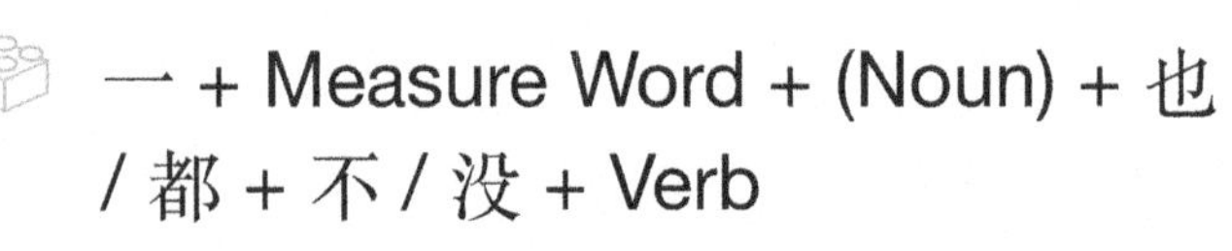

Examples

- 他 一 句话 都 没说。
  Tā yī jù huà dōu méi shuō.
  He didn't say a thing.
- 他 一 句中文 都 不会说。
  Tā yī jù Zhōngwén dōu bù huì shuō.
  He can't speak one sentence of Chinese.
- 为什么这里 一 个人 都 没有?
  Wèishénme zhèlǐ yī gè rén dōu méiyǒu?
  Why is there not a single person here?
- 我 一 口 都 没吃。
  Wǒ yī kǒu dōu méi chī.
  I haven't had a single bite.
- 来上海以前，他 一 个外国朋友 都 没有。
  Lái Shànghǎi yǐqián, tā yī gè wàiguó péngyou dōu méiyǒu.
  He didn't have a single foreign friend before coming to Shanghai.

- 她 一 瓶可乐 也 没喝。
  Tā yī píng kělè yě méi hē.
  She didn't drink a single bottle of cola.
- 我 一 点消息 都 不知道。
  Wǒ yī diǎn xiāoxi dōu bù zhīdào.
  I don't know a single thing.

Advanced Pattern

Structure

If you want to put the topic of your conversation at the beginning of the sentence, make sure the comment which follows has a strong emphasis or some kind of extreme quality.

> Topic + Subj. + 一 + Measure Word + (Noun) + 也 / 都 + Verb

Examples

- 这个人 我 一 次 都 没见过。
  Zhège rén wǒ yī cì yě méi jiàn guo.
  I've never met this person even once.
- 这样的菜 我 一 次 也 没吃过。
  Zhèyàng de cài wǒ yī cì yě méi chī guo.
  I've never eaten this kind of food before.
- 这次活动 我们公司 一 个人 也 没参加。
  Zhè cì huódòng wǒmen gōngsī yī gè rén yě méi cānjiā.
  Not one person in our company has participated in this activity.

Dictionaries

Similar to

- Advanced uses of "lian" (HSK4)
- Expressing "even" with "lian" and "dou" (HSK4)
- Expressing "not at all" with "yidianr ye bu" (HSK4)

Expressing "the more... the more..." with "yue... yue..."

More than "putting stuff" after two instances of 越 (yuè) in a sentence, there are a number of very specific patterns you will notice if you want to get more sophisticated with 越 (yuè) and go beyond using the simpler 越来越 (yuèláiyuè)[1].

Pattern with a Single Subject

Structure

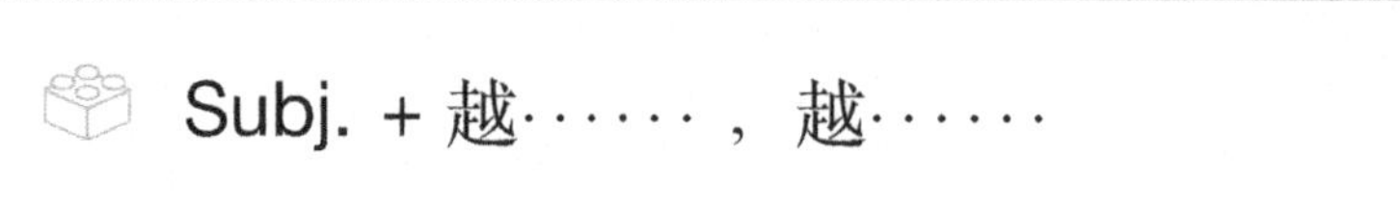

Subj. + 越……，越……

It's normally verbs or verb phrases following each 越, but adjectives are also possible (typically after the second 越).

Examples

- 我们 越 想 越 生气。
  Wǒmen yuè xiǎng yuè shēngqì.
  The more we think about it, the angrier we get.
- 我 越 看 越 喜欢。
  Wǒ yuè kàn yuè xǐhuan.
  The more I look at it, the more I like it.

Sometimes this pattern is best translated into English as "more and more," which is similar to 越来越 (yuèláiyuè)[1].

- 他 越 跑 越 快。
  Tā yuè pǎo yuè kuài.
  He ran faster and faster. / The more he ran, the faster he got.
  "faster and faster" = "more and more fast"
- 雨 越 下 越 大。
  Yǔ yuè xià yuè dà.
  The rain got heavier and heavier. / The more it rained, the heavier it got.
  "heavier and heavier" = "more and more heavy"

---

1. Expressing "more and more" with "yuelaiyue" (Grammar), page 189

Pattern with Two Different Subjects

Structure

What follows the first 越 is mostly the reason why the second 越 phrase happens.

> Subj. 1 + 越……, Subj. 2 + 越……

Again, it's normally verbs or verb phrases following each 越, but adjectives are also possible (typically after the second 越).

Examples

- 她越说，我越生气。
  Tā yuè shuō, wǒ yuè shēngqì.
  The more she talks, the angrier I get.
- 你们越看我，我越紧张。
  Nǐmen yuè kàn wǒ, wǒ yuè jǐnzhāng.
  The more you look at me, the more nervous I am.
- 我越走，腿越痛。
  Wǒ yuè zǒu, tuǐ yuè tòng.
  The more I walk, the more my legs hurt.

The More... the Less...

This is actually the same pattern as the last one, but it's different English translation makes it worth paying attention to.

Structure

Examples

- 你越让孩子学，孩子越不想学。
  Nǐ yuè ràng háizi xué, háizi yuè bù xiǎng xué.
  The more you push the kid to study, the less he wants to learn.
- 他越问，我越不想说。
  Tā yuè wèn, wǒ yuè bù xiǎng shuō.
  The more he asks, the less I want to tell him.
- 你越这样说，他越不听。
  Nǐ yuè zhèyàng shuō, tā yuè bù tīng.
  The more you talk this way, the less he listens.

Colloquial Saying

This pattern involves the same verb repeated after each 越. It is limited to a small number of single-syllable verbs related to sensory perception, but you do hear it used.

Structure

Examples

- 这本书我越看越想看。
  Zhè běn shū wǒ yuè kàn yuè xiǎng kàn.
  The more I read this book, the more I want to read.
- 这种零食让人越吃越想吃。
  Zhè zhǒng língshí ràng rén yuè chī yuè xiǎng chī.
  The more you eat it, the more you will want to eat.
- 我吃了这个药以后总是想睡觉，而且越睡越想睡。
  Wǒ chī le zhè gè yào yǐhòu zǒngshì xiǎng shuìjiào, érqiě yuè shuì yuè xiǎng shuì.
  I'm always so sleepy after taking this medicine. And also, the more I sleep, the more I want to sleep.

Similar to

- Expressing "more and more" with "yuelaiyue" (HSK3), page 189

Using "ba" sentences

Also known as: 把字句 ("bǎ"zìjù), 把 construction, preposition 把, disposal construction and pre-transitive 把.

The 把 (bǎ) sentence is a useful structure for constructing longer sentences which focus on the result or influence of an action. One of its key features is that it brings the object of the verb closer to the front of the sentence and precedes it with a 把. It's really common in Mandarin but can feel a bit awkward at first for English speakers.

What is a 把 sentence?

A basic sentence in Mandarin is formed with a subject-verb-object (SVO) word order, as in English:

Subj. + [Verb Phrase] + Obj.

A 把 sentence shakes things up a bit, and you get this structure:

Subj. + 把 + Obj. + [Verb Phrase]

Note that the **object has moved**, and is preceded by 把. You now have SOV word order.

This is all well and good, but most students of Chinese, on learning about 把 sentences for the first time, have the same reaction: *"Why the heck would I ever use this structure? The SVO word order always works just fine, right?"* The answer is: well, no… not always. It's true that 把 sentences are often used to achieve somewhat subtle differences in emphasis, but there are also very good reasons to use 把 sentences when a regular sentence just won't do. Take this sentence for example:

- 把书放在桌子上。
  Bǎ shū fàng zài zhuōzi shàng.
  Put the book on the table.

How would you say this without the 把 construction? You might try this:

✖ 放书在桌子上。
Fàng shū zài zhuōzi shàng.

The problem is that the above Chinese sentence is not grammatical. *You can't put an object right after a verb, and then put other modifiers of the verb after the object.* Here are other examples of how to successfully use 把 and 放 in the same sentence.

- 她 把 我的手机 放 在 她的包 里 了。
  Tā bǎ wǒ de shǒujī fàng zài tā de bāo lǐ le.
  She put my cell phone in her bag.
- 他 把 脏衣服 放 在 床 下面 了。
  Tā bǎ zāng yīfu fàng zài chuáng xiàmiàn le.
  He put his dirty laundry under the bed.
- 你是不是 把 护照 放 在 行李箱 里 了？
  Nǐ shì bu shì bǎ hùzhào fàng zài xínglixiāng lǐ le?
  Did you put your passport in your suitcase?

For each of these, the sentence would be ungrammatical if you tried to do away with the 把 and put the object right after the verb.

Key Things to Keep in Mind When Using 把

- The object should be known. So it has already been mentioned or discussed previously.
- 把字句 are most often used to describe what happened to the object in some detail. The verb is not just "bare"; there's "more stuff" after it. Often the "stuff" is related to some kind of manipulation of the object.
- 把字句 are not tied to any particular time. You can use them when talking about events in the past, or for making a request.

把 Sentences with Two Objects

The usual structure for 把 sentences, as described above, puts the object right after 把. For certain verbs, however, you can have two objects in a 把 sentence. Their use in a 把 sentence will also involve prepositions.

They use the following structure:

> Subj. + 把 + Obj. 1 + Verb + 给 + Obj. 2

Common verbs that take two objects include: 送 (sòng), 拿 (ná), 递 (dì), 卖

(mài), 借 (jiè), 还 (huán), 介绍 (jièshào).

Subject	把	Object 1	Verb	Preposition	Object 2		
我们	把	礼物	送	给	客人	了	。
把	盐	递	给	我	。		
他	把	房子	卖	给	谁	了	?
我	把	他	介绍	给	我老板	了	。

把 Sentences with Complements

Because 把 sentences are all about "doing stuff" to the object, and complements in Mandarin often handle this issue, it's good to be aware of how these two grammar features interact.

Result complements work particularly well in 把 sentences. When you consider that both structures deal with the result or outcome of an action, this makes sense. The majority of result complements (except for perception verbs) fit in very well in a 把 construction. For example:

- 我 把 作业做 完 了。
  Wǒ bǎ zuòyè zuò wán le.
  I finished doing my homework.
- 老师 把 我的名字读 错 了。
  Lǎoshī bǎ wǒ de míngzi dú cuò le.
  The teacher read my name wrong.

Direction complements[1] also work well in 把 constructions, for similar reasons. For example:

- 请 把 客人带 进去 。
  Qǐng bǎ kèrén dài jìnqù .
  Please take the guests inside.
- 把 我的眼镜拿 过来 。
  Bǎ wǒ de yǎnjìng ná guòlái .
  Please bring my glasses over here.

1. Direction complement (Grammar), page 133

Note that potential complements[1] do not appear in 把 sentences. This is because they are hypothetical, whereas a 把 sentence must describe what actually happens.

Forming 把 Sentences

Since the basic structure has already been given above, we can jump right into some more exciting patterns!

Negating 把 Sentences

To negate a 把 sentence, insert 不要 or 别 (present or future) or 没有 (past) directly in front of 把. You can't put it after 把, 'inside' the 把 construction, as this would break the rule about describing what actually happened to the object. It would be like saying "What happened to… was nothing." It doesn't sound natural.

Subject	Negative	把	Object	Verb Phrase	
阿姨	没有	把	房间	打扫干净	。
我	没	把	钱	借给他	。
你们	不要	把	这件事	告诉她	。

Question Forms of 把 Sentences

You can make 把 sentences into questions in the usual three ways to form questions in Mandarin:

- With a question particle
- With a question word
- With positive-negative verbs

Some examples:

- 你们 把 那个问题 解决了吗?
  Nǐmen bǎ nàge wèntí jiějué le ma?
  Did you solve that problem?
- 你 把 我手机 放在哪儿了?
  Nǐ bǎ wǒ shǒujī fàng zài nǎr le?
  Where did you put my cell phone?

1. Potential complement (Grammar), page 140

- 他 把 钱 借给谁了?
  Tā bǎ qián jiè gěi shéi le?
  Who did he lend the money to?
- 你能不能 把 你房间 打扫干净?
  Nǐ néng bu néng bǎ nǐ fángjiān dǎsǎo gānjìng?
  Can you clean your room or not?

Be careful how you form questions with 把 sentences though. Remember that you have to have a definite object, and you have to describe what was done to that object. A question form could easily get in the way of one of these conditions.

Adverbs in 把 Sentences

Adverbs can usually be placed before 把 or before the verb (the exception is negative adverbs, as described above). Adverbs in each of these positions can change the meaning in slightly different ways, as demonstrated with 都 in the examples below.

Subj.	Adv.	把	Object	Adv.	Verb Phrase
我们	都	把	作业	做完了	。
他	把	咖啡	都	喝完了	。
他	已经	把	钱	还给我了	。
我	可能	把	手机	忘在朋友家了	。

In the first sentence, 都 modifies 我们 to express "we all finished the homework." In the second sentence, 都 modifies 咖啡 to express "he finished all the coffee".

把 Sentences and Quantity Phrases

As mentioned above, the object of a 把 sentence must be something specific and definite. This might involve noun measure words, which will come after the 把 and before the object.

Subject	把	Quantity Phrase	Noun	Verb Phrase	
我	把	那 两件	脏衣服	洗干净了	。

他	把	最后 三块	蛋糕	吃完了	。
你	把	这 几句	话	读一下	。

Verb measure words are frequently used in 把 sentences and come at the end of a 把 sentence.

Subject	把	Object	Verb	Quantity Phrase	
把	课文	读	一遍	。	
她	把	这个字	写了	十遍	。
他	把	手机	摔坏过	两三次	。

Note that in all of these sentences, the object is something specific and definite.

Verbs for 把 Sentences

Some verbs generally can't indicate what happened *to* the object. They only describe what the subject did. Below are some examples of verbs that do not generally work in 把 sentences.

Psychological verbs: 爱 (ài) "to love," 喜欢 (xǐhuan) "to like," 想 (xiǎng) "to miss," 了解 (liǎojiě) "to know well," 害怕 (hàipà) "to fear," 恨 (hèn) "to hate."

Perception verbs: 看 (kàn) "to look at," 听 (tīng) "to listen to," 闻 (wén) "to smell," 像 (xiàng) "to resemble."

Other Uses of 把

It's important to note that 把 is a word with other uses. The most common is as a measure word for things with handles, or things that you hold. Examples include 一把伞 ("an umbrella"), 一把枪 ("a gun"), and 一把椅子 ("a chair"). So, you've got to look at how 把 is being used in a sentence before you can understand its meaning.

To demonstrate the difference, here's a sentence with both kinds of 把:

- 请你 把 那 把 伞拿给我。
  Qǐng nǐ bǎ nà bǎ sǎn ná gěi wǒ.
  Please give me that umbrella.

Similar to

- Advanced uses of “ba” (HSK5)
- Using “jiang” as a formal “ba” (HSK5)

Using "bei" sentences

被 (bèi) sentences, which are called 被字句 (bèizìjù) in Chinese, are a key way to express the passive voice in modern Mandarin Chinese. In passive sentences, the *object* of an action becomes the subject of the sentence, and the "doer" of the action, which would have been the subject of the normal (active voice) sentence, becomes secondary and may or may not be mentioned in the passive sentence.

What is a 被 sentence?

被 (bèi) sentences are simply sentences which use a passive verb and the word 被. 被 sentences are not the only way to create the passive verb form in Chinese, but they are the most common and definitely the type to tackle first.

For the sake of clarity, take these sentences for example:

- 男孩吃了 热狗 。
  Nánhái chī le règǒu .
  The boy ate the hot dog.
  active voice sentence: "the hot dog" is the object of the verb "ate"
- 热狗 被 男孩吃了。
  Règǒu bèi nánhái chī le.
  The hot dog was eaten by the boy.
  "the hot dog" is now the subject, and "the boy" is the "doer"
- 热狗 被 吃了。
  Règǒu bèi chī le.
  The hot dog was eaten.
  passive voice with the "doer" omitted

Why use them?

First, passive sentences indicate that one has been negatively affected. For example:

- 他 被 打了。
  Tā bèi dǎ le.
  He was beaten.

Second, passive sentences shift emphasis from the "doer" of the action to the one affected by that action. For example:

- 你 被 公司炒鱿鱼了？
  Nǐ bèi gōngsī chǎo yóuyú le?
  You got fired by the company?

Third, passive sentences allow one to avoid having to mention the "doer" of the action, either because it is unknown, or for other reasons. For example:

- 我的手机 被 偷了。
  Wǒ de shǒujī bèi tōu le.
  My cell phone got stolen.

How to Use 被 Sentences

Normal use of 被 has a few preconditions:

- The verb to be used with 被 needs to have an object (this will become the new subject of the 被 sentence). Verbs that take objects are called transitive verbs.
- If you're going to state *who the verb was done by* (the "doer"), then the subject doing the original action must be known.
- The verb can't be too simple (for example, a one-character verb like 吃). Put simply, *something needs to come after the verb*. That "something" can be a particle like 了, a complement, or sometimes even an additional object.

Structure

Subj. + 被 (+ Doer) + Verb + 了

Examples

被 sentences with a doer:

- 我 被 他 骗 了 。
  Wǒ bèi tā piàn le .
  I was deceived by him.
- 他 被 警察 抓 了 。
  Tā bèi jǐngchá zhuā le .
  He was caught by the police.
- 他 被 父母 骂 了 。
  Tā bèi fùmǔ mà le .
  He was scolded by his parents.

被 sentences without a doer:

- 我的车 被 撞 了 。
  Wǒ de chē bèi zhuàng le .
  My car was hit.
- 他们做的坏事 被 发现 了 。
  Tāmen zuò de huàishì bèi fāxiàn le .
  The bad things they've done were discovered.
- 文件 被 删 了 。
  Wénjiàn bèi shān le .
  The files were deleted.

Common Errors

✗ 咖啡 被 我喝。
Kāfēi bèi wǒ hē.

Remember: you need SOMEthing after the verb.

✓ 咖啡 被 我喝 了 。
Kāfēi bèi wǒ hē le .
The coffee was drunk by me.

✓ 咖啡 被 我喝 完了 。
Kāfēi bèi wǒ hē wán le .
The coffee was finished by me.

✗ 他 被 打。
Tā bèi dǎ.

Remember: you need SOMEthing after the verb.

✓ 他 被 打 了 。
Tā bèi dǎ le .
He was beaten.

✓ 他 被 打 伤了 。
Tā bèi dǎ shāng le .
He was beaten and wounded.

Forming 被 Sentences

You know the basic pattern already, so it's time to go deeper…

Negating 被 Sentences

There's just one other complication. What if you want to make a sentence in the *negative*? To negate a 被 sentence, you need to insert 没 or 没有 (past) directly in front of 被. For the present and future, use 不.

Doer	Negative	被	Subject	Verb Phrase	
他	没有	被	打伤	。	
他	没	被	炒鱿鱼	。	
她的想法	不	被	父母	理解	。

Question Forms of 被 Sentences

You can make 被 sentences into questions in the usual three ways to form questions in Mandarin:

- With a question particle
- With a question word
- With positive-negative verbs

Some examples:

- 那些书 被 借 走了 吗?
  Nàxiē shū bèi jiè zǒu le ma?
  Have those books been borrowed?
- 他 被 谁打 的 ?
  Tā bèi shéi dǎ de ?
  Who was he beaten by?
- 你是不是 被 公司炒鱿鱼 了 ?
  Nǐ shì bu shì bèi gōngsī chǎo yóuyú le ?
  Did you get fired by the company or not?

被 Sentences with Aspect Particles

The particles 了 and 过 can both be used with 被 constructions, while 着 cannot. 着 indicates an action is "ongoing," which is not appropriate for a 被 construction, which should refer to an already complete action.

Subject	被	Object	Verb	Aspect particle	
他	被	老师	打	过	。
你	被	他	骗	了	!

我的车	被	撞	过	。	
她	被	男朋友	甩	了	。

被 Sentences with Complements

Both result complements and direction complements[1] work well in 被 sentences.

Some examples:

- 花瓶 被 摔 碎 了。
  Huāpíng bèi shuāi suì le.
  The vase was broken into pieces.
- 那个人 被 车撞 死 了。
  Nàge rén bèi chē zhuàng sǐ le.
  That man got hit and killed by a car.
- 那个男人 被 警察赶 出去 了。
  Nàge nánrén bèi jǐngchá gǎn chūqù le.
  The man was kicked out by the policeman.
- 孩子 被 他父母送 回去 了。
  Háizi bèi tā fùmǔ sòng huíqù le.
  The child was sent back by his parents.

Sorry if these example sentences all seem like downers, but 被 sentences tend to be negative (or even tragic!).

Adverbs in 被 Sentences

What if you want to include adverbs in your 被 sentence? Where should those go? They go in the same place as the *negative* adverb 没有, above.

Subject	Adv.	被	Doer	Verb Phrase		
他	刚才	被	同学	打	了	。
我们	都	被	老师	骂	了	。

1. Direction complement (Grammar), page 133

手机	又	被	偷	了	?
小偷	终于	被	抓住	了	!

Alternative existential sentences

Expressing something's existence in a certain place or location is not just limited to 在 (zài) and 有 (yǒu). The word order may be a little different from what you are used to, but 着 (zhe) and 是 (shì) are also ways to make everyday statements such as, "There is a book lying on the desk."

Pattern with 着

Verbs that are paired with 着 are usually stative verbs. So unlike with action verbs, you're going to be describing an action that is kind of like just sitting there. It could be standing there, lying there, sitting there hanging there... the point is it isn't actively expending energy *doing* anything.

Structure

Place + Verb + 着 + [Noun Phrase]

Examples

- 桌子上放 着 一本书。
  Zhuōzi shàng fàng zhe yī běn shū .
  There is a book on the desk.
- 大厅里站 着 一些警察。
  Dàtīng lǐ zhàn zhe yīxiē jǐngchá.
  There are several policemen standing in the hall.
- 教室里坐 着 两百多个学生。
  Jiàoshì lǐ zuò zhe liǎng bǎi duō gè xuéshēng.
  There are more than two hundred students sitting in the classroom.
- 地下室里堆 着 很多旧东西。
  Dìxiàshì lǐ duī zhe hěn duō jiù dōngxi.
  There is lots of old stuff piled up in the basement.
- 楼下停 着 几辆车。
  Lóuxià tíng zhe jǐ liàng chē.
  A few cars are parked downstairs.

Note that in English we sometimes use a verb in its "-ing" form, and sometimes use the passive "-ed" form of the verb.

Pattern with 是

The subject in the 是 sentence pattern indicates the location or area. The object that comes after 是 is the only thing (worth mentioning) in that area. It's worth noting that there's no real time indication for most sentences like this. It could be setting a scene in a story (in the past), or it could be describing the current state of things (in the present).

Structure

Place + 是 + [Noun Phrase]

Examples

- 洗衣机里 是 一些脏衣服。
  Xǐyījī lǐ shì yīxiē zāng yīfu.
  There are dirty clothes inside the washing machine.
  There is nothing in the washing machine other than the dirty clothes.
- 袋子里 是 我的午饭。
  Dàizi lǐ shì wǒ de wǔfàn.
  My lunch is in the bag.
  The only thing in the bag is my lunch.
- 墙上都 是 他家人的照片。
  Qiáng shàng dōu shì tā jiārén de zhàopiàn.
  His family's photos are hanging on the wall.
  His family's photos are all over the wall, and nothing else is on he wall.
- 盒子里 是 你的礼物。
  Hézi lǐ shì nǐ de lǐwù.
  Your gift is in the box.
  Other than your gift, there is nothing else in the box.
- 桌子上 是 昨天没吃完的菜。
  Zhuōzi shàng shì zuótiān méi chī wán de cài.
  The food that was left over from yesterday is on the table.
  The food that was left over from yesterday is the only thing on the table.

Note that 是 is used to describe a singular object existing somewhere, while 有 can refer to multiple objects/people.

Expressing "as one likes" with "jiu"

When we want to express "to do something as one pleases," we can use the "想 (xiǎng) *verb* 就 (jiù) *verb*" pattern.

Basic Pattern

This structure is similar to how we would say in English, "whatever I want to eat, I eat" or, "wherever I want to go, I go." The verb that comes after the 想 and the 就 are the same verb.

Structure

 想 + Verb + 就 + Verb

Examples

- 想吃就吃。
  Xiǎng chī jiù chī.
  If you want to eat, help yourself.
- 想走就走吧。
  Xiǎng zǒu jiù zǒu ba.
  Leave if you want to.
- 想买就买，不用问我。
  Xiǎng mǎi jiù mǎi, bùyòng wèn wǒ.
  If you want to buy it, go ahead. You don't need to ask me.
- 别害怕，想说就说。
  Bié hàipà, xiǎng shuō jiù shuō.
  Don't be afraid. If you want to say, say it.
- 想做就做，考虑那么多干吗?
  Xiǎng zuò jiù zuò, kǎolǜ nàme duō gànmá?
  If you want to do it, do it. Why do you need to think about it so much?

Advanced Pattern

You can also add in a question word, like 什么, 哪儿, or 怎么. When this is the case, the pronouns don't necessarily refer to anything specific. They can be seen more as words like “whatever” or “wherever.” This way, question pronouns (什么, 谁, 什么时候,etc) serve as “indefinite references.”

Structure

想 + Verb + [Question Word] + 就 + Verb + [Question Word]

Examples

- 想去哪儿就去哪儿。
  Xiǎng qù nǎr jiù qù nǎr.
  You can go wherever you'd like to go.
- 想请谁就请谁。
  Xiǎng qǐng shéi jiù qǐng shéi.
  You can invite whoever you like.
- 想什么时候来就什么时候来。
  Xiǎng shénme shíhou lái jiù shénme shíhou lái.
  You can come whenever you like.
- 想点什么就点什么，我请客。
  Xiǎng diǎn shénme jiù diǎn shénme, wǒ qǐngkè.
  You can order whatever you like. I'm buying.
- 这些钱我想怎么花就怎么花。
  Zhèxiē qián wǒ xiǎng zěnme huā jiù zěnme huā.
  I will spend this money however I like.

Similar to

- Expressing “then” with “jiu” (HSK2)
- Conditions with “yao” and “jiu” (HSK5)

Expressing "every" with question words

This grammar point is not about how to use 每 (měi) to mean "every," but rather how to combine question words with 都 (dōu) to make words and phrases like "everywhere" or "everyone." You may have learned this same pattern for expressing "everything," but now it's time to extend it.

"Everyone" with 谁都

谁都 (shéi dōu) is a pattern used to express "everyone" (or possibly "anyone") in Chinese. The placement of the question word 谁 is very similar to the way 什么 (shénme) can be used to express "every", along with other question words like 哪儿 (nǎr) and 多少 (duōshao).

Structure

谁 + 都 + Predicate

The predicate part of the pattern can be a verb or an adjective.

Examples

- 谁 都 喜欢美食。
  Shéi dōu xǐhuan měishí.
  Everyone likes delicious food.
- 谁 都 可以进。
  Shéi dōu kěyǐ jìn.
  Everyone can come in.
- 谁 都 不相信他说的话。
  Shéi dōu bù xiāngxìn tā shuō de huà.
  No one believes what he said.

"Everywhere" with 哪儿都

This pattern works with both 哪儿 (nǎr) and 哪里 (nǎlǐ).

Structure

哪儿 / 哪里 (+ Verb) + 都 + Predicate

Examples

- 他的房间里 哪儿 都 是脏衣服。
  Tā de fángjiān lǐ nǎr dōu shì zāng yīfu.
  His dirty laundry is all over his room.
- 我太累了，哪儿 都 不想去。
  Wǒ tài lèi le, nǎr dōu bù xiǎng qù.
  I'm too tired. I don't want to go anywhere.
- 在 哪里 见面 都 行。
  Zài nǎlǐ jiànmiàn dōu xíng.
  I'm fine with meeting anywhere.

"Whenever" with 什么时候都

什么时候 (shénme shíhou) combines with 都 (dōu) to mean "whenever" or "anytime."

Structure

什么时候 (+ Verb) + 都 + Predicate

Examples

- 什么时候 都 可以。
  Shénme shíhou dōu kěyǐ.
  Anytime is fine.
- 你 什么时候 来 都 欢迎。
  Nǐ shénme shíhou lái dōu huānyíng.
  You're welcome to come anytime.

- 什么时候 开始 都 不晚。
  Shénme shíhou kāishǐ dōu bù wǎn.
  It's never too late to start.

"However Much" with 多少都

多少 (duōshao) also works with 都 in this case.

Structure

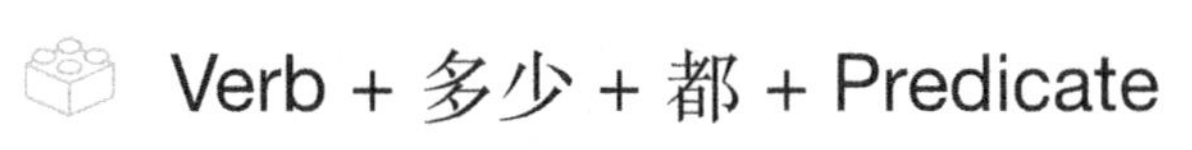

Verb + 多少 + 都 + Predicate

Examples

- 你想吃 多少 都 可以。
  Nǐ xiǎng chī duōshao dōu kěyǐ.
  You can eat however much you want.
- 这些是免费的，我们拿 多少 都 没问题。
  Zhèxiē shì miǎnfèi de, wǒmen ná duōshao dōu méi wèntí.
  These are all free. We can take as much as we want.
- 我跟他说 多少 遍 都 没有用。
  Wǒ gēn tā shuō duōshao biàn dōu méiyǒu yòng.
  It doesn't matter how many times I tell him.

"However" with 怎么都

怎么 (zěnme) also works with 都.

Structure

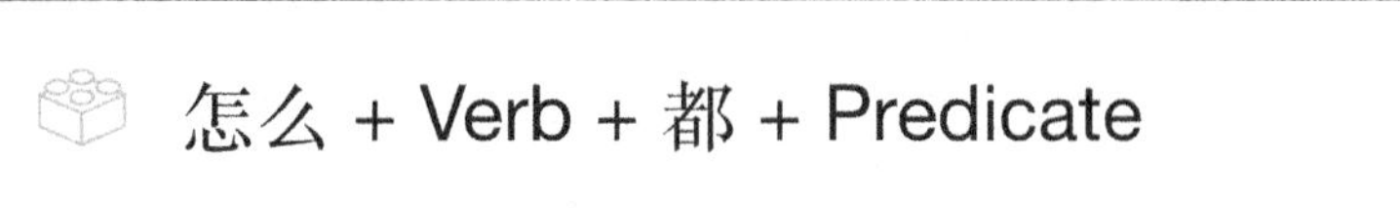

怎么 + Verb + 都 + Predicate

Examples

- 怎么 做 都 可以吗?
  Zěnme zuò dōu kěyǐ ma?
  It's OK if I do it however I want?

- 这些钱你 怎么 花 都 行。
  Zhèxiē qián nǐ zěnme huā dōu xíng.
  You can spend this money however you like.
- 别人 怎么 想 都 不重要。
  Biérén zěnme xiǎng dōu bù zhòngyào.
  It's not important what other people think.

Similar to

- Expressing “everything” with “shenme dou” (HSK2)
- Expressing “some” with question words (HSK3), page 191

Expressing "more and more" with "yuelaiyue"

越来越 (yuèláiyuè) is used frequently in Chinese to express that some quality or state is increasing with time and is often translated into English as "more and more." This is the simple form of this pattern, which uses 来, but there is also a more complex one (which uses two different adjectives/verbs)[1].

Used with Adjectives

This structure expresses that something is becoming more and more *adjective* over time, with the latter adjective changing with the verb. The most common structure is:

Structure

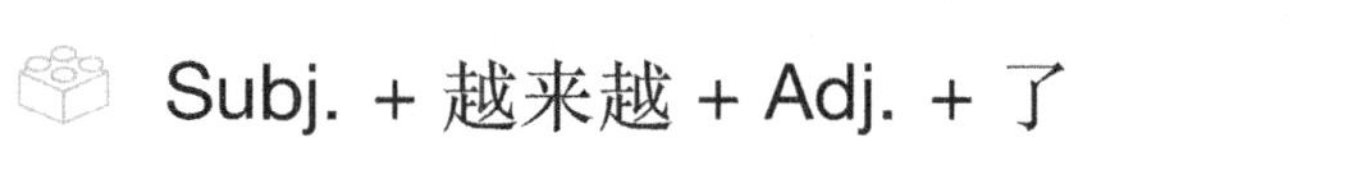

Subj. + 越来越 + Adj. + 了

Examples

- 天气 越来越 冷 了 。

  Tiānqì yuèláiyuè lěng le .

  The weather is getting colder and colder.

- 你女儿 越来越 漂亮 了 。

  Nǐ nǚér yuèláiyuè piàoliang le .

  Your daughter is getting more and more beautiful.

- 你说得 越来越 好 了 。

  Nǐ shuō de yuèláiyuè hǎo le .

  You speak better and better.

- 技术 越来越 发达 了 。

  Jìshù yuèláiyuè fādá le .

  Technology is getting more and more developed.

- 空气污染 越来越 严重 了 。

  Kōngqì wūrǎn yuèláiyuè yánzhòng le .

  The air pollution is getting worse and worse.

---

1. Expressing "the more... the more..." with "yue... yue..." (Grammar), page 164

Used with Verbs

Structure

 Subj. + 越来越 + Verb + 了

Examples

- 我 越来越 喜欢上海 了 。
  Wǒ yuèláiyuè xǐhuan Shànghǎi le .
  I like Shanghai more and more.
- 你 越来越 了解我 了 。
  Nǐ yuèláiyuè liǎojiě wǒ le .
  You know me better and better.
- 我 越来越 理解我的父母 了 。
  Wǒ yuèláiyuè lǐjiě wǒ de fùmǔ le .
  I understand my parents more and more.

When the verb is negative in Chinese, a translation like "less and less" with a positive verb might be more appropriate in English than sticking with a "more and more" translation. The Chinese pattern doesn't change, though.

- 我 越来越 不 相信他 了 。
  Wǒ yuèláiyuè bù xiāngxìn tā le .
  I believe him less and less.
- 你 越来越 不 懂我 了 。
  Nǐ yuèláiyuè bù dǒng wǒ le .
  You understand me less and less.

Similar to

- Expressing "the more… the more…" with "yue· · · yue· · ·" (HSK3), page 164

Expressing "some" with question words

Chinese question words can play a double role. As we know, they are used in questions, but they can also mean "some." The "some" we refer to is the vague, undefined "some," as in "somewhere," "someone," "something," or "sometime."

"Somewhere" with 哪儿

This one is often used with Verb + 过.

Examples:

- 这个人我在 哪儿 见过。
  Zhège rén wǒ zài nǎr jiàn guo.
  I've met this person somewhere before.
- 这首歌我在 哪儿 听过。
  Zhè shǒu gē wǒ zài nǎr tīng guo.
  I've heard this song somewhere.
- 这篇文章我们在 哪儿 看过。
  Zhè piān wénzhāng wǒmen zài nǎr kàn guo.
  I've read this article somewhere before.

"Someone" with 谁

Examples:

- 你让 谁 来帮我一下。
  Nǐ ràng shéi lái bāng wǒ yīxià.
  Ask someone to help me with this.
- 这件事我听 谁 说过。
  Zhè jiàn shì wǒ tīng shéi shuō guo.
  I've heard somebody talk about this before.
- 你找 谁 带你进去吧。
  Nǐ zhǎo shéi dài nǐ jìnqù ba.
  You should find someone to take you inside.

"Something" with 什么

This one is often used with 点 (儿) before the verb.

Examples:

- 我们应该做点儿 什么 。
  Wǒmen yīnggāi zuò diǎnr shénme.
  We should do something.
- 老大，你不说点儿 什么 ？
  Lǎodà, nǐ bù shuō diǎnr shénme?
  Boss, aren't you going to say something?
- 我想喝点儿 什么 。
  Wǒ xiǎng hē diǎnr shénme.
  I want to drink something.

"Sometime" with 什么时候

Careful with this one! If you're not paying attention, you might think that it's a question asking "when," but in reality it might just be polite noise. If the lack of question intonation isn't enough, the 吧 on the end is also a clue that these sentences aren't actually questions.

Examples:

- 什么时候 我们见面谈吧。
  Shénme shíhou wǒmen jiànmiàn tán ba.
  Let's meet and talk about this sometime.
- 什么时候 来我新家玩吧。
  Shénme shíhou lái wǒ xīn jiā wán ba.
  You should come to my new house to hangout sometime.
- 我们 什么时候 去看看他吧。
  Wǒmen shénme shíhou qù kànkan tā ba.
  Let's pay him a visit sometime.

Similar to

- Expressing "every" with question words (HSK3, HSK4), page 185

Expressing purpose with "weile"

为了 (wèile) is most often used to indicate the purpose of an action or the person that will benefit from some act of kindness. In the "purpose" sense, it almost exactly corresponds to "in order to" or "for the purpose of" in English.

Basic Usage

When 为了 indicates the purpose of an action, it's usually acting as a preposition. In this role, the *whole* "为了 phrase" should come **before** the verb.

Structure

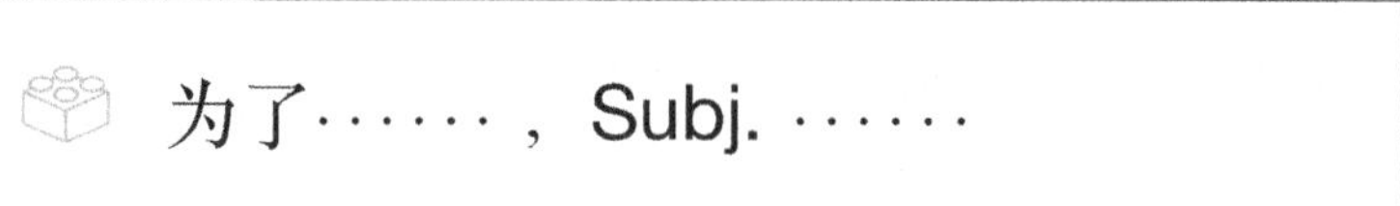

Note also that 为了 is a single word; the 了 here is not serving its role as a particle in this case.

Examples

- 为了钱，他什么都愿意做。
  Wèile qián, tā shénme dōu yuànyì zuò.
  He's willing to do anything for money.
- 为了孩子的未来，他决定搬到上海。
  Wèile háizi de wèilái, tā juédìng bāndào Shànghǎi.
  He decided to move to Shanghai for his children's future.
- 为了这个面试，他买了一套很贵的西服。
  Wèile zhège miànshì, tā mǎi le yī tào hěn guì de xīfú.
  He bought a very expensive suit for this job interview.
- 为了找灵感，那个作家搬到了农村。
  Wèile zhǎo línggǎn, nàge zuòjiā bān dào le nóngcūn.
  In order to find inspiration, that writer moved to the countryside.
- 五年前，为了女朋友，他放弃了上海的工作。
  wǔniánqián, Wèile nǚpéngyǒu, tā fàngqì le Shànghǎi de gōngzuò.
  Five years ago he passed up a job in Shanghai for his girlfriend.

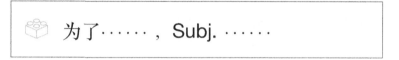

- 为了 奖励大家，公司明年带你们去日本旅行。
  Wèile jiǎnglì dàjiā, gōngsī míngnián dài nǐmen qù Rìběn lǚxíng.
  In order to reward everyone, the company will take you all on a trip to Japan next year.

Expressing "the Reason Why"

Sometimes you will see 为了 following 是. In this case, 为了 mean "for." Note that 为了 and 因为 both have the character 为 in them, and they have sort of similar meanings. You will also see 因为 following 是, instead of 为了. It literally means "is because (of)."

Structure

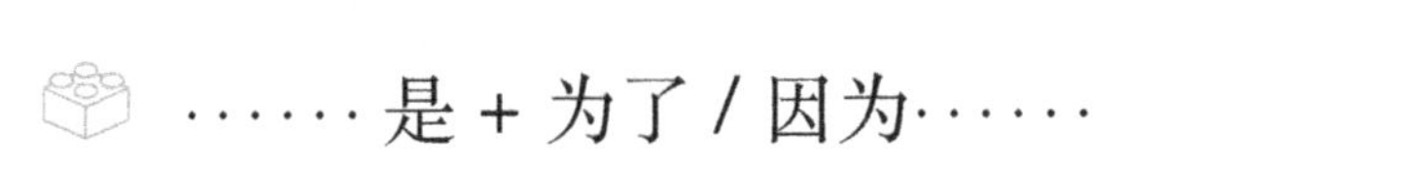

Example

- 我这么做 是为了 帮你。
  Wǒ zhème zuò shì wèile bāng nǐ.
  I did all this to help you.
- 他做兼职 是为了 多赚点钱。
  Tā zuò jiānzhí shì wèile duō zhuàn diǎn qián.
  The reason why he has a part time job is to make a little more money.
- 你学中文 是因为 你的中国女朋友吗?
  Nǐ xué Zhōngwén shì yīnwèi nǐde Zhōngguó nǚpéngyou ma?
  Are you studying Chinese because of your Chinese girlfriend?
- 我们之所以反对 是因为 风险太大。
  Wǒmen zhī suǒyǐ fǎnduì shì yīnwèi fēngxiǎn tài dà.
  The reason why we oppose it is because the risk is too high.

Note that 之所以 is a more difficult pattern, which means "the reason why" in a more formal way.

Similar to

- Explaining purpose with "wei… er…" (HSK4)
- Using "lai" to connect two verb phrases (HSK4)
- Expressing "for" with "wei" (HSK5)

- Expressing purpose with “hao” (HSK5)
- Stating the effect before the cause (HSK5)

Expressing "compared with" using "gen"

If you want to do a straight-up comparison statement, go ahead and use the classic 比 (bǐ) structure. But if you want to lead with a "compared with..." phrase, you'll need a 跟 (gēn) and a slightly different word order.

Used with Two Subjects

This sentence structure is used for comparing one thing *as it relates to* another.

Structure

These patterns are for making a comment about B, *as it relates to* A.

跟 + A + 比 (起来)， B……

B can also come at the beginning of the sentence:

B + 跟 + A + 比 (起来)，……

For both of these structures, you could swap out 跟 (gēn) for 和 (hé) with no real difference, but using 跟 (gēn) is slightly more common.

Examples

- 跟 上海 比，我老家的物价很低。
  Gēn Shànghǎi bǐ, wǒ lǎojiā de wùjià hěn dī.
  Compared to Shanghai, prices in my hometown are very low.
- 跟 东部 比，我更喜欢美国西部。
  Gēn dōngbù bǐ, wǒ gèng xǐhuan Měiguó xībù.
  Compared to the eastern USA, I like the western USA more.
- 跟 他 比，你最大的优势是什么?
  Gēn tā bǐ, nǐ zuì dà de yōushì shì shénme?
  Compared to him, what is your biggest advantage?

- 妹妹 跟 姐姐 比起来 有点害羞。
  Mèimei gēn jiějie bǐ qǐlái yǒudiǎn hàixiū.
  Compared to the older sister, the younger sister is a bit shy.
- 新版本 跟 旧版本 比起来 ，多了一些功能。
  Xīn bǎnběn gēn jiù bǎnběn bǐ qǐlái , duō le yīxiē gōngnéng.
  Compared with the old version, the new version has a few more features.

Used with a Single Subject

比 (bǐ) can also be used for comparing one subject over two different time periods.

Structure

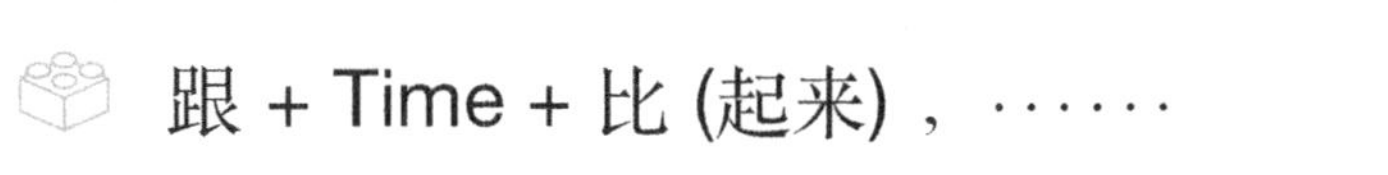

跟 + Time + 比 (起来) , ……

Again, you could use 和 (hé) instead of 跟 (gēn) here, but using 跟 (gēn) is more common.

Examples

- 跟 去年 比 ，你的中文进步了很多。
  Gēn qùnián bǐ , nǐ de Zhōngwén jìnbù le hěn duō.
  Compared to last year, your Chinese has improved a lot.
- 跟 十年前 比起来 ，中国人的生活水平提高了很多。
  Gēn shí nián qián bǐ qǐlái , Zhōngguó rén de shēnghuó shuǐpíng tígāo le hěn duō.
  Compared to ten years ago, the standard of living for Chinese people has gotten much better.
- 跟 上个月 比 ，这个月的工作很轻松。
  Gēn shàngge yuè bǐ , zhège yuè de gōngzuò hěn qīngsōng.
  Compared with last month, this month our work is a lot more relaxed.
- 跟 前几周 比 ，这个星期的天气舒服多了。
  Gēn qián jǐ zhōu bǐ , zhège xīngqī de tiānqì shūfu duō le.
  Compared to the past few weeks, the weather has been much more comfortable this week.

- 跟 刚毕业的时候 比起来 ，他成熟了很多。
  Gēn gāng bìyè de shíhou bǐ qǐlái , tā chéngshú le hěn duō.
  Compared to when he first graduated, he's much more mature.

Similar to

- Expressing "much more" in comparisons (HSK2, HSK3), page 201
- Expressing "even more" with "geng" or "hai" (HSK3), page 199
- Expressing comparable degree with "you" (HSK3), page 203

Expressing "even more" with "geng" or "hai"

When used in a comparison, 更 (gèng) or 还 (hái) can kick up an adjective to an even higher degree. For example, New York City is America's biggest city with a population of around 9 million. Shanghai is China's biggest city, with a population of more than 20 million. So even though NYC's population is big, Shanghai's is even bigger. You'd use 更 or 还 to express this in Chinese.

Structure

Noun 1 + 比 + Noun 2 + 更 / 还 + Adj.

Examples

- 上海 比 纽约人口 更 多。
  Shànghǎi bǐ Niǔyuē rénkǒu gèng duō.
  Shanghai's population is even bigger than New York's.
- 我妹妹 比 我 更 瘦。
  Wǒ mèimei bǐ wǒ gèng shòu.
  My younger sister is even skinnier than me.
- 我的猫 比 我的狗 更 淘气。
  Wǒ de māo bǐ wǒ de gǒu gèng táoqì.
  My cat is even naughtier than my dog.
- 有时候动物 比 人类 更 聪明。
  Yǒushíhou dòngwù bǐ rénlèi gèng cōngming.
  Sometimes animals are even smarter than human beings.
- 大城市的工作机会 比 我老家 更 多。
  Dà chéngshì de gōngzuò jīhuì bǐ wǒ lǎojiā gèng duō.
  There are even more job opportunities in big cities than in my hometown.
- 他 比 姚明 还 高。
  Tā bǐ Yáo Míng hái gāo.
  He is even taller than Yao Ming.

- 昨天 38 度，今天 比 昨天 还 热。

  38 °C = 100 °F

  Zuótiān sānshí-bā dù, jīntiān bǐ zuótiān hái rè.

  It was 38 degrees yesterday, and it's even hotter today.

- 这个外国人的汉语说得 比 中国人 还 地道。

  Zhège wàiguó rén de Hànyǔ shuō de bǐ Zhōngguó rén hái dìdao.

  This foreigner speaks even more authentic Chinese than native speakers do.

还 has a more intense tone, and it usually carries a tone of surprise and skepticism. Therefore, using the form of a rhetorical question with 还 can be understood as "how can it be?"

Also note that 更 can be used with 了 in this pattern, indicating change of situation or state, while 还 can't be used in this way.

✘ 这个地方 比 以前 还 热闹 了 。

Zhège dìfang bǐ yǐqián hái rènao le .

✔ 这个地方 比 以前 更 热闹 了 。

Zhège dìfang bǐ yǐqián gèng rènao le .

This place is even livelier than before.

Similar to

- Expressing "much more" in comparisons (HSK2, HSK3), page 201
- Expressing "compared with" using "gen" (HSK3), page 196
- Expressing comparable degree with "you" (HSK3), page 203

Expressing "much more" in comparisons

If you want to up the contrast of your comparisons, you might want to express "much more." You can do this using 多 (duō), but did you know there are actually three different ways to do it?

Structure

As well as expressing that two things differ, you might want to go further and say that they differ **a lot** by adding 很多 (hěn duō), 多了 (duō le), or 得多 (de duō). This is like saying that one thing is *much more Adj.* than another in English.

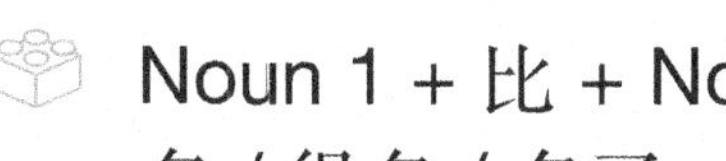

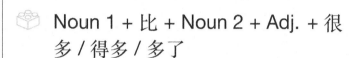

Noun 1 + 比 + Noun 2 + Adj. + 很多 / 得多 / 多了

Examples

- 拼音 比 汉字容易 很多 。
  Pīnyīn bǐ Hànzì róngyì hěn duō .
  Pinyin is much easier than Chinese characters.
- 坐高铁 比 坐飞机方便 很多 。
  Zuò gāotiě bǐ zuò fēijī fāngbiàn hěn duō .
  It's much more convenient to take the high-speed train than the airplane.
- 这个女老师 比 那个男老师严格 得多 。
  Zhège nǚ lǎoshī bǐ nàge nán lǎoshī yángé de duō .
  This female teacher is much stricter than that male teacher.
- 我老婆的工资 比 我高 得多 。
  Wǒ lǎopo de gōngzī bǐ wǒ gāo de duō .
  My wife's salary is much higher than mine.
- 你 比 我有经验 多了 。
  Nǐ bǐ wǒ yǒu jīngyàn duō le .
  You're much more experienced than me.

- 你们 比 我们幸运 多了 。

  Nǐmen bǐ wǒmen xìngyùn duō le .

  You're much luckier than us.

- 他打篮球 比 我厉害 多了 。

  Tā dǎ lánqiú bǐ wǒ lìhai duō le .

  He plays basketball much better than I do.

Short Form with 多了

Given sufficient context, it's possible to use 多了 without the full comparison pattern. 多了 is the only one of the three "much more" phrases introduced in this article which can be used this way.

Subj. + Adj. + 多了

A few examples:

- 我的感冒好 多了 。

  Wǒ de gǎnmào hǎo duō le .

  My cold is getting much better.

  We both know I've had this bad cold.

- 最近天气暖和 多了 。

  Zuìjìn tiānqì nuǎnhuo duō le .

  It's been much warmer lately.

  We're both aware of recent weather, obviously.

- 上大学以后，她成熟 多了 。

  Shàng dàxué yǐhòu, tā chéngshú duō le .

  She became much more mature after she went to college.

  We both know how immature she used to be.

Similar to

- Basic comparisons with "bi" (HSK2)
- Expressing "a little too" with "you dian" (HSK2)
- Expressing "compared with" using "gen" (HSK3), page 196
- Expressing "rather" with "bijiao" (HSK3), page 44
- Basic comparisons with "bu bi" (HSK5)
- Expressing "a bit too" (HSK5)

Expressing comparable degree with "you"

有 (yǒu), besides just meaning "to have," can also be used in comparisons. It's what you use instead of 比 (bǐ) if something is "as [Adj.] as" something else.

Basic Pattern

The structure literally means, "A has B's [Adj.]." The meaning is "A is as [Adj.] as B." This pattern is often used in questions. Think of the jealous girl asking, "is she as pretty as me?" or the insecure weightlifter bro asking, "is he as jacked as me?" Note that for this kind of question, B is usually the one that the speaker prefers.

Structure

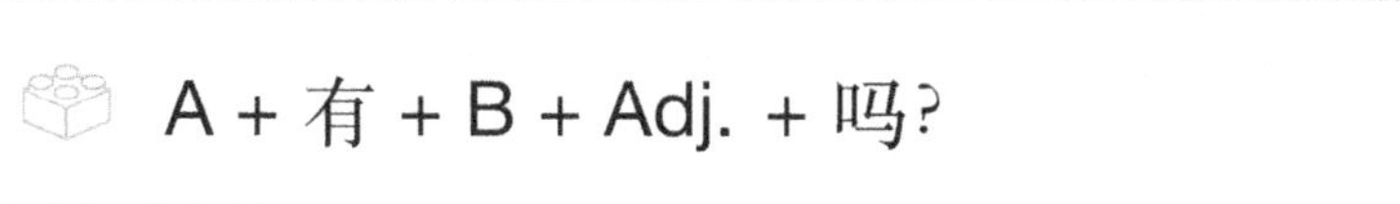

This comparison pattern is generally only used in questions, not statements.

Examples

- 他 有 我帅吗?
  Tā yǒu wǒ shuài ma?
  Is he as handsome as me?
- 你 有 老板忙吗?
  Nǐ yǒu lǎobǎn máng ma?
  Are you as busy as the boss?
- 他 有 姚明高吗?
  Tā yǒu Yáo Míng gāo ma?
  Is he as tall as YaoMing?
- 纽约人口 有 上海人口多吗?
  Niǔyuē rénkǒu yǒu Shànghǎi rénkǒu duō ma?
  Is the population of New York city as big as that of Shanghai?

Pattern Including a Verb

If a verb is included in this pattern to talk about an action, it's probably going to involve a degree complement using this structure below:

Structure

A + 有 + B + Verb + 得 + Adj. + 吗?

Examples

- 他 有 我做 得 好吗?
  Tā yǒu wǒ zuò de hǎo ma?
  Can he do it as well as I do?
- 你 有 Bolt 跑 得 快吗?
  Nǐ yǒu Bolt pǎo de kuài ma?
  Can you run as fast as Bolt does?

Advanced Pattern Using 这么 / 那么

This form is often used with 这么 or 那么, which in this case means "as much." And it indicates that B is already very [Adj.]. When B is absent, 那么 means "so" or "that".

Structure

A + 有 (+ B) + 这么 / 那么 + Adj. + 吗?

Examples

- 她 有 那么 漂亮吗?
  Tā yǒu nàme piàoliang ma?
  Is she really that pretty?
- 这个药 有 这么 神奇吗?
  Zhège yào yǒu zhème shénqí ma?
  Is this medicine really that magical?

- 他 有 姚明 那么 高吗?
  Tā yǒu Yáo Míng nàme gāo ma?
  Is he really as tall as YaoMing?
- 你 有 Bill Gates 那么 有钱吗?
  Nǐ yǒu Bill Gates nàme yǒuqián ma?
  Are you as rich as Bill Gates?

Similar to

- Basic comparisons with "bi" (HSK2)
- Expressing "much more" in comparisons (HSK2, HSK3), page 201
- Basic comparisons with "yiyang" (HSK3), page 40
- Expressing "compared with" using "gen" (HSK3), page 196
- Expressing "even more" with "geng" or "hai" (HSK3), page 199
- Comparisons with "buru" (HSK5)

Expressing "except" and "in addition" with "chule... yiwai"

Using 除了 (chúle)–often with 以外 (yǐwài)–will help you spruce up your sentences when you want to express the meanings of "except," "besides," or "in addition." You may feel that "except" has a pretty different meaning from the other two. Well, read on!

Used as "Except"

除了…… (以外), 都…… is a pattern used to express "except." Make a special note of the 都 (dōu)!

Structure

> 除了……(+ 以外)，Subj. + 都……

以外 can be omitted from the pattern without changing its meaning.

Examples

- 除了 他，我们 都 去过。
  Chúle tā , wǒmen dōu qù guo.
  Except for him, we've all been there.
- 除了 白酒，别的酒他 都 喝。
  Chúle báijiǔ, biéde jiǔ tā dōu hē.
  He drinks all kinds of alcohol except baijiu.
- 除了 周末，老板每天 都 加班。
  Chúle zhōumò, lǎobǎn měi tiān dōu jiābān.
  Except for weekends, the boss works overtime every day.
- 除了 价格 以外 ，其他方面我们 都 很满意。
  Chúle jiàgé yǐwài , qítā fāngmiàn wǒmen dōu hěn mǎnyì.
  We're satisfied with all aspects except for the price.
- 除了 政治新闻 以外 ，其他新闻我 都 看。
  Chúle zhèngzhì xīnwén yǐwài , qítā xīnwén wǒ dōu kàn.
  I read all types of news except for political news.

Used as "in Addition"

除了…… (以外), 也/还…… is used to express "in addition." Make a special note of the 也 or 还!

Structure

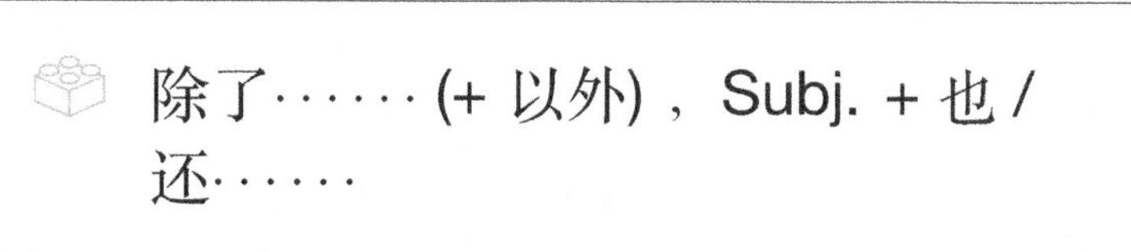

除了…… (+ 以外)，Subj. + 也 / 还……

Examples

- 除了 英语，我 也 会说法语和西班牙语。
  Chúle Yīngyǔ, wǒ yě huì shuō Fǎyǔ hé Xībānyáyǔ.
  In addition to English, I can also speak French and Spanish.
- 除了 运动 以外，你 还 有什么爱好？
  Chúle yùndòng yǐwài, nǐ hái yǒu shénme àihào?
  In addition to sports, what other hobbies do you have?
- 除了 猫和狗，我 还 养过兔子。
  Chúle māo hé gǒu, wǒ hái yǎng guo tùzi.
  In addition to a cat and a dog, I also had a rabbit.
- 除了 海鲜，你 还 对什么过敏？
  Chúle hǎixiān, nǐ hái duì shénme guòmǐn?
  In addition to seafood, what else are you allergic to?
- 中国的功夫明星，除了 李小龙和成龙 以外，李连杰 也 很有名。
  Zhōngguó de gōngfu míngxīng, chúle Lǐ Xiǎolóng hé Chéng Lóng yǐwài, Lǐ Liánjié yě hěn yǒumíng.
  In addition to Bruce Lee and Jackie Chan, Jet Li is also a very famous Chinese kung fu star.

Similar to

- Expressing "and also" with "hai" (HSK2)
- Expressing "in addition" with "haiyou" (HSK4)
- Expressing "in addition" with "lingwai" (HSK4)

Expressing "if" with "ruguo... dehua"

如果…… 的话 (rúguǒ... dehuà) is a pattern commonly used in Chinese to express "if." An easy way to remember the pattern's format is that in the full form, the condition is "sandwiched" between 如果 and 的话.

Fuller Pattern

Structure

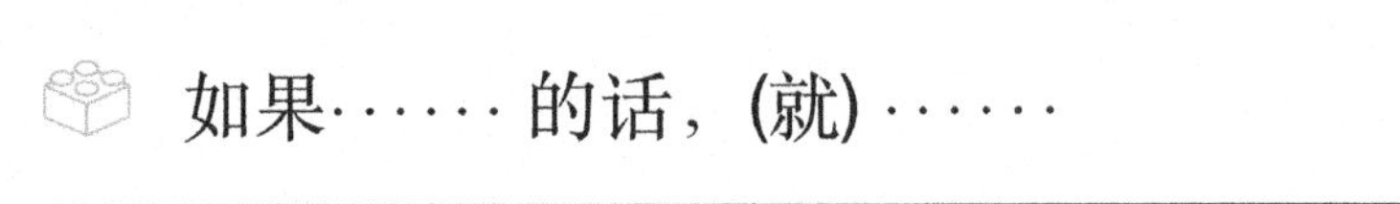

Note that 就 (jiù) is often optional. For more on using 如果 with 就, check out the "if…, then…" two-part pattern with 如果…… 就……[1].

Examples

- 如果 明天下雨 的话 ，我们 就 不去了。
  Rúguǒ míngtiān xiàyǔ dehuà, wǒmen jiù bù qù le.
  If it rains tomorrow, we won't go.
- 别点那么多菜。 如果 吃不完 的话 ，就 太浪费了。
  Bié diǎn nàme duō cài. Rúguǒ chī bu wán dehuà, jiù tài làngfèi le.
  Don't order so much. It will be a big waste of food if we can't finish it all.
- 如果 有人帮他 的话 ，他 就 不会出事了。
  Rúguǒ yǒu rén bāng tā dehuà, tā jiù bù huì chūshì le.
  If someone had helped him, he would't have had this accident.
- 如果 你们不来 的话 ，一定会后悔的。
  Rúguǒ nǐmen bù lái dehuà, yīdìng huì hòuhuǐ de .
  If you don't come, you'll definitely regret it.
- 如果 他不同意 的话 ，你怎么办?
  Rúguǒ tā bù tóngyì dehuà, nǐ zěnmebàn?
  What will you do if he doesn't agree?

Simple Pattern

Colloquially, it's also possible to drop the 如果 and just use the 的话 instead

1. Expressing "if... then..." with "ruguo... jiu..." (Grammar), page 210

to mean “if.” 的话 is optional.

Structure

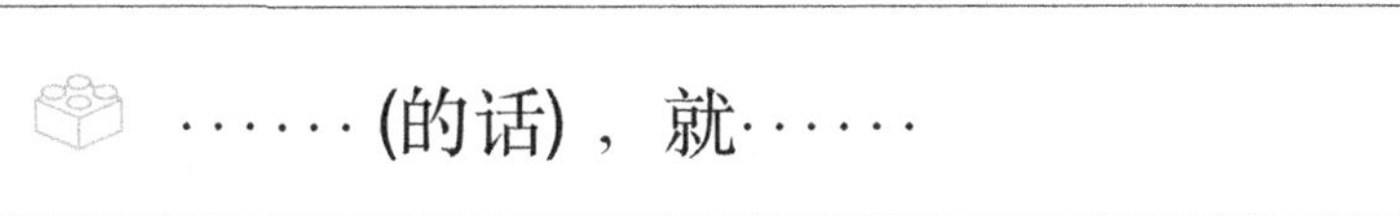

……(的话)，就……

Examples

- 不想去 的话 就 别去了。

  Bù xiǎng qù dehuà jiù bié qù le.

  Don't go if you don't feel like going.

- 好吃 的话 ， 就 多吃点。

  Hǎochī dehuà, jiù duō chī diǎn.

  If you think it's tasty, eat some more.

- 喜欢 就 拿走吧。

  Xǐhuan jiù názǒu ba.

  Take it if you like it.

It's even possible to use neither 的话 nor 就, and let the “if” be completely implied.

- 有事给我打电话。

  Yǒu shì gěi wǒ dǎ diànhuà.

  Give me a call if you need anything.

- 有空来我家玩。

  Yǒu kòng lái wǒ jiā wán.

  If you're free, come to my place and hang out.

Note that 如果 can be switched out for the various other terms for “if,” including the common 要是 (yàoshi) and the formal 假如 (jiǎrú), among others.

Similar to

- Expressing “then” with “jiu” (HSK2)
- Expressing “if… then…” with “ruguo… jiu…” (HSK3), page 210
- Expressing “only if” with “zhiyou” (HSK3), page 154
- Expressing “if··· then···” with “yaoshi” (HSK4)
- Marking a topic with “de hua” (HSK5)

Expressing "if... then..." with "ruguo... jiu..."

The 如果……, 就…… (rúguǒ..., jiù...) two-part structure is very logical and concise, meaning "if... then...."

Standard Pattern

Structure

如果……, 就…… is an often-used pattern that is utilized in the same way that "*If…, then…*" is in English. In English we sometimes drop then "then" in the second half of the sentence, and you can do the same in Chinese, dropping the 就.

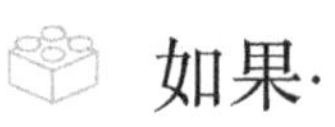 如果……，就……

Examples

- 如果 有困难， 就 给我打电话。
  Rúguǒ yǒu kùnnan, jiù gěi wǒ dǎ diànhuà.
  If there is any difficulty, give me a call.
- 如果 你输了， 就 给我一百块。
  Rúguǒ nǐ shū le, jiù gěi wǒ yī bǎi kuài.
  If you lose, give me 100 kuai.
- 如果 真的找不回来， 就 再买一个吧。
  Rúguǒ zhēnde zhǎo bu huílái, jiù zài mǎi yī gè ba.
  If you can't find it, then buy a new one.
- 如果 他再来，我们 就 报警。
  Rúguǒ tā zài lái, wǒmen jiù bàojǐng.
  If he keeps showing up, we'll call the police.
- 如果 你们已经不相爱了， 就 分手吧。
  Rúguǒ nǐmen yǐjīng bù xiāngài le, jiù fēnshǒu ba.
  If you no longer love each other, just break up.

Alternate Pattern Using 那么

Sometimes 那么 (nàme) is used instead of 就 (jiù), imparting a more relaxed, informal feel to the sentence. Sometimes just 那 (nà) will be used instead of

那么 (nàme).

Structure

 如果……，那么 / 那……

Examples

- 如果 他知道，那 他一定会告诉我。
  Rúguǒ tā zhīdào, nà tā yīdìng huì gàosu wǒ.
  If he knew, he would definitely tell me.
- 如果 大家都不感兴趣，那 我不说了。
  Rúguǒ dàjiā dōu bù gǎn xìngqù, nà wǒ bù shuō le.
  If none of you are interested, I will stop talking.
- 如果 你们真的想合作，那么 我们应该找时间好好谈谈。
  Rúguǒ nǐmen zhēnde xiǎng hézuò, nàme wǒmen yīnggāi zhǎo shíjiān hǎohǎo tántan.
  If you really want to work with us, then we should schedule a day to discuss it.
- 如果 能找到投资，那 下个月就可以开始做了。
  Rúguǒ néng zhǎodào tóuzī, nà xià gè yuè jiù kěyǐ kāishǐ zuò le.
  If we can find the investment, we'll be able to get on it next month.
- 如果 你想申请，那么 现在就要开始准备。
  Rúguǒ nǐ xiǎng shēnqǐng, nàme xiànzài jiù yào kāishǐ zhǔnbèi.
  If you want to apply, you need to start to prepare right away.

Adding in 的话

This article is focused on the two-part "if… then…" pattern 如果……，就……. But it's also possible to take the first half and make it into a "sandwich pattern" using 如果……的话.

Similar to

- Expressing "then" with "jiu" (HSK2)
- Expressing "as one likes" with "jiu" (HSK3), page 183
- Expressing "if" with "ruguo… dehua" (HSK3), page 208
- Expressing "only if" with "zhiyou" (HSK3), page 154

- Events in quick succession with “yi… jiu…” (HSK4)
- Expressing “if· · · then· · ·” with “yaoshi” (HSK4)
- Expressing “if· · · then· · ·” with “jiaru” (HSK5)
- Expressing “if· · · then· · ·” with “jiashi” (HSK5)
- Expressing “once…then…” with “yidan…jiu…” (HSK5)
- Marking a topic with “de hua” (HSK5)
- Use “tangruo” to express “if” (HSK6)

Expressing "not only... but also"

不但……，而且……(bùdàn…, érqiě…) is a very commonly used pattern that indicates "not only, … but also…."

Used with Single Subject

Structure

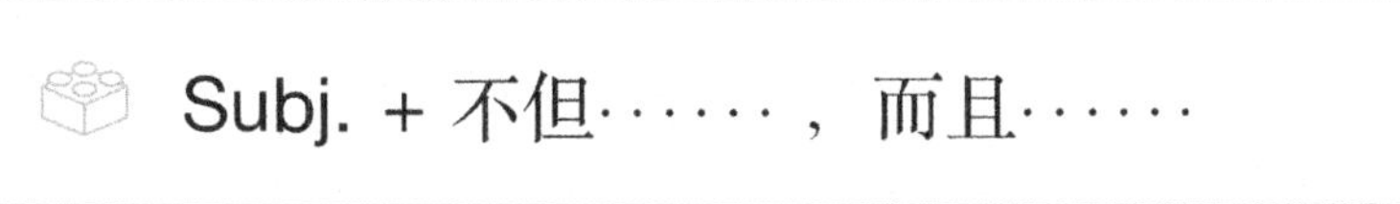

The same subject should apply to both the first part and the second part (the part after 而且). The pattern can also be used omitting 而且, and instead using adverbs like 也 and 还 in its place.

Examples

- 这个东西 不但 贵，而且 难买。
  Zhège dōngxi bùdàn guì, érqiě nán mǎi .
  This thing is not only expensive, but also hard to buy.
- 这道菜 不但 好看，也 好吃。
  Zhè dào cài bùdàn hǎokàn, yě hǎochī.
  This dish is not only attractive, but also delicious.
- 她 不但 聪明，而且 很幽默。
  Tā bùdàn cōngming, érqiě hěn yōumò.
  She is not only smart, but also very humorous.
- 她 不但 离开了我，还 拿走了我所有的钱。
  Tā bùdàn líkāi le wǒ, hái názǒu le wǒ suǒyǒu de qián.
  Not only did she leave me, but she also took all my money.
- 他 不但 提前做完了，而且 做得很好。
  Tā bùdàn tíqián zuò wán le, érqiě zuò de hěn hǎo.
  Not only did he finish it in advance, but he did it very well.

Used with Two Subjects

When there is only one subject with 不但…… 而且……, the subject has to come at the beginning of the sentence, before both 不但 and 而且. When using two different subjects, however, you need to put one after 不但 and one after 而且.

Structure

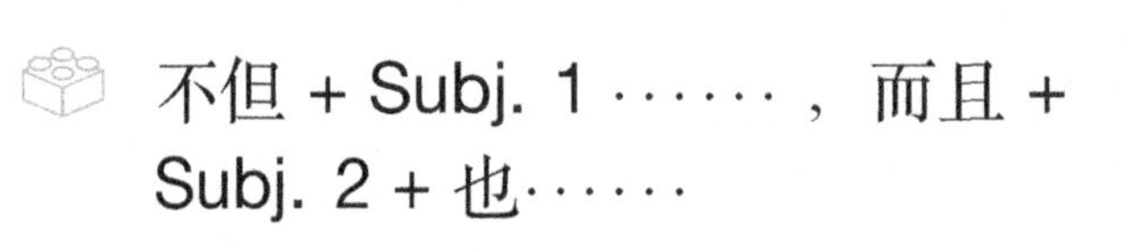

不但 + Subj. 1 ……，而且 + Subj. 2 + 也……

The pattern can also be used omitting 而且, and instead using adverbs like 也 in its place.

Examples

- 不但大学生找工作难，而且研究生也不容易。
  Bùdàn dàxuéshēng zhǎo gōngzuò nán, érqiě yánjiūshēng yě bù róngyì.
  Not only is it hard to find a job for undergraduates, but it's also hard for graduate students.
- 这个电影不但孩子们喜欢，大人也很喜欢。
  Zhège diànyǐng bùdàn háizimen xǐhuan, dàren yě hěn xǐhuan.
  Not only do children like this movie, but adults like it too.
- 不但员工压力大，老板压力也很大。
  Bùdàn yuángōng yālì dà, lǎobǎn yālì yě hěn dà.
  Not only are the employees under a lot of pressure, but the boss is under a lot of pressure too.
- 老师发现，不但学生说谎，而且家长也说谎。
  Lǎoshī fāxiàn, bùdàn xuéshēng shuōhuǎng, érqiě jiāzhǎng yě shuōhuǎng.
  The teacher found that not only did the student lie, but his parents did too.
- 不但老百姓害怕这些人，而且警察也害怕。
  Bùdàn lǎobǎixìng hàipà zhèxiē rén, érqiě jǐngchá yě hàipà.
  Not only do ordinary folk fear these people, but the police fear them too.

Similar to

- Expressing “and” with “he” (HSK1)
- Expressing “and also” with “hai” (HSK2)
- Expressing “both A and B” with “you” (HSK3), page 42

- Expressing "except" and "in addition" with "chule··· yiwai" (HSK3), page 206
- Expressing "in addition" with "haiyou" (HSK4)
- Expressing "in addition" with "lingwai" (HSK4)
- Expressing "in addition" with "zaishuo" (HSK4)
- Many types of "not only... but also..." (HSK4)
- Using "budan... geng" to express "not only... but also"
- Using "er" to explain contrasting ideas (HSK4)
- Expressing "and" with "he" (advanced) (HSK5)
- Expressing "not only..., even..." using "budan······, shenzhi lian" (HSK5)
- Expressing "not only··· but also" with "bujin" (HSK5)

Comparing "cai" and "jiu"

Both 才 (cái) and 就 (jiù) are adverbs that have to do with expressing time, and they are both placed before verbs. However, they typically have opposite effects on the tone of the sentence, with 才 (cái) implying a sense of lateness, and 就 (jiù) imparting a sense of earliness.

Emphasis with 才

Expressing Lateness with 才

才 indicates[1] that the speaker feels that the events discussed happened later than expected. Sometimes it also expresses anxiety, impatience, anger, or other related emotions.

Structure

Subj. + Time Word + 才 + Verb

Examples

- 我等了两个小时 才 买到票。

  Wǒ děng le liǎng gè xiǎoshí cái mǎi dào piào.

  I waited two hours before I could buy the ticket.

- 老板十一点 才 到办公室。

  Lǎobǎn shíyī diǎn cái dào bàngōngshì.

  The boss didn't come to the office until 11 o'clock.

- 这个项目最少要花两个月 才 能做完。

  Zhège xiàngmù zuì shǎo yào huā liǎng gè yuè cái néng zuò wán.

  It's going to take at least two months to complete this project.

Expressing Small Quantity with 才

才 can also mean "only" in the sense of a small quantity.

1. Expressing lateness with "cai" (Grammar), page 27

Structure

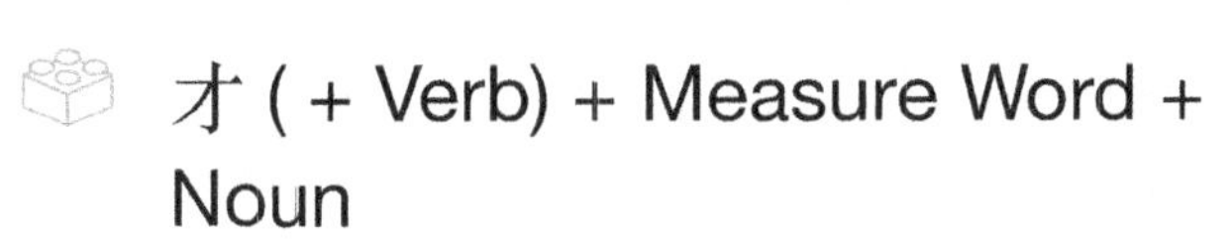

才 (+ Verb) + Measure Word + Noun

The key thing to pay attention to here is that the 才 goes *before* the *verb*, and not the "small quantity" that follows it.

Examples

- 我们有这么多人，你 才 点了三个菜。
  Wǒmen yǒu zhème duō rén, nǐ cái diǎn le sān gè cài.
  We have so many people and you only ordered three dishes.
- 我买了这么多东西， 才 花了五百块。
  Wǒ mǎi le zhème duō dōngxi, cái huā le wǔ bǎi kuài.
  I bought this many things, and I only spent 500 RMB.

Expressing "Not Late" with 才 and Time

When 才 is followed by a time, it can express the idea of "only," as in, "it's only 9 o'clock," expressing the idea that "9 o'clock is not late." This would seem to be the opposite of the 才 expressing "lateness," but it's important to remember that this 才 precedes a *time*, and not an *action*.

Structure

(现在) + 才 + Time

Examples

- 现在 才 九点，再玩一会儿。
  Xiànzài cái jiǔ diǎn, zài wán yīhuìr.
  It's only nine o'clock. Stay and hang out a little bit more.
- 才 六点，起那么早干吗?
  Cái liù diǎn, qǐ nàme zǎo gànmá?
  It's only six. Why did you get up so early?

Emphasis with 就

Expressing Earliness with 就

就 indicates that something has occurred earlier than the speaker expected. There may be an accompanying feeling of surprise or amazement.

Structure

Subj. + Time + 就 + Verb + Obj. + 了

Examples

- 她十九岁 就 结婚了。
  Tā shíjiǔ suì jiù jiéhūn le.
  She got married when she was only 19.
- 你妹妹十五岁 就 上大学了?
  Nǐ mèimei shíwǔ suì jiù shàng dàxué le?
  Your younger sister started college when she was only fifteen?
- 他下午四点 就 吃晚饭了。
  Tā xiàwǔ sì diǎn jiù chī wǎnfàn le.
  He ate dinner at four in the afternoon.
- 你们这么早 就 下班了?
  Nǐmen zhème zǎo jiù xiàbān le?
  You guys getting off work this early?
- 我八点 就 出门了，路上堵车，我还是迟到了十分钟。
  Wǒ bā diǎn jiù chūmén le, lù shàng dǔchē, wǒ háishi chídào le shí fēnzhōng.
  I left at eight o'clock, but there was a traffic jam, so I was still ten minutes late.

Expressing Small Quantity with 就

就 can be used to mean "only," in the sense of a small quantity.

If you're thinking, "*didn't we just learn to use 才 to also mean small quantity??*" then you're very perceptive, and the answer is *yes*. For this "small quantity" emphasis, both 才 and 就 can be used before the verb to express essentially the same thing. (If you really want to split hairs, native speakers might say that there's a tiny difference in emphasis between the two, but that level of nuance goes beyond the scope of this grammar point.)

Structure

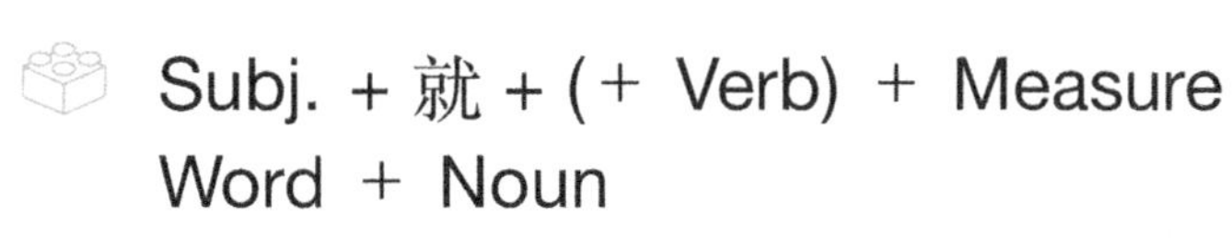

Examples

- 我们有这么多人，你 就 买了一瓶可乐？
  Wǒmen yǒu zhème duō rén, nǐ jiù mǎi le yī píng kělè?
  We have all these people, and you just bought that one bottle of cola?
- 你们每天 就 睡四个小时？
  Nǐmen měi tiān jiù shuì sì gè xiǎoshí?
  Do you only sleep four hours every day?
- 每个人都写了五页纸，你 就 写了一页纸！
  Měi gè rén dōu xiě le wǔ yè zhǐ, nǐ jiù xiě le yī yè zhǐ!
  Everyone wrote five pages, but you wrote just one?
- 那时候中国人都生四五个孩子，他们家 就 一个孩子？
  Nà shíhou Zhōngguó rén dōu shēng sì wǔ gè háizi, tāmen jiā jiù yī gè háizi?
  At that time Chinese people all had four or five children, but their family only had one?

Using 才 and 就 Together

They're not matter and anti-matter; these two "opposite" words can actually be used together. When used together, they're the "just recently" meaning of 才 and the "early" meaning of 就. Together, they indicate that one thing *just happened recently*, and then the other happened *soon after*.

Structure

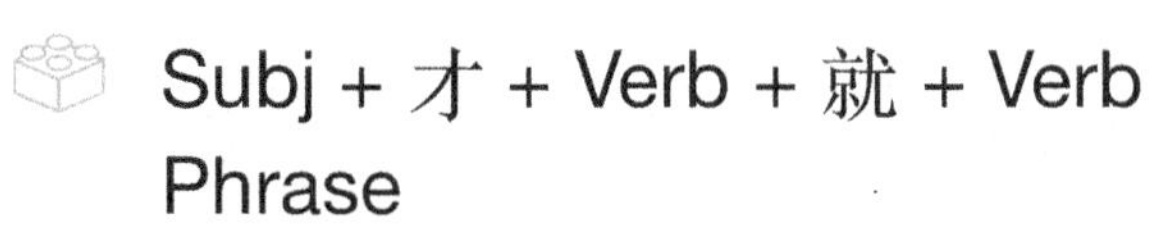

Examples

- 你 才 来 就 要走？不多坐一会儿？
  Nǐ cái lái jiù yào zǒu? bù duō zuò yīhuìr?
  You only just came and you're leaving already? Are you not going to sit a little longer?
- 电影 才 开始你 就 不想看了？
  Diànyǐng cái kāishǐ nǐ jiù bù xiǎng kàn le?
  The movie just started and you don't want to watch it anymore?
- 他 才 毕业 就 找到了这么好的工作？
  Tā cái bìyè jiù zhǎodào le zhème hǎo de gōngzuò?
  He just graduated and already found such a good job?

Similar to

- Expressing earliness with "jiu" (HSK2)
- Expressing lateness with "cai" (HSK3), page 27

Comparing "gang" and "gangcai"

刚 (gāng) and 刚才 (gāngcái) have similar meanings of "just (now)," but they differ on a few key uses.

刚 as "Just Happened"

刚 is actually an adverb, and it is placed in front of the verb. It emphasizes that the action *just* happened a short time ago. Unsurprisingly, it is similar to the English "just." 刚刚 and 刚 are interchangeable in this case.

The key here is that "a short time ago" is relative and determined by the speaker. For this reason, 刚 can indicate that something "just" happened 1 second ago, 5 minutes ago, 2 hours ago, 3 weeks ago, or even a year ago. The absolute time is flexible, but from the speaker's perspective, it *feels* recent.

刚 Before a Verb

One thing that confuses a lot of learners is that when you use 刚 with a verb, *you normally don't need 了*. Keep that in mind while reading the following examples, and look for the explanation below.

A few examples:

- ✔ 他 **刚** 到。
  Tā **gāng** dào.
  He just arrived.

This gives the impression that not only did he just get here, but he should still be here.

- ✔ 我们昨天 **刚** 到。
  Wǒmen zuótiān **gāng** dào.
  We just arrived yesterday.
- ✔ 真不巧，老板 **刚** 走。
  Zhēn bùqiǎo, lǎobǎn **gāng** zǒu.
  What bad timing. The boss just left.

It would be wrong to use 刚才 instead:

- ✘ 他 **刚才** 到。
  Tā **gāngcái** dào.
- ✘ 我们昨天 **刚才** 到。
  Wǒmen zuótiān **gāngcái** dào.

刚才 should be used for events a lot closer in time than 昨天.

- ✘ 真不巧，老板 **刚才** 走。
  Zhēn bùqiǎo, lǎobǎn **gāngcái** zǒu.

And if you mean to say "when I first arrived in Shanghai," use 刚 instead of 刚才:

- 我 刚 到上海的时候，谁都不认识。

  Wǒ gāng dào Shànghǎi de shíhou, shéi dōu bù rènshi.

  I didn't know anyone when I had just arrived in Shanghai.

刚 or 刚刚 before An Adjective

刚, as an adverb, can also be placed in front of a verb, while 刚才 can't be used this way. 刚 can also be used interchangeably with 刚刚.

A few examples:

- 他的感冒 刚刚 好。

  Tā de gǎnmào gānggāng hǎo.

  He just recovered from his cold.

- 天 刚 晴。

  Tiān gāng qíng.

  The sky just became clear.

- 牛肉 刚 熟。

  Niúròu gāng shú.

  The beef just got cooked.

刚才 as "Just Now"

刚才 is a time noun (like 今天 and 现在), and it expresses that the time elapsed is really short, in near-absolute terms. We're talking no more than 1-30 minutes in most situations, and often less than 5 minutes. When used before a verb, 刚才 emphasizes something happened "*just now*."

A few examples:

- 他 刚才 哭 了 。

  Tā gāngcái kū le .

  He was crying just now.

  He was crying a moment ago but he stopped.

- 我 刚才 看到他 了 。

  Wǒ gāngcái kàndào tā le .

  I just now saw him.

  Sounds like he's not here anymore; I just saw him, but don't see him now.

- 现在我感觉比 刚才 好一点 了 。

  Xiànzài wǒ gǎnjué bǐ gāngcái hǎo yīdiǎn le .

  I feel a little better now than just before.

刚才, as a time noun, can directly modify a noun to indicate it is that one from "just now" or "just before," while 刚 can't be used this way.

- ✘ 刚 的事情 太让人生气了。
  Gāng de shìqing tài ràng rén shēngqì le.
  What just happened is really upsetting.
- ✔ 刚才 的事情 太让人生气了。
  Gāngcái de shìqing tài ràng rén shēngqì le.
  What just happened is really upsetting.

刚 and 刚才 with 了

You may have noticed that something interesting is going on with regards to 了 in the sentences with 刚 and 刚才. Namely, 了 is not usually required in sentences with 刚, but it is usually required in sentences with 刚才. This is because 刚才 refers to a time in the *recent past*, and you're usually indicated that something *happened just now* (started and finished).

Take these sentences for example:

- 我昨天看了。
  Wǒ zuótiān kàn le.
  I looked at it yesterday.
- 我 刚才 看了。
  Wǒ gāngcái kàn le.
  I looked at it just now.

So these are both simple "subject + verb" sentences. Notice that when they refer to the *past* (including the one with 刚才), the action is completed and you need 了. You don't need 了 for things that haven't happened yet (they're just plans, and nothing is completed). And remember that 刚才 *always refers to the past.*

OK, now what about 刚? *Why does it not need 了?* The key is that you don't need a 了 in a sentence with 刚 if the verb *already indicates a clear result*. So, to use the 看 example from above:

- ✔ 我 刚 看到 。
  Wǒ gāng kàndào .
  I just saw it.
  Adding a 到 to 看 gives the verb a meaning of the result of "looking at."
- ✘ 我 刚 看到 了 。
  Wǒ gāng kàndào le .
  I just saw it.
  了 is not needed here as 看到 includes the result of "looking at."

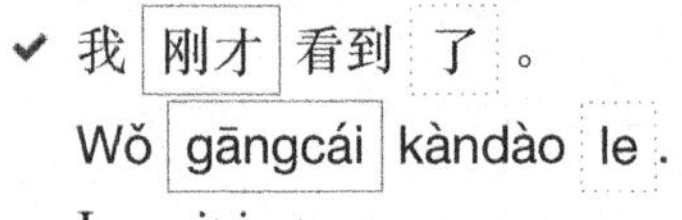

I saw it just now.

了 is needed with 刚才 because it feels so recent and unresolved.

A few more examples:

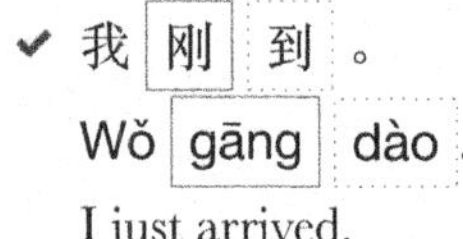

I just arrived.

The verb 到 includes a clear result.

✔ 你 刚 知道 吗?
Nǐ gāng zhīdào ma?
You just found out?

The verb 知道 always includes the result of "knowing."

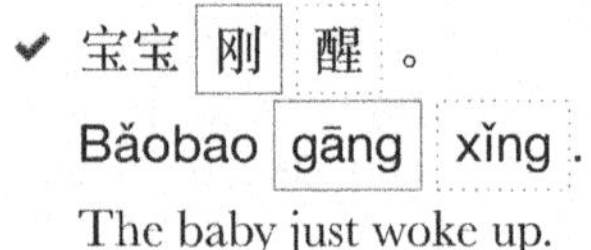

The baby just woke up.

The verb 醒 includes a clear enough indication of result.

刚 and 刚才 with 没

There's also something going on with 没 in sentences with 刚 and 刚才. The deal here is that you can say something *didn't happen* ***just now*** (刚才), but you can't say that something ***just*** *didn't happen* (刚). [Saying that something "just didn't happen" only works in English if you interpret "just" to mean "simply."]

The takeaway? Just don't use 刚 in sentences where you use 没 to negate the past.

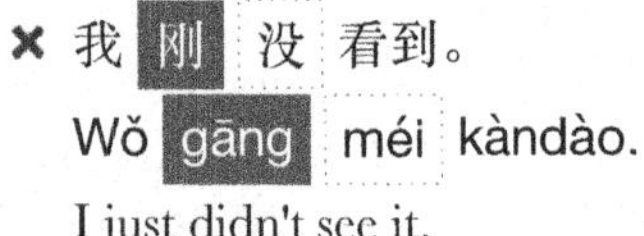

I just didn't see it.

Don't use 刚 with 没 in the past.

✘ 我 刚 没 听懂。
Wǒ gāng méi tīngdǒng.
I didn't understand just now.

Use 没 with 刚才 (and no 了) to negate the past.

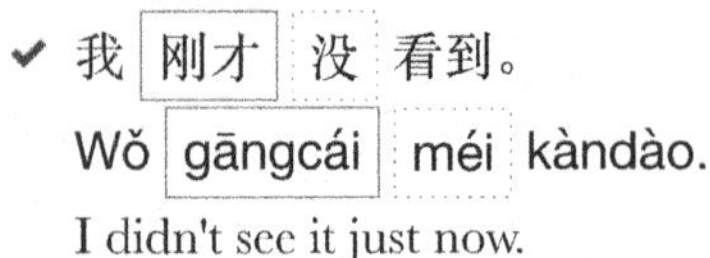

I didn't see it just now.

✔ 我 刚才 没 听懂。

Wǒ gāngcái méi tīngdǒng.

I didn't understand just now.

Example Dialog

A: 你 刚才 去哪儿了?

Nǐ gāngcái qù nǎr le?

Where did you go just now?

B: 我去上厕所了。刚 回来。

Wǒ qù shàng cèsuǒ le. Gāng huílái.

I went to the bathroom. I just got back.

Similar to

- Expressing "just now" with "gangcai" (HSK3), page 66
- Expressing "just" with "gang" (HSK4)

Comparing "youdian" and "yidian"

一点 (yīdiǎn) and 有点 (yǒudiǎn), usually pronounced 一点儿 (yīdiǎnr) and 有点儿 (yǒudiǎnr) in northern China, mean pretty much the same thing on the surface — "a little" or "a bit" — but they have different uses in sentences.

Both Can Be Used for Describing Degree

Usage of 有点

有点 is placed before an adjective, and while used for descriptions, it also expresses a tone of complaint by the speaker, or some other form of negative impression. It doesn't just mean "a bit," but rather "a bit *too*" (for the speaker's liking).

A few examples:

- 今天我 有点 累 。 *This is a complaint.*
  Jīntiān wǒ yǒudiǎn lèi .
  I am a little tired today.
- 这个菜 有点 咸 。 *This is a complaint.*
  Zhège cài yǒudiǎn xián .
  This dish is a bit salty.

Usage of 一点

一点 can't be placed before an adjective. Instead, it is placed *after* adjectives. The adjectives that can be used are particularly limited. 一点 is often used when comparing, requesting, or expressing the speaker's expectation. In this usage, 一点 can also be shortened to just 点。

A few examples:

- 请说 慢 一点 。 *This is a request.*
  Qǐng shuō màn yīdiǎn .
  Please speak a little more slowly.
- 快 点 ，要迟到了。 *This is a request.*
  Kuài diǎn , yào chídào le.
  Hurry up a bit, we're going to be late.
- 老板， 便宜 点 吧。 *This is a request.*
  Lǎobǎn, piányi diǎn ba.
  Boss [shop owner], a little cheaper, please.

- 这个比那个 重 一点 。
  Zhège bǐ nàge zhòng yīdiǎn.
  This one is a bit heavier than that one.

This is a comparison.

Use 有 (一) 点 for Describing Quantity

一点 can be placed before a noun to mean "small quantity," like 一点水，一点钱 while 有点 can't be used this way. Note that 有点 is also a shortened form of 有一点, which means "there is a little" of something.

A few examples to help you understand:

- 你脸上 有一点 番茄酱 。
  Nǐ liǎn shàng yǒu yī diǎn fānqiéjiàng .
  There's a little ketchup on your face.
- 你碗里还 有点 饭 ，吃完吧。
  Nǐ wǎn lǐ hái yǒu diǎn fàn , chī wán ba.
  There's still a little rice in your bowl. Finish eating it.

Negative Forms

Use 有点 Before Just 不 or 没

After 有点, you can use 不 or 没 before the adjective, however the adjective should have a positive connotation, like 高兴 (gāoxìng), 舒服 (shūfu), 喜欢 (xǐhuan), etc. This makes the overall emotion expressed negative still.

Some examples:

- 孩子们 有点 不 喜欢我们的新家。
  Háizi men yǒudiǎn bù xǐhuan wǒmen de xīn jiā.
  The children don't really like our new home.
- 她 有点 不 舒服。
  Tā yǒudiǎn bù shūfu.
  She doesn't feel very well.
- 我 有点 不 相信那个人。
  Wǒ yǒudiǎn bù xiāngxìn nàge rén.
  I don't really believe that guy.
- 我们 有点 没 听懂。
  Wǒmen yǒudiǎn méi tīngdǒng.
  We didn't really understand what was said.

Use 一点 Before 也不 or 也没

一点 can also be used in the 一点也不 or 一点也没 structure to mean "not at all."

Some examples:

- 这个菜 一点也 不 辣。
  Zhège cài yīdiǎn yě bù là.
  This dish is not spicy at all.
- 作业你 一点也 没 做?
  Zuòyè nǐ yīdiǎn yě méi zuò?
  You didn't do any homework at all?

Common Mistakes

✗ 今天 一点 热。
Jīntiān yīdiǎn rè.

✔ 今天 有点 热。
Jīntiān yǒudiǎn rè.
It's a little hot today.

This is a complaint.

✗ 我 一点 饿。
Wǒ yīdiǎn è.

✔ 我 有点 饿。
Wǒ yǒudiǎn è.
I'm a little hungry.

This is a complaint.

Similar to

- Expressing "a little too" with "you dian" (HSK2)
- Expressing "not at all" with "yidianr ye bu" (HSK4)
- Expressing "a bit too" (HSK5)

Comparing "zai" and "you"

Both 再 (zài) and 又 (yòu) express the repeating of an action and can be roughly translated in English to "again." However, 再 is used to express actions that have not yet occurred (the "future again") and 又 is used for actions that have already occurred (the "past again"). They're not interchangeable. In addition, each word has some additional special usages.

再 is used to express repetition of an action in the future

再 is used to express something that has already happened and will happen again.

Structure

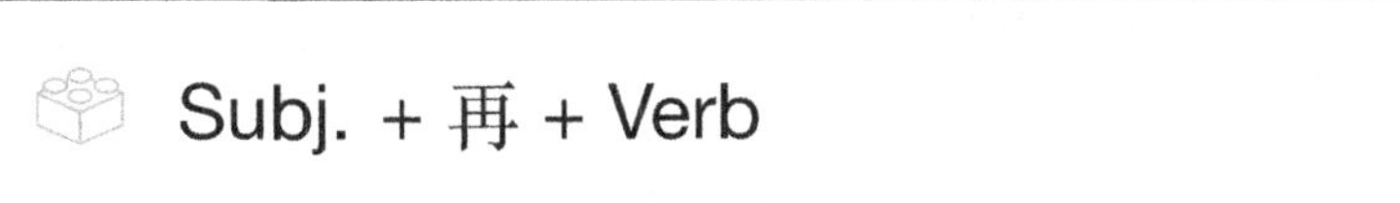

Examples

- 我们下次 再 来吧。
  Wǒmen xiàcì zài lái ba.
  We will come here again next time.
- 我想 再 看一下。
  Wǒ xiǎng zài kàn yīxià.
  I want to take a look again.

You need to use 再 for this usage; you can't use 又:

✘ 请 又 说一次。
Qǐng yòu shuō yī cì.

Since it is asking about a future action, you can't use "又"

✔ 请 再 说一次。
Qǐng zài shuō yī cì.
Please say it one more time.

再 can be used to say "another"

Aside from expressing the repetition of an action, 再 can also be used to express the equivalent of the English word "another."

Structure

 Subj. + 再 + Verb + Obj.

Note that the "Object" mentioned above is usually also going to have an 一 and a measure word in front of it. You'll see that in the examples below.

Examples

- ✔ 我要 再 看一部电影。
  Wǒ yào zài kàn yī bù diànyǐng.
  I want to watch another movie.
- ✔ 你可以 再 做一碗面条吗?
  Nǐ kěyǐ zài zuò yī wǎn miàntiáo ma?
  Can you make another bowl of noodles?
- ✘ 我得 又 写一篇作文。
  Wǒ děi yòu xiě yī piān zuòwén.
  I have to write another essay.
  Since it is about the future, you can't use "又"
- ✘ 我要 又 吃一块蛋糕。
  Wǒ yào yòu chī yī kuài dàngāo.
  I want to eat another piece of cake.
  Since it is about the future, you can't use "又"

再 can be used to say "and then"

再 can be used with 先 to express sequential order[1]. (ex. Do this....and then this....) In some cases, 再 can appear by itself to simply mean "and then." While this doesn't sound so easy to confuse with 又, it's actually quite common for intermediate learners to misunderstand this use of 再 as meaning "again," so it's definitely worth mentioning here.

Structure

 Subj. + (先) + Action 1 + 再 + Action 2

---

1. Sequencing with "xian" and "zai" (Grammar), page 29

Examples

✔ 我们 先 做作业 再 去酒吧。
Wǒmen xiān zuò zuòyè zài qù jiǔbā.
First we'll do our work, then we'll go to the bar.

✔ 我 先 买房子 再 结婚。
Wǒ xiān mǎi fángzi zài jiéhūn.
First I'll buy a house, then I'll get married.

✔ 我们吃完饭 再 看电影。
Wǒmen chī wán fàn zài kàn diànyǐng ba.
After we buy a drink, then we'll go to a movie.

✔ 我们回家 再 讨论好吗？
Wǒmen huíjiā zài tǎolùn, hǎo ma?
We discuss it after we go home, OK?

✘ 我要看完书 又 睡觉。
Wǒ yào kàn wán shū yòu shuìjiào.
I want to read the book and go to sleep.

"' 又"can not be used as the action"go to bed" haven't occured yet.

✘ 你 先 吃饭 又 打电话给父母。
Nǐ xiān chīfàn yòu dǎ diànhuà gěi fùmǔ.
You should eat before you call your parents.

"又" does not sequence events.

又 is used to express repetition of an action that has already occurred in the past

又 is used in declarative sentences and describes the simple repetition of actions. This repeated action has already occurred once in the past.

Structure

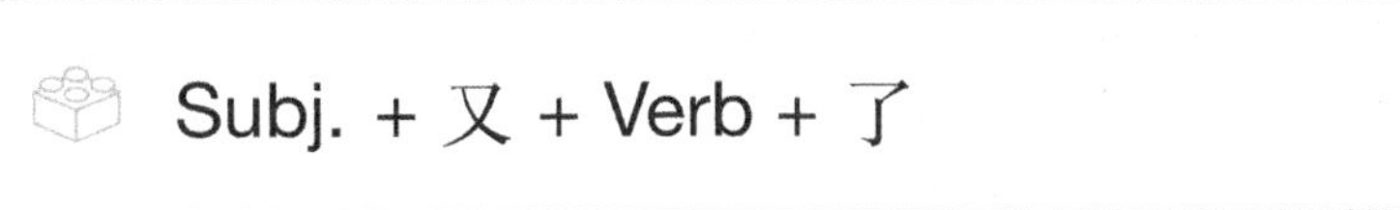

Example

✔ 你怎么 又 给我打电话了，什么事？
Nǐ zěnme yòu gěi wǒ dǎ diànhuà le, shénme shì?
You keep calling me, what's the matter?

- ✔ 这个人 又 来了。
  Zhège rén yòu lái le.
  This man is here again.
- ✔ 他 又 不来上课了，老师可能罚他。
  Tā yòu bù lái shàngkè le, lǎoshī kěnéng fá tā.
  He didn't come to class again. The teacher is probably going to punish him.
- ✔ 你为什么 又 看这本书了？你已经看过了。
  Nǐ wèishénme yòu kàn zhè běn shū le? nǐ yǐjīng kàn guò le.
  Why are you reading that book again? You already read it.
- ✘ 昨天他 再 喝醉了。
  Zuótiān tā zài hēzuì le.
  He was drunk again yesterday.
  "再" is not used for past events.
- ✘ 昨天我 再 看电影了。
  Zuótiān wǒ zài kàn diànyǐng le.
  I watched the movie again yesterday.
  "再" is not used for past events.

又 adds emotional coloring to events recurring in the future

又 is sometimes used to express that something that has happened before is going to happen in the immediate future. In this case, it usually appears with 要 (yào), 可以 (kěyǐ), 能 (néng), or 是 (shì). This usage often expresses exasperation or impatience with something happening *yet **again***, but sometimes it's more neutral, or even happy.

Structure

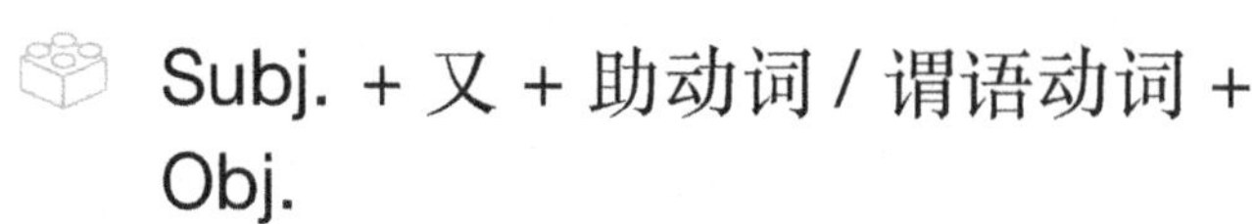
Subj. + 又 + 助动词 / 谓语动词 + Obj.

Example

- 明天 又 是 星期一！
  Míngtiān yòu shì Xīngqīyī!
  Tomorrow is Monday again.

- 明天 又 要 开会，真烦人。
  Míngtiān yòu yào kāi huì, zhēn fán rén.
  We're having another meeting tomorrow. So annoying!
- 你 又 要 辞职了？为什么？
  Nǐ yòu yào cízhí le? wèishénme?
  You're going to resign again? Why?
- 夏天快到了，又 可以 吃冰淇淋了！
  Xiàtiān kuài dào le, yòu kěyǐ chī bīngqílín le!
  It's almost summer, and we can eat ice cream again!
- 如果我能瘦一些，我就 又 能 穿我最喜欢的牛仔裤啦！
  Rúguǒ wǒ néng shòu yīxiē, wǒ jiù yòu néng chuān wǒ zuì xǐhuan de niúzǎikù la!
  If I can slim down a bit, I can wear my favorite jeans again!

Both 再 and 又 have other uses as well

The comparisons above are the cases where 又 and 再 are most easily confused. This wiki also has other uses of both, however:

- All uses of 又
- All uses of 再

Similar to

- Expressing "again" in the future with "zai" (HSK2)
- Expressing "again" in the past with "you" (HSK3), page 14
- Sequencing with "xian" and "zai" (HSK3, HSK4), page 29
- Advanced use of "you" (HSK5)

Comparing "haishi" and "huozhe"

Both 还是 (háishì) and 或者 (huòzhě) mean "or" and are used to present a choice. However, 还是 is normally used when asking a question, and 或者 is mostly for declarative sentences.

还是 for Providing Choices as a Question

When asking a question, 还是 can be used to provide choices or options.[1]

Structure

Option A + 还是 + Option B ?

Examples

- 你喜欢他 还是 我?
  Nǐ xǐhuan tā háishì wǒ?
  Do you like him or me?
- 你喝茶 还是 喝咖啡?
  Nǐ hē chá háishì hē kāfēi?
  Do you drink tea or coffee?
- 你中午出去吃 还是 叫外卖?
  Nǐ zhōngwǔ chūqù chī háishì jiào wàimài?
  Are you going out for lunch or ordering take-out?

或者 for Giving Options as a Statement

或者 is used in a statement in which options are presented.

Structure

Possibility 1 + 或者 + Possibility 2

The structure for 或者 and 还是 is the same, but the meaning, as well as the context in which 或者 is needed, is different. 或者 drops the "A or B, PICK

1. Offering choices with "haishi" (Grammar), page 59

ONE" attitude in favor of a more open, "maybe A, perhaps B… (or maybe both or neither?)" So it's less exclusive and less demanding of a choice RIGHT NOW.

Examples

- 周末我想在家看书 或者 看电影。
  Zhōumò wǒ xiǎng zài jiā kànshū huòzhě kàn diànyǐng.
  This weekend, I want to stay home and read or watch movies.
- 你可以坐 1 号线 或者 2 号线去人民广场。
  Nǐ kěyǐ zuò yī hào xiàn huòzhě èr hào xiàn qù Rénmín Guǎngchǎng.
  You can take Line 1 or Line 2 to People's Square.
- 我们可以电话 或者 邮件联系。
  Wǒmen kěyǐ diànhuà huòzhě yóujiàn liánxì.
  We can contact each other by phone or email.

还是 for Questions That Are Embedded in Sentences

Deciding whether or not to use 还是 becomes difficult with sentences that contain statements like "I don't know," "I want to know," "I'm not sure," etc. Alone, these statements are not technically questions. However, when used in a sentence that contains choices, these statements imply that a question must be answered. Therefore, you must use 还是.

A few examples:

- 我 不知道 这本书是他的 还是 我的。
  Wǒ bù zhīdào zhè běn shū shì tā de háishì wǒ de.
  I don't know if this book is his or mine.
- 我 想知道 他们是支持 还是 反对。
  Wǒ xiǎng zhīdào tāmen shì zhīchí háishì fǎnduì.
  I want to know if they support or oppose.
- 老板 不确定 是这个周末出差 还是 下个周末出差。
  Lǎobǎn bù quèdìng shì zhège zhōumò chūchāi háishì xià gè zhōumò chūchāi.
  The boss isn't sure if he's going on a business trip this weekend or next weekend.

Incorrect Examples

- ✕ 我们打车 或者 坐地铁？ *Since it is a question, it should use 还是*
  Wǒmen dǎchē **huòzhě** zuò dìtiě?
  Shall we take a taxi or take the metro?
- ✕ 明天 **还是** 后天都行。 *Since it is a statement, it should use 或者*
  Míngtiān **huòzhě** hòutiān dōu xíng.
  Either tomorrow or the day after is fine.
- ✕ 我 想知道 那个人是男的 **或者** 女的。 *It's an embedded question, so it should use 还是*
  Wǒ xiǎng zhīdào nàge rén shì nánde **huòzhě** nǚde.
  I'd like to know if that person is male or female.

Similar to

- Expressing "or" in statements (HSK3), page 51
- Offering choices with "haishi" (HSK3), page 59

Keyword Index

Look up grammar points based on keywords they contain.

Glossary

We strive to avoid unnecessarily technical terms on the Chinese Grammar Wiki, but occasionally it's sort of necessary, and sometimes even useful (yes, really!). So to help you out, we've placed all of the grammatical terms related to Mandarin Chinese in one place. Each term has a page on the wiki with a more complete description, and many pages also have lists of grammar points related to the term.

List of Mandarin Grammar Terms

Action verb — *Also known as: 动作动词 (dòngzuò dòngcí) and 行为动词 (xíngwéi dòngcí).* Action verbs describe what a subject did, is doing, or will do, physically.

Adjective — *Also known as: 形容词 (xíngróngcí).* Adjectives are the "describing" words of a language. In Chinese, they have some characteristics that they don't have in English.

Adjectival phrase — *Also known as: 形容词性词组 (xíngróngcí-xìng duǎnyǔ) and adjective phrase.* Adjectival phrases often consist of just an adjective and the adverbs modifying it, but they might also have other structures, such as an adjective and complement.

Adjectival predicate sentence — *Also known as: 形容词谓语句 (xíngróngcí wèiyǔ jù) and 形容词性谓语句 (xíngróngcí-xìng wèiyǔ jù).* A fancy name for a sentence where the predicate consists of an adjective.

Adverb — *Also known as: 副词 (fùcí).* Adverbs are words that modify verbs and adjectives. In Chinese, word order of adverbs is much stricter than in English. Chinese adverbs normally come before the main verb of a sentence, but in some cases come right at the beginning of a sentence.

Adverbial — *Also known as: 状语 (zhuàngyǔ).* An adverbial is a sentence element that functions like an adverb, modifying a verb or adjective.

Adverbial phrase — *Also known as: 副词短语 (fùcí duǎnyǔ) and adverb phrase.* An adverbial phrase is a phrase with two or more words that act like an adverb, modifying a verb or adjective.

Affirmative-negative question — *Also known as: 正反问句 (zhèng-fǎn wènjù) and alternative questions.* A common way to form questions in Chinese is to first use a verb in the positive, then repeat the same verb in its negative form, similar to how in English we can say, "Do you have money or not?" or "Have you or have you not been to the park?" This sentence pattern feels a lot more natural in Chinese than those admittedly awkward English equivalents, however.

Affix — *Also known as: 词缀 (cízhuì).* An affix is a linguistic unit added to the beginning, middle or end of a word to change its meaning (e.g. prefix, infix, suffix).

Aspect — *Also known as: 动作状态 (dòngzuò zhuàngtài).* Chinese does not use the concept of formal tenses. Instead, it employs what is called "grammatical aspect." Rather than conjugating its verbs, Chinese uses particles to indicate how a verb works within a particular timeframe, or how the verb relates to the flow of time. The particles most often used to indicate aspect in Chinese are 了 (le), 过 (guo), and 着 (zhe).

Aspectual particle — *Also known as: 动态助词 (dòngtài zhùcí).* These words are added to verbs to indicate aspect (not the same as tense). The particles most often used to indicate aspect in Chinese are 了 (le), 过 (guo), and 着 (zhe).

Attributive — *Also known as: 定语 (dìngyǔ).* An attributive is the word or phrase that directly precedes the noun it describes. Frequently it is linked to the noun with the structural particle 的 (de).

Auxiliary verb — *Also known as: modal verb, 助动词 (zhùdòngcí), 情态动词 (qíngtài dòngcí) and 能愿动词 (néngyuàn dòngcí).* Auxiliary verbs are "helping" verbs that come before main verbs and help express a tone or mood. (The word "modal" comes from "mood.") In English, auxiliary verbs include words like "should," "will," and "can," which all change something about the situation and the speaker's attitude. Auxiliary verbs express capability, possibility, necessity, obligation or willingness.

Cardinal number — *Also known as: 基数词 (jīshùcí).* Cardinal numbers are numbers such as 1, 2, or 3 used to indicate quantity. They contrast with ordinal numbers.

Causative verb — *Also known as: 使令动词 (shǐlìng dòngcí) and 使役动词 (shǐyì dòngcí).* A causative verb is a kind of verb that is used to indicate that someone or something causes something else to do or be something. In Chinese, 让 (ràng) is a major player in this space.

Complement — *Also known as: 补语 (bǔyǔ) and objective complement.* A complement is a word or phrase following a verb (or sometimes an adjective) that provides additional meaning to the verb phrase. Complements are not the same as objects, and can be as short as one character, or practically as long as a sentence. Complements provide additional information associated with verbs, such as degree, result, direction or possibility, and are extremely common. Complements are not a form of flattery (those are compliments); they're much more versatile than that!

Complex sentence — *Also known as: 复句 (fùjù).* A complex sentence is a sentence with one main clause and one or more subordinate clauses.

Conjunction — *Also known as: 连词 (liáncí).* Conjunctions in Chinese do exactly what they do in English: connect things. They help make the transition between ideas smoother and also show the relationships between those ideas.

Content word — *Also known as: 实词 (shící).* Content words refer to real objects in the real world, whether solid and palpable, or observable in some other way. These words refer to objects, actions, concepts, and even emotions, which exist in some real way as more than just grammatical tools. Words that serve purely grammatical roles are called function words.

Coverb — *Also known as: 副动词 (fùdòngcí) and 伴动词 (bàndòngcí).* A coverb is a verb that modifies the main verb of a sentence when used with its own object.

Degree adverb — *Also known as: 程度副词 (chéngdù fùcí) and adverb of degree.* Degree adverbs intensify or in some other way modify the degree of expression of the adjective (or verb).

Degree complement — *Also known as: 程度补语 (chéngdù bǔyǔ) and complement of degree.* While most complements follow verbs, degree complements can follow both verbs and adjectives. These complements intensify or modify the degree of expression of the verb or adjective.

Demonstrative pronoun — *Also known as: 指示代词 (zhǐshì dàicí).* A demonstrative pronoun is a pronoun used in the place of a noun and specifies what is being referred to.

Dependent clause — *Also known as: 从句 (cóngjù).* A dependent clause is dependent on and modifies an independent clause. Dependent clauses have a subject and verb, but also start with a subordinate conjunction, making it clear that they are not meant to stand on their own.

Direct object — *Also known as: 直接宾语 (zhíjiē bīnyǔ).* A direct object is what is being acted upon, thus receiving the action of a verb. In Chinese grammar, direct objects are often simply referred to as "objects."

Direction complement — *Also known as: 趋向补语 (qūxiàng bǔyǔ), directional complement and complement of direction.* A direction complement is a complement used to describe the direction of a verb. Verbs often already have some inherent movement implied, but by adding a direction complement, it becomes clearer where, exactly, that action is going.

Directional verb — *Also known as: 趋向动词 (qūxiàng dòngcí).* Directional verbs can be added to other verbs in a direction complement, illustrating which direction the verb is going.

Directional complement — See **direction complement**

Distinguishing word — *Also known as: 区别词 (qūbiécí) and attributive adjective.* "Distinguishing words" are rather foreign to the English speaker. On the surface they may seem like regular adjectives, but distinguishing words cannot have degree, so they cannot be modified by adverbs. Unlike normal adjectives, sentences involving distinguishing words use 是 (shì), and usually 的 (de) as well. Common words include the Chinese words for "male," "female," "real," "fake," and colors.

Existential verb — *Also known as: 存现动词 (cúnxiàn dòngcí).* Existential verbs declare the existence or nonexistence of things.

Function word — *Also known as: 虚词 (xūcí).* Function words do not refer to real objects in the real world; rather they serve purely grammatical roles in sentences, drawing relationships and logical connections between the content words in a sentence. Words that refer to real objects in the real world are called content words.

Judgment verb — *Also known as: 关系动词 (guānxì dòngcí) and 判断动词 (pànduàn dòngcí).* Judgment verbs are verbs used to express the speaker's judgment. This can be as simple as the verb "to be," but also covers a wide range of other verbs.

Indirect object — *Also known as: 间接宾语 (jiànjiē bīnyǔ).* Indirect objects occur when there are two objects in a sentence. The indirect object is for/to whom/what the action of the verb is done and who/what is receiving the direct object. In Chinese grammar, indirect objects are often referred to as second objects.

Independent clause — *Also known as: 主句 (zhǔjù).* An independent clause is a clause that has a subject and a predicate that modifies the subject, allowing it to stand alone as a sentence.

Independent phrase — *Also known as: 独立语 (dúlì yǔ).* An independent phrase has no subject acting out the verb in the sentence.

Interjection — *Also known as: 叹词 (tàncí) and 感叹词 (gǎntàncí).* This type of word is used in exclamations or various kinds of emotional response.

Interrogative pronoun — See **question word**

Intransitive verb — *Also known as: 不及物动词 (bùjíwù dòngcí).* Intransitive verbs are verbs which take no direct object.

Location word — *Also known as: 方位名词 (fāngwèi míngcí), 方位词 (fāngwèi cí) and noun of locality.* Location words are nouns showing direction and location.

Main clause — See **independent clause**

Measure word — *Also known as: 量词 (liàngcí) and classifier.* Measure words are used together with numerals to indicate the quantity of a noun, and sometimes even of an action. The general term for "measure word" in linguistics is "classifier," because measure words involve some kind of classification of the noun (or action) being counted.

Mimetic word — See **onomatopoeia**

Modal adverb — *Also known as: 语气副词 (yǔqì fùcí) and tone adverb.* Modal adverbs express likelihood with adverbs such as probably, possibly, evidently, certainly, etc.

Modal particle — *Also known as: 语气助词 (yǔqì zhùcí), 语气词 (yǔqì cí), Sentence-final particle and Sentential particle.* Modal particles are words used at the end of sentences to indicate mood, or attitude. They tend to be neutral tone and hard to translate, but they add a bit of "flavor" to a sentence. See also particles.

Modal verb — See **auxiliary verb**

Negative adverb — *Also known as: 否定副词 (fǒudìng fùcí).* Negative adverbs negate verbs and adjectives to make a negative statement. The main ones in Chinese are 不 (bù) and 没 (méi).

Noun — *Also known as: 名词 (míngcí).* You may have learned these as "person, place, or thing." Nouns often act as subjects, are modified by adjectives, and can be counted with measure words in Chinese.

Noun measure word — *Also known as: 名量词 (míngliàngcí) and nominal measure word.* As the name suggests, these are measure words that are only used for nouns.

Noun phrase — *Also known as: 名词性短语 (míngcí-xìng duǎnyǔ).* A noun phrase is a phrase with a noun or pronoun as a head word that has any sort of modifier.

Numeral — *Also known as: 数词 (shùcí).* A numeral is a symbol that represents a number.

Nominal predicate sentence — *Also known as: 名词谓语句 (míngcí wèiyǔjù).* Nominal predicate sentences are sentences with a noun phrase that functions as the main predicate of the sentence.

Object — *Also known as: 宾语 (bīnyǔ).* The object is the receiver of the action of the verb.

Onomatopoeia — *Also known as: 象声词 (xiàngshēngcí) and 拟声词 (nǐshēngcí).* Onomatopoeia are words which represent sounds and noises.

Ordinal number — *Also known as: 序数词 (xùshù cí).* Ordinal numbers are numbers used to express rank or sequence. Think "1st," "2nd," etc. Ordinal numbers contrast with cardinal numbers.

Particle — *Also known as: 助词 (zhùcí).* Particles are function words that depend on other words or phrases to impart meaning. They're kind of like prepositions, but more abstract. In Chinese, the key ones are aspectual particles (for indicating aspect), structural particles (for indicating relationships between words), and modal particles (for indicating mood). Chinese particles are also special words because they tend to always take the neutral tone.

Passive voice — *Also known as: 被动结构 (bèidòng jiégòu), 被动句式 (bèidòng jùshì), 被动语态 (bèidòng yǔtài) and the passive.* "Passive voice" is a grammatical term used to refer to sentences in which the "recipient" of an action (often referred to as the "direct object" or simply "object") becomes the subject of the sentence, and the "doer" of the action is demoted to secondary importance or omitted altogether.

Passive structure — See **passive voice**

Personal pronoun — *Also known as: 人称代词 (rénchēng dàicí).* Personal pronouns include 我 (wǒ), 你 (nǐ), 他 (tā), and 她 (tā). To make them plural, all you need to do is add the suffix -们 (-men) to them. There is also a polite second person form 您 (nín), which cannot normally take the -们 (-men) suffix.

Place noun — *Also known as: 处所名词 (chùsuǒ míngcí).* Place nouns are nouns describing the position or place of something.

Place adverb — *Also known as: 处所副词 (chùsuǒ fùcí), location adverb, adverb of place and adverb of location.* Place adverbs modify the location of a verbs or adjective.

Placement verb — See **existential verb**

Phrase — *Also known as: 短语 (duǎnyǔ) and 词组 (cízǔ).* A phrase is a group of words that expresses a concept. It can be focused on fleshing out a particular word, as in a noun phrase or verb phrase. See also clause, which expresses a more complete thought.

Possessive pronoun — *Also known as: 物主代词 (wùzhǔ dàicí).* Possessive pronouns take the place of a noun and show ownership.

Potential complement — Verbs can take potential complements to indicate whether or not an action is possible. Potential complements contain a 得 (de) or a 不 (bu) immediate after the verb being modified, and are quite common in everyday spoken Mandarin.

Predicate — *Also known as: 谓语 (wèiyǔ).* Predicates are the main verb or verb phrase of a sentence, and state something about the subject. Aside from verbs, adjectives and sometimes even nouns can be predicates as well.

Preposition — *Also known as: 介词 (jiècí).* Prepositions are words that indicate location or direction. They are called "pre"-positions because they are positioned *before* the words that they modify.

Prepositional phrase — *Also known as: 介词短语 (jiècí duǎnyǔ).* A prepositional phrase is a phrase beginning with a preposition that precedes the word it modifies and clarifies that word's relationship with another word in the sentence.

Pronoun — *Also known as: 代词 (dàicí).* Pronouns substitute in for regular nouns and proper nouns to avoid unnecessary repetition of the same words over and over again.

Proper noun — *Also known as: 专有名词 (zhuānyǒu míngcí).* A proper noun is specific person, place or thing. Proper nouns are generally capitalized (e.g. Anubis, Asgard, AllSet Learning), both in English and in pinyin.

Psychological verb — *Also known as: 心理动词 (xīnlǐ dòngcí) and psych verb.* A psychological verb is a verb that conveys the speaker's mental state or attitude.

Qualitative adjective — *Also known as: 性质形容词 (xìngzhì xíngróngcí).* Qualitative adjectives describe the quality or nature of something.

Quantitative phrase — *Also known as: 数量短语 (shùliàng duǎnyǔ).* Quantitative phrases express a measurement of amount.

Quantity complement — *Also known as: 数量补语 (shùliàng bǔyǔ), quantitative complement and complement of quantity.* A quantity complement follows a verb and supplies information regarding an amount.

Question pronoun — See **question word**

Question word — *Also known as: 疑问代词 (yíwèn dàicí), question pronoun, interrogative pronoun.* A **question word** refers to a special kind of pronoun used to ask questions. These would include 什么 (shénme), 什么时候 (shénme shíhou), 谁 (shéi), 哪儿 (nǎr) / 哪里 (nǎlǐ), 哪个 (nǎge), 为什么 (wèishénme), 怎么 (zěnme). Beginners should pay attention to the placement of question words.

Reduplication — It is one of the great ironies of linguistics that the term for repeating a word is overly repetitive itself. You'd think that the word "duplication" would work just fine, but the linguistic term really is reduplication. In Chinese, verbs and adjectives are often reduplicated.

Relational verb — See **judgment verb**

Result complement — *Also known as: 结果补语 (jiéguǒ bǔyǔ), complement of result, resultative complement and result compound.* Result complements are a kind of verbal complement that appears very frequently in Chinese. Surprisingly enough, they're used to describe the result of a verb.

Scope adverb — *Also known as: 范围副词 (fànwéi fùcí).* Scope adverbs modify and expand a verb or adjective.

Sentence with a nominal predicate — See **nominal predicate sentence**

Sentence with a verbal predicate — *Also known as: 动词谓语句 (dòngcí wèiyǔ jù).* A sentence with a verb as the main element of its predicate is called a sentence with a verbal predicate. This type of sentence is extremely common.

Sentence with an adjectival predicate — See **adjectival predicate sentence**

Sentence with a subject-predicate structure as predicate — *Also known as: 主谓谓语句 (zhǔ-wèi wèiyǔ jù).*

Sentence-final particle — See **modal particle**

Sentential particle — See **modal particle**

Separable verb — *Also known as: 离合词 (líhécí) and verb-object phrase.* "Separable verbs" get their name from their ability to "separate" into two parts (a verb part and an object part), with other words in between. In fact, you could also simply call separable verbs "verb-object phrases."

Subject — *Also known as: 主语 (zhǔyǔ).* A subject is a noun or pronoun that the sentence centers around. It is the actor of the verb and is what something is said about.

Subject-predicate construction — *Also known as: 主谓结构 (zhǔ-wèi jiégòu).* The subject-predicate construction consists of a subject and a predicate, and may be part of a larger sentence, or may serve as a sentence on its own.

Subject-predicate sentence — *Also known as: 主谓句 (zhǔ-wèi jù).* A sentence composed of a subject and a predicate. The vast majority of sentences fit this description.

Subordinate clause — See **dependent clause**

State complement — *Also known as: 状态补语 (zhuàngtài bǔyǔ), 情态补语 (qíngtài bǔyǔ) and complement of state.* State complements describe an achieved state of an action. State complements are usually adjective phrases (adverb + adjective) but can take the form of verb phrases, subject-predicate phrases, or other complements. State complements that are adjective phrases often look the same as degree complements and thus are often lumped together with degree complements in textbooks.

Stative adjective — *Also known as: 状态形容词 (zhuàngtài xíngróngcí).* A stative adjective is an adjective describing a relatively unchanging or permanent condition/state.

Stative verb — *Also known as: 状态动词 (zhuàngtài dòngcí), 静态动词 (jìngtài dòngcí), state verb and static verb.* A stative verb is a verb describing a relatively unchanging or permanent condition/state. Stative verbs in Mandarin are usually translated as adjectives in English.

Structural particle — *Also known as: 结构助词 (jiégòu zhùcí).* A structural particle is a function word that denotes the structural/grammatical relationship between elements of a sentence.

Time adverb — *Also known as: 时间副词 (shíjiān fùcí).* Adverbs of time express the when, how long, or how often of a verb.

Time phrase — *Also known as: 时间短语 (shíjiān duǎnyǔ).* A time phrase occurs before the verb phrase and indicates the when, how long, or how often of a situation.

Time noun — *Also known as: 时间名词 (shíjiān míngcí), 时间词 (shíjiāncí), time nominal and temporal noun.* Time nouns are nouns that provide information regarding time. One reason they're noteworthy in Chinese is that words indicating time in English are often adverbs, whereas their Chinese counterparts are nouns.

Time-measure complement — *Also known as: 时量补语 (shí-liàng bǔyǔ).* Time-measure complements show the state or duration of an action.

Tone adverb — See **modal adverb**

Topic-comment structure — *Also known as: 主题句 (zhǔtí-jù), 主题结构 (zhǔtí jiégòu), 主题评论结构 (zhǔtí-pínglùn jiégòu), 主题述题结构 (zhǔtí-shùtí jiégòu) and 主题评述结构 (zhǔtí-píngshù jiégòu).* A topic-comment structure is an alternative to the typical subject-predicate sentence structure, whereby a topic (or theme) is followed by the speaker's comment on that topic. The topic is not the "doer" (subject) of the sentence, but rather sets the scope of the comments (some thoughts related to the topic).

Transitive verb — *Also known as: 及物动词 (jíwù dòngcí).* A transitive verb is an verb which takes a direct object.

Verb — *Also known as: 动词 (dòngcí).* Verbs are the "action" words which make up the predicates of most sentences, but may also simply indicate relationships, changes, or mental activity rather than physical actions. Verbs may take objects, and can also be reduplicated in Chinese. They can be negated, as well as modified by particles.

Verb measure word — *Also known as: 动量词 (dòng liàngcí), verbal measure word and verbal classifier.* A verb measure word accompanies the number of times a verb occurred to count the frequency or re-occurrence of an action. See: Measure words for verbs

Verb phrase — *Also known as: 动词性短语 (dòngcí-xìng duǎnyǔ) and verbal phrase.* A verb phrase is a phrase with a verb as a head word that has any sort of modifier. It commonly includes modal verbs before it and objects after it.

Verbal measure word — *Also known as: 动量补语 (dòng-liàng bǔyǔ), verb measure word, verbal classifier and action-measure complement.* This type of measure word is not used to count nouns. Rather, it is placed after verbs to show the frequency of an action.

Verbal predicate sentence — See **sentence with a verbal predicate**

Acknowledgments

The Chinese Grammar Wiki may have been pioneered by AllSet Learning, but it would not be possible without the hard work of many selfless individuals, including AllSet Learning interns, students, teachers, and regular users. Thank you!

AllSet Interns

• Donna Yee • Lucas Simons • Hugh Grigg • Greg McAndrews • Jonathan Pope • Pavel Dvorak • Parry Cadwallader • Jack Overstreet • Dan Emery • Erick Garcia • Mei Tong • Ben Slye • Brandon Sanchez • Logan Pauley • Ashlyn Weber • Michelle Birkenfeldt • Zach Herzog • Jazlyn Akaka • Salomé Vergne • Natalie Kuan • Jack Du • Erick Garcia • Cai Qingyang • Michael Moore • Liza Fowler • Mike Blood • Jacob Rodgers • Dominic Pote • Amani Core • Michelle Guerra • Amanda Gilbride • Callan Mossman • Jenna Salisbury • Audrey Brady • Jocelyn Kwong • Natalia Tun • Jake Liu

Volunteer Editors

Some of these editors did tons of work on their own, while others emailed in issues they found. We thank them all for the hard work and valuable contributions!

• Nicholas Fiorentini • Noémi Németh • Betsy • HuaWei • Kryby • Jay • Luolimao • Trackpick • Morris • Philip Harding • Gintaras Valentukonis • Benedikt Rauh

AllSet Teachers and Staff

• 马丽华 (Mǎ Lìhuá) • 李炯 (Lǐ Jiǒng) • 陈世霜 (Chén Shìshuāng) • 刘倖倖 (Liú Xìngxìng) • 赵以华 (Zhào Yǐhuá) • 于翠 (Yú Cuì) • 杨仁君 (Yáng Rénjùn) • 毛思平 (Máo Sīpíng) • 吴蒙蒙 (Wú Méngméng) • 贾贝茜 (Jiǎ Bèixī) • Parry Cadwallader • Michael Moore • John Pasden

Big props also go to full-time staff 李炯 (Lǐ Jiǒng) and 马丽华 (Mǎ Lìhuá) for their unflinching dedication to repeated proofreading tasks as we completed the final checks of the print book.

Sincere thanks to Parry Cadwallader for making both the original wiki itself as well as the ebook version of the Chinese Grammar Wiki possible technically, with very little extra production work needed from the academic team. A big thank you also to Adam Abrams for all the layout work that went into creating the print version.

Other Credits

The Chinese Grammar Wiki website and ebook both make use of the **Silk** icon set **FamFamFam.com**. The Chinese Grammar Wiki BOOK (print edition) uses a "structure" icon from **Pixeden.com**, as well as several icons from **Icomoon.io**. The HSK Grammar series uses graphics from Pablo Stanley's outstanding **Humaaans** vector art library.

References

This page is a bibliography for the Chinese Grammar Wiki. It lists all sources referenced extensively when researching the content of the Chinese Grammar Wiki grammar points.

- Chen, Ru 陈如, and Xiaoya Zhu 朱晓亚. *Hanyu Changyong Geshi 330 Li 汉语常用格式 330 例 [Common Chinese Patterns 330]*. Beijing: Beijing Foreign Languages Printing House, 2010. Print.
- Fang, Yuqing 房玉清. *Shiyong Hanyu Yufa 实用汉语语法 [A Practical Chinese Grammar]*. Beijing: Beijing Yuyan Daxue Chubanshe, 2008. Print.
- General Information on the HSK. *Hanyu Kaoshi Fuwu Wang*, http://www.chinesetest.cn. Web.
- Herzberg, Qin Xue, and Larry Herzberg. *Basic Patterns of Chinese Grammar: A Student's Guide to Correct Structures and Common Errors*. Berkeley, CA: Stone Bridge, 2011. Print.
- Ho, Yong. *Intermediate Chinese*. New York: Hippocrene, 2004. Print.
- Jiang Liping 姜丽萍, ed. Wang Fang 王芳, Wang Feng 王枫, and Liu Liping 刘丽萍. *标准课程 Standard Course: HSK 1*. Beijing: Beijing Language and Culture University Press, 2014. Print.
- Jiang Liping 姜丽萍, ed. Wang Feng 王枫, Liu Liping 刘丽萍, and Wang Fang 王芳. *标准课程 Standard Course: HSK 2*. Beijing: Beijing Language and Culture University Press, 2014. Print.
- Jiang Liping 姜丽萍, ed. Yu Miao 于淼, and Li Lin 李琳. *标准课程 Standard Course: HSK 3*. Beijing: Beijing Language and Culture University Press, 2014. Print.
- Jiang Liping 姜丽萍, ed. Dong Zheng 董政 and Zhang Jun 张军. *标准课程 Standard Course: HSK 4 上*. Beijing: Beijing Language and Culture University Press, 2014. Print.
- Jiang Liping 姜丽萍, ed. Zhang Jun 张军 and Dong Zheng 董政. *标准课程 Standard Course: HSK 4 下*. Beijing: Beijing Language and Culture University Press, 2014. Print.
- Jiang Liping 姜丽萍, ed. Liu Chang 刘畅 and 鲁江 Lu Jiang. *标准课程 Standard Course: HSK 5 上*. Beijing: Beijing Language and Culture University Press, 2014. Print.
- Jiang Liping 姜丽萍, ed. 鲁江 Lu Jiang and Liu Chang 刘畅. *标准课程 Standard Course: HSK 5 下*. Beijing: Beijing Language and Culture University Press, 2015. Print.
- Jiang Liping 姜丽萍, ed. Yao Shujun 么书君 and Yang Huizhen 杨慧真. *标准课程 Standard Course: HSK 6 上*. Beijing: Beijing Language and

Culture University Press, 2015. Print.

- Jiang Liping 姜丽萍, ed. Yang Huizhen 杨慧真 and Yao Shujun 么书君. *标准课程 Standard Course: HSK 6 下*. Beijing: Beijing Language and Culture University Press, 2016. Print.
- Li, Charles N., and Sandra A. Thompson. *Mandarin Chinese: A Functional Reference Grammar*. Berkeley: U of California, 1981. Print.
- Li, Dejin 李德津, and Meizhen Cheng 程美珍, eds. *Waiguoren Shiyong Hanyu Yufa 外国人实用汉语语法 [A Practical Chinese Grammar for Foreigners]*. Beijing: Beijing Yuyan Daxue Chubanshe, 1998. Print.
- Li, Luxing 李禄兴, Ling Zhang 张玲, and Juan Zhang 张娟. *Hanyu Yufa Baixiang Jianglian: Chuzhongji 汉语语法百项讲练：初中级 [Chinese Grammar–Broken Down Into 100 Items]*. Beijing: Beijing Language and Culture UP, 2011. Print.
- Li, Xiaoqi 李晓琪, ed. *Xiandai Hanyu Xuci Shouce 现代汉语虚词手册 [Modern Chinese Function Words Handbook]: A Guide to Function Words in Modern Chinese*. Beijing: Beijing Daxue Chubanshe, 2003. Print.
- Liu, Delian 刘德联, and Xiaoyu Liu 刘晓雨. *Hanyu Kouyu Changyong Jushi Lijie 汉语口语常用句式例解 [Exemplification of Common Sentence Patterns in Spoken Chinese]*. Ed. Liwen Song 宋立文. Beijing: Beijing Daxue Chubanshe, 2005. Print.
- Liu, Xun 刘珣, ed. *Xin Shiyong Hanyu Keben 新实用汉语课本 [New Practical Chinese Reader Textbook 1]*. Beijing: Beijing Language and Culture UP, 2002. Print.
- Liu, Xun 刘珣. *Xin Shiyong Hanyu Keben 新实用汉语课本 [New Practical Chinese Reader Textbook 2]*. Beijing: Beijing Language and Culture UP, 2002. Print.
- Liu, Xun 刘珣. *Xin Shiyong Hanyu Keben 新实用汉语课本 [New Practical Chinese Reader Textbook 3]*. Beijing: Beijing Language and Culture UP, 2003. Print.
- Liu, Yuehua 刘月华, Wenyu Pan 潘文娱, and Wei Gu 故桦. *Shiyong Xiandai Hanyu Yufa 实用现代汉语语法 [Practical Modern Chinese Grammar]*. Beijing: Shangwu Yinshuguan Chuban, 2001. Print.
- Liu, Yuehua, and Tao-chung Yao. *Zhongwen Tingshuo Duxie 中文听说读写 [Integrated Chinese Textbook Simplified Characters Level 1 Part 2]*. 3rd ed. Boston: Cheng & Tsui, 2009. Print.
- Liu, Yuehua, and Tao-chung Yao. *Zhongwen Tingshuo Duxie 中文听说读写 [Integrated Chinese Textbook Simplified Characters Level 2 Part 2]*. 3rd ed. Boston: Cheng & Tsui, 2009. Print.
- Liu, Yuehua, and Tao-chung Yao. *Zhongwen Tingshuo Duxie 中文听说读写 [Integrated Chinese Textbook Simplified Characters Level 1 Part 1]*.

3rd ed. Boston: Cheng & Tsui, 2009. Print.

- Liu, Yuehua, and Tao-chung Yao. *Zhongwen Tingshuo Duxie 中文听说读写 [Integrated Chinese Textbook Simplified Characters Level 2 Part 1]*. 3rd ed. Boston: Cheng & Tsui, 2009. Print.
- Lü, Shuxiang 吕叔湘, comp. *Xiandai Hanyu Babai Ci 现代汉语八百词 [800 Modern Chinese Words]*. Beijing: Shangwu Yinshuguan, 1980. Print.
- Ma, Jing-heng Sheng, and Claudia Ross. *Modern Mandarin Chinese Grammar: A Practical Guide*. London: Routledge, 2006. Print.
- Mu, Ling, Rongzhen Li, and Peisong Xu. *Chinese Usage Dictionary*. Center for Language Study, Yale University, 2004. Web.
- "Qingwen." Podcast audio content. *ChinesePod*. Web.
- Ross, Claudia. *Schaum's Outline of Chinese Grammar*. New York: McGraw-Hill, 2004. Print.
- Teng, Wen-Hua. *Yufa!: A Practical Guide to Mandarin Chinese Grammar*. London: Hodder Education, 2011. Print.
- *Xiandai Hanyu Xuci Lishi 现代汉语虚词例释 [Modern Chinese Function Words Examples and Explanations]*. Beijing: Shangwu Yinshuguan, 1957. Print.
- Yip, Po-ching, and Don Rimmington. *Chinese: An Essential Grammar*. London: Routledge, 1997. Print.
- Yip, Po-ching, Don Rimmington, Xiaoming Zhang, and Rachel Henson. *Basic Chinese: A Grammar and Workbook*. London: Routledge, 1998. Print.
- Zhang, Jing 张婧, ed. *Yufa Jingjiang Jinglian 语法精讲精练 [Practicing HSK Grammar]*. 1st ed. Beijing: Sinolingua, 2008. Print.
- Zhu, Xiaoxing 朱晓星, ed. *Jianming Hanyu Yufa Xuexi Shouce 简明汉语语法学习手册 [Simple Chinese Grammar Study Handbook]: Chinese Grammar without Tears*. Beijing: Beijing Daxue Chubanshe, 2002. Print.

Made in the USA
Coppell, TX
23 December 2022